THE TWO FRANKLINS

BY BERNARD FAŸ

FRANKLIN: The Apostle of Modern Times

SINCE VICTOR HUGO: French Literature of To-day

THE TWO FRANKLINS: Fathers of American Democracy

HIGH STREET, from Ninth Street, PHILADELPHIA

A VIEW OF PHILADELPHIA, HIGH STREET SEEN
FROM NINTH STREET, IN 1800, MADE BY BIRCH

BERNARD FAŸ's

THE
TWO
FRANKLINS:

Fathers of

American Democracy.

With Illustrations.

BOSTON:

Published by LITTLE, BROWN, AND
COMPANY, MCMXXXIII.

PREFACE

A REVOLUTION is a change of mind. There have been few more radical changes of mind than the one which took place in America between 1790 and 1800.

But when historians describe the downfall of the Federalists and the victory of the new Democratic-Republican Party during these years they always speak in terms of Jefferson and Hamilton. They do not exhibit a change of mind. They merely stage a picturesque fight between two very great men, and two very attractive men.

I find these two men very attractive myself, and well worth presenting. But I cannot overlook the fact that they began by collaborating in revolutionary organization (1776–1783, 1790–1793), and ended by coöperating even more closely. Jefferson would never have been elected President without Hamilton's final help.

So, in this study of the second American Revolution, I shall necessarily deal with these men; but I shall also deal, more especially, with the change of mind of the American nation and the leaders who influenced it.

As I see the matter, while Hamilton opposed this change and Jefferson made use of it, it was other men who effected this change of mind. I propose to deal mostly with these other men, and, above all, with the one of them who strikes me as the most outspoken, the most reckless, the most generous, and the most neglected. His name was Bache.

He may have been wrong. In any case, he died too soon

[v]

PREFACE

to be right. But he was a good fighter and he took the side
which found favor with the American nation in the end.

Here is the story as I have found it in old archives and
dusty pamphlets. It is the story of the birth of a new nation and the death of a young man.

FOREWORD

THIS book would never have been written without the generosity of Mr. Franklin Bache, who placed at my disposal not only his family archives, but also his vast knowledge of his family in the history of Philadelphia. In fact, I owe him much of the personal affection and respect I feel for Benjamin Franklin and for Benjamin Franklin Bache.

I also wish to express my appreciation to Northwestern University, which permitted me, through the lectures which I gave on the Norman Wait Harris Foundation, to present the point of view that I am developing in these pages.

This point of view may seem somewhat novel, but I came to it through the good fortune that I had in being authorized to see a great deal of unpublished and hitherto neglected material in the William L. Clements Library at Ann Arbor, in the collections of MM. Lucien and Philibert Cramer, in Geneva, Mr. G. S. Eddy in New York, MM. de Marignac in Geneva, Mr. W. S. Mason in Evanston, Ill., Doctor A. S. W. Rosenbach in New York and Philadelphia, Madame la Duchesse de La Rochefoucauld in Paris, Miss E. F. Ward in Evanston, and also in the departments of manuscripts of the American Antiquarian Society in Worcester, Massachusetts, in the American Philosophical Society in Philadelphia, the Massachusetts Historical Society in Boston, the Morgan Library in New York, the Pennsylvania Historical Society in Philadelphia, the New York Historical Society, the New York Public Library,

FOREWORD

the Wisconsin Historical Society, the Manuscript Division
of the Library of Congress, the Archives du Ministère des
Affaires Etrangères in Paris, the Archives de Genève, the
Manuscript Department of the Bibliothèque Nationale in
Paris, the Public Record Office in London, and many others,
though I am unfortunately unable to mention all. But to all
of them I wish to state my indebtedness and to express my
gratitude.

I am no less grateful to the great libraries of Europe and
America for having placed at my disposal the services of
their staffs and the wealth of their collections. I am particularly grateful to the Bibliothèque Nationale and the American Library of Paris, the British Museum Library, the Morgan Library in New York, the Library of Congress, the
libraries of Columbia University, Harvard University,
Northwestern University, the University of Chicago, the
American Antiquarian Society, the New York Historical
Society, the Pennsylvania Historical Society, the Grosvenor
Public Library in Buffalo, the Library Company of Philadelphia, and the Newberry Library in Chicago.

Furthermore, I wish to express my appreciation to fellow
workers in this field, who have been kind enough to let me
use the information they had collected, and particularly to
Mr. E. P. Kilroe, the historian of Tammany, to Mr.
Clarence Brigham of the American Antiquarian Society, to
Professors Isaac J. Cox of Northwestern University, M. W.
Jernegan of the University of Chicago, Frank Monaghan
of New York University, S. E. Morison of Harvard University, D. R. Fox of Columbia University, and to Mr.
Raymond Carey of Northwestern University, all of whom
have made very valuable suggestions and have helped me
to discover many documents.

I am greatly indebted also to Mr. Rupert Hughes, the

historian of Washington, who was kind enough to send me some rare books and interesting data.

I shall add that whatever literary qualities may exist in the English version of this book are due to the very kind and understanding collaboration of Mr. Warren B. Wells.

Finally I thank Mr. Walter H. Murphey. Without him I should never have been able to collect, digest and use all the material I needed.

Without him, I should not have written *this* book.

CONTENTS

CONTENTS

ILLUSTRATIONS

[xiii]

ILLUSTRATIONS

ILLUSTRATIONS

ILLUSTRATIONS

Book One

THE GRANDSON OF "POOR RICHARD"

A GREAT MAN'S SMALL FAMILY

"LAST Thursday evening, Mr. Richard Bache of this city, merchant, was married to Miss Sally Franklin, the only daughter of the celebrated Dr. Franklin, a young lady of distinguished merit. . . . The next day, all the shipping in the harbor displayed their colors on the happy occasion."

So said the newspapers of Philadelphia, on November 2, 1767.

They omitted to recall that the young lady of distinguished merit had nearly been burned alive or lynched in her father's house two years before, when Doctor Franklin was held responsible for the measures taken by England to impose taxes on the Americans. Luckily Mrs. Franklin was a resourceful woman. She had barricaded the house, she had assembled arms and ammunition, she had gathered together a few neighbors and cousins of hers, and so she had given people's minds time to calm down.

People's minds had calmed down, time had passed, and the English Parliament had repealed the hateful laws. The elections of October, 1766, had given the victory to Franklin's partisans.

Sally wrote to her brother: " 'The old ticket forever! We have it by 34 votes! God bless our worthy and noble Agent and all his family!' were the joyfull words we were awak'd with at 2 or 3 o'clock this morning by the White Oaks;

[3]

they then gave us 3 hurras and a blessing, then march'd off. How strong is the curse of the Truth! We have beat three parties — the Proprietary, the Presbyterians, and the half and half."

Poor Sally, daughter of a great man! They had good reason to run up the flags for her; for her marriage was a real victory. Hitherto she had had more glory than joy, more honors than peace. But this time she had got what she wanted.

No doubt Doctor Franklin was a famous philosopher, a sage, and a perfect philanthropist. No doubt he had lavished upon his family, as upon his friends and the world at large, the treasures of his philosophy; but philosophy alone cannot make a girl contented and happy.

Sally had received an excellent education. Her mother had taught her cooking and the art of housekeeping. Her father had provided her with a tailor to teach her the difficult technique of making buttonholes, one day when he saw her fumbling at it, and later he had taught her to play the harmonica. Finally, she had received from Heaven robust health, imperturbable good nature, plenty of common sense, and a fine, strong body, which was well matched by a face radiant with sincerity. Sally played with her cards on the table and never stopped playing with them on the table.

It was not always easy. Her father was a great man, but there were plenty of little dark corners in his life. Nobody knew exactly how he and Mrs. Franklin had got married or whether there had been any benefit of clergy in the matter. People gossiped about it. Nobody knew exactly how William, Franklin's only son, and Sarah's only brother, had got into the family, and Mrs. Franklin seemed to know less about it than anybody else; which sometimes put her

SILHOUETTE OF DOCTOR FRANKLIN
MADE BETWEEN 1785 AND 1790 BY
CHARLES WILSON PEALE

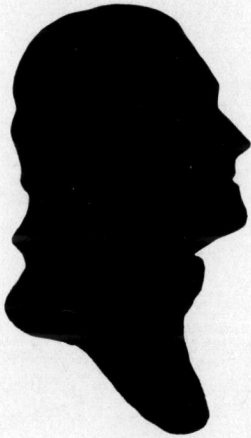

SILHOUETTE OF THOMAS JEFFERSON
MADE BEFORE 1790

Both silhouettes are from the collection of Franklin Bache

out of temper with William and with "Pappy", as she called her illustrious spouse. Philadelphia, a small and purse-proud pious town, did not by any means fail to make the Franklin family pay for these breaches of accepted usage, and, as people often needed the Doctor, his wife and his daughter paid more than he did.

They kept on paying, while he, with his fortune made and his fame established, set out for England to represent Pennsylvania and defend the interests of the Province against the King and the Parliament. Was not this his duty? He performed it with address, courage, and perseverance. From 1757 to 1775 he spent only two years in America, and during this time he made many journeys away from Philadelphia.

He was always away, and Mrs. Franklin could not reconcile herself to his absence. There was nothing philosophical about her; she had been very beautiful in her youth, but her beauty was of the material, plebeian kind. She had never learned to give the first place to intellect, as he had done since he became a gentleman.

For his part, he experienced a melancholy, profound pleasure in writing fine, long, affectionate letters to his faithful Debby, while in London a thoughtful and assiduous hostess was taking great care of him. Mrs. Franklin labored over drafting, as best she could, uncouth letters in which she poured out her whole heart, and all her little troubles and bothers. Then, when night came, in her big, empty bed, she trembled as she heard the clocks striking in the deserted study, and the tinkling of the mysterious bells which the Doctor had fitted up to reveal the passage of electricity. The melancholy chant of the town crier announcing the time of night reminded her only that she was an old woman, abandoned by her husband.

She did her best to forgive him. She thanked him for all the handkerchiefs, the fine China porcelain, the Turkey carpets, the Lyons silks, the demijohns, the Kashmir shawls and all the other fine things that he sent her from London. In return she sent him apples, and big Pennsylvania cakes, and little striped squirrels, and pretty nuts. And they kept on exchanging letters — affectionate, kindly, sweet, weary, wearisome.

She had kept her daughter, and she would have fought to keep her. When the great man had tried to take Sally away from her, she had refused to let her go, and he had not dared to insist. For once she had stood up to him. So, instead of becoming a fine English young lady, mixing in high society with her father, Sally had stayed in Philadelphia, a quite simple and very good girl, who helped her mother to entertain her father's friends in his absence and get on with William, kept an eye on the servants and did the shopping, worked at furnishing the new house and doing errands for her father, and filled the empty hours of her mother's long grass widowhood with her cheerfulness.

She had a strong character and a soft heart. When her dear friend, Elizabeth Ross, died, Sally was beside her, in floods of tears, but still anxious to console Elizabeth's betrothed. Before Elizabeth closed her eyes for the last time, she entrusted them to each other.

So it was that, beside a death-bed, amid the tumult of rioting, far away from her father, and without her mother having much to do with it, Sarah Franklin became betrothed to Richard Bache.

She loved him very much. Without needing to eat it, he resembled Franklin after a good dinner. He was a stout fellow, friendly and jovial, with nothing of a great man about him. He had a big mouth and a capacious smile, and he was given to making coarse jokes. He was a simple-minded man. You could depend on him.

He was in business and was not making much of a success of it; but Sally had discovered that success does not mean happiness. For the rest, he came of an honorable and very prolific family in the north of England, and his brother had made a fine fortune in New York. Sally could adapt herself to all this very well, and so could Mrs. Franklin. They dealt with Bache as roundly as his own rotundity.

William Franklin, who was angular and aristocratic, had something to say about it. He had just been appointed Royal Governor of New Jersey, he had married a charming and distinguished English girl from the West Indies, he mixed in high society and corresponded with the English aristocracy, and he did not like the idea of his sister marrying a merchant who was headed for bankruptcy. He wrote to his father that the young couple would become a burden on him if he gave his consent. Doctor Franklin, upset and anxious about his daughter's future, wrote his wife some very positive letters; but he was a long way off, his daughter and his wife had made up their minds, and, for the rest, he was reaching the age when peace seems more essential to happiness than even joy itself.

Without any more than the minimum of consent or ceremony, Sarah Franklin and Richard Bache got married, and Philadelphia ran up the flags in honor of Doctor Franklin.

Sally had got what she wanted. She knew how to get other people to make the best of it. She proved to her father that Richard would cost him scarcely anything, and that he might even bring him in something, since he was

[7]

prepared to concern himself with small interests which the great man neglected. She made use of the influence which was exercised over Franklin by his good hostess in London, Mrs. Stevenson, who, anxious as she was to keep her famous guest, saw clearly that some concessions must be made to his far-off family.

Finally Bache went to England, his father-in-law opened his arms to him, they embraced, they had a long talk, they drank together like good fellows, and Richard Bache went back with three hundred pounds which Benjamin Franklin had lent him. Franklin gave his daughter his blessing, and there was nothing more to be said.

Sarah had got what she wanted. Mrs. Franklin got what she wanted too.

On August 12, 1769, in the course of one of those heavy, torrid Pennsylvanian summers which overpower plants, animals and human beings, in Doctor Franklin's house in Market Street, between Third Street and Fourth Street, opposite Market, was born a very small child, with big, dark eyes, who was christened Benjamin Franklin.

Benny might be tiny, but he was well-made from his birth, and from the very first moment he was a god to his grandmother. She never got tired of gazing at him, petting him and kissing him. She called him "her little kingbird", and sought in the sparkling of his child's eyes for the character of his expression, as though it were given to a human being to possess any before he has suffered. She was delighted to discover blue in his eyes, and even reconciled herself to the darker shades which she found in them.

Benny was her very own. She had had a son once, but he was dead. She had accepted another son, but he was not hers. She had a husband, but he did not belong to her any

[8]

more. Though even yet . . . Finally, she had a daughter, but this daughter of hers was married, happy, busy.

Only this little soul, a prisoner like herself, and solitary like herself, was near to her. He belonged to the same world, the same joys and the same sorrows, as herself. An instinct united them. She spent endless hours gazing at him, and never got tired of this happiness, secure at last, which was her own possession. At the sight of her the good Richard burst out laughing, and Sarah smiled.

In his cradle the child prattled.

He was baptized on August 30, 1769, in Christ Church. For godmothers he had his grandmother and his aunt, and for godfathers his grandfather, who was represented by Mr. Baynton, and his uncle.

Henceforth all the old woman's attention was concentrated upon him. Around her Revolution was rising. In the streets, noises became louder and more clamorous; in the market-place, people assembled in denser groups; but she neither saw nor understood. From London word came that her husband was threatened, then — at the end of the winter of 1774 — that he had been dismissed from his high office of Deputy-Postmaster General of America. It was said that he was in danger, and that perhaps he would never come back to America; but she had ceased either to fear or to hope for him.

Her eyes, which grew a little dimmer every day, her hands, which trembled now when they picked things up, no longer turned anywhere except towards the child; and her poor heart, at which pain was gnawing, no longer beat with joy except at the sight of the little one.

He was pretty, affectionate and gentle. When people played music, he beat time with his hands; then, sometimes he started sobbing soundlessly. Later, as he grew older, he had charming ways. He made his bow in the English style, and he made a conquest of his schoolmistress. "Ben Bache is the Commodore over the Madam," the other children said; but the little girls forgave him for it.

One day when Mrs. Franklin was entertaining a captain, the boy stood up, glass in hand, and gave a toast: "Your health, Master Soldier." He was so fond of his mother that if he had displeased her during the day, he could not eat his supper in the evening. She used to shrug her shoulders and say, "I can assure you I often have to mortify myself, for fear of spoiling him." She would add, "I look upon Ben to be of a temper that will be easy to govern. He will do a great deal out of affection."

When she was staying with her brother in New Jersey and was writing to her mother, Ben leaned over her shoulder and asked, "Mrs. Bache, have you sent my duty to Grandmamma?" So a new link, stronger, more supple and more charming than the old, was forged between mother and daughter.

One last gleam was shedding its rays on Mrs. Franklin's fading life, and for anything else she did not care. She had written to her husband that if he wanted ever to see her again, he must come home at once; and he, full of affection, multiplied his promises, set dates, and underlined those fine words of his. They had ceased to mean anything to her. She could see only the young life, fresh and flourishing, of her grandson.

On December 14, 1774, she had a stroke. Her body lingered a few days longer, but finally, on December 19th, she breathed her last sigh.

Very politely, William went to her funeral, and he wrote to his father that he really ought to have been there.

[10]

The good Richard consoled Franklin, pointing out to him that she had slipped away "without a groan or even a sigh; she was released from a troublesome world, and happily relieved from all future Pain and Anxiety."

In an armchair Sarah sobbed, and little Ben, with his head in his mother's lap, sobbed with her.

He had lost his first friend, and his moist eyes began to see life as it was — those big, black eyes of his.

CHAPTER II

THE SCHOOL OF REVOLUTION

What Benny Bache's eyes saw first in this world was tumult. In his already noisy home, where he romped with his little brother William, born on May 31, 1773, for a playmate, his sister Sarah made her appearance on December 1, 1774. They had barely got over this joyful emotion when his grandmother fell ill, on the fourteenth of December. On the nineteenth she was dead. She was buried in Christ Church cemetery, in the midst of a great gathering of old friends headed by Richard Bache, jovial even in his mourning, and William Franklin, more correct than ever in the presence of death.

Then there was no time for tears, or for rest after tears. The house was invaded. Visitors never stopped coming and going. Some of them brought letters from Doctor Franklin. Others of them wanted news of him. All of them were nervous and restless.

Among them was a man with a long nose drooping over a loose mouth, in a flabby face lit up by two extraordinarily dark and shining eyes. His name was Thomas Paine. He had been recommended by Doctor Franklin. He wanted a little money, a lot of glory, and other things besides, for which his eyes asked, but not his lips. Richard Bache gave him a drink, Sarah listened to him, and they introduced him to their friends.

So it was that Thomas Paine established himself as a writer in Philadelphia.

Rumor kept on swelling all the time. In that soundbox of a city, everything set a clamor going, and the clamor penetrated into everybody's house. People went to bed in a fever of expectation, to awaken avidly curious. They hurried out into the streets, just as before they had been in the habit of hurrying home.

On the evening of April 24th, when a breathless, radiant, and mud-spattered courier pulled up outside the City Tavern, a crowd flocked at once to hear the great news that the messenger brought. It had been on its way since the evening of April 19th, carried from committee to committee, from town to town, from village to village, by messengers who rode day and night, and it was the great news that everybody was awaiting — war. In the towns of Concord and Lexington, the English troops and the American militia had exchanged the first shots. It meant the end of waiting.

Forthwith nervousness was transformed into exaltation. The next morning, eight thousand persons thronged into the City Hall and the square which surrounded it. Moved by a common impulse, without many words being wasted, they swore to stand together, to take up arms, and to defend themselves against any attack. Then, without loss of time, they started drilling, and from that date the "Confederates", as they were called, held the city. They obeyed only the Committee of Safety, an organization as revolutionary as themselves, and the order which they maintained was a revolutionary order.

Henceforth everything was revolutionary in Philadelphia. From south and north, on horseback, in coaches, in pinnaces, delegates to Congress arrived, and at every arrival the Confederates organized a procession, a parade, a trooping. Fifes and drums were to be heard in all directions. Volleys and musket shots resounded ceaselessly. Men kept on enrolling, apprentices jostled one another for a better view of what was going on, and at home, under the anxious eyes of mothers, children played at soldiers.

But, of all these arrivals, the most moving was that of May 5th. That evening the *Pennsylvania Packet*, Captain Osborn, coming from London, which she had left six weeks before, entered the port of Philadelphia, and Doctor Franklin disembarked. A crowd flocked to meet him, escorted him home, acclaimed him and besieged him.

For the first time Benny Bache saw his grandfather. Hitherto all he knew of him was his armchair, his mysterious apparatus, his innumerable books, and his portrait. Franklin was taller, stouter, stronger-looking than his portrait; but, above all, his eyes were different, and the light in them made everything around them, everything to do with him, different too. Grandfather and grandson had a long look at each other. They both had the same way of looking.

Together with Franklin arrived a boy with fine features, keen eyes, a short, stubborn chin, and ready, assured manners. He resembled Uncle William, and they told Benny that he was a cousin of his, but did not explain to him just how he came to be so. A shy friendship was struck up at once between the adolescent from London and the boy of Philadelphia. The one was proud to find a family that belonged to him and to lord it over younger children, the other to have a big cousin and to take orders from him. But Temple did not make a long stay. He went off to New Jersey to rejoin his father, who recognized him as his legitimate son.

In the Bache household tumult kept on growing. Every-

[14]

thing was given up to the Revolution. On the morrow of his arrival, it had snapped up Benjamin Franklin, for he was immediately elected to Congress and took his seat there. He was appointed Postmaster-General of the American Colonies some weeks later, and elected to the Committee of Public Safety of his home town, which now controlled the city, the county, and the province. In November he was also elected to the Municipal Council, to the Provincial Assembly, and to the Committee of Correspondence of Congress.

Morning, noon, and night, in Congress, on the Committee of Safety, at the Philosophical Society, he never stopped drafting documents, taking part in debates, giving his advice to committees or presiding over them. His house was never empty of beggars and disciples, admirers and electors.

Everywhere people discussed revolution. Everybody was excited and all in favor of revolution; but everybody wanted his own revolution, and it was very difficult to pick one's way among all these revolutions and make a success of one of them. People talked revolution day and night, wrote revolution, drafted revolution.

Food itself turned revolutionary. People spared salt, in order to avoid having to buy it. They did without lamb and mutton in order to let the wool grow on the sheep's back and so encourage American manufactures. They dressed themselves, revolutionary style, in cloth woven at home, in order to avoid buying anything that came from England.

Ideas and sentiments were revolutionary. Servants had to be so too. Sarah Bache had a maid who was suspected of being lukewarm, and finally of being a spy. She was denounced and accused. She protested, then confessed, and in

[15]

the end burst into floods of tears. The papers talked about it, for the house had become a public place.

Doctor Franklin sat in his big armchair in the middle of the room, surrounded by his friends, gesticulating and debating while the children played in a corner. William, still babyish, imitated the tumult of the streets. He marched back and forth with a little wooden gun, whistling by way of a fife. But Benny, already serious, sitting in his little chair at his little table, with his elbows on the top of it and his face intent, like grown-ups, filled long sheets of writing paper, making a mess of them with his scrawls and his erasures.

His grandfather told him one day that he had a little friend in England, Elizabeth Hewson, who would make a fine wife for him; but Benny at once asked what age she was and decided that Elizabeth was too young. They laughed at this. So difficult is it for grown-ups to understand that, young or old, all men play the same game!

As a rule, Benny stayed in his corner without anybody taking notice of him, or needing to. He was a wise child in a world where everything had gone mad. His grandfather belonged to the revolution. For its sake he strove in Congress and toiled on the Committee of Safety. For its sake he traveled as far as New England in order to inspect the army outside Boston, and spent all of the fall on the dusty roads of New Jersey, New York and New England.

Benny's father, Richard Bache, though with a more ponderous and temperate zeal, followed Franklin's example. He was on the City Committee. He helped his father-in-law, interviewed callers for him, looked after the mail, and served to the best of his ability. Sarah Bache served too, but on occasion she knew how to give orders as well. She ran the household, backed her father, guided the neighbors, and rallied patriotic women around her. She had strength of character, and, like Franklin, a capacity for keeping calm along with it.

She needed it. Everything was going to pieces around them. Horrible scenes were staged in the streets. One day they saw the good Mr. Hunt, a friend and neighbor of theirs, hoisted onto a wagon and compelled to make his public confession. He was accused of having defended England. A shrill band played burlesque airs. Boys threw stones at him, men cursed him, and women, fearing the worst, hurried away. Some of the crowd shouted that he ought to be tarred and feathered, since he deserved nothing better; but strong measures were averted, thanks to his coolness and his humility.

It was not the same with Doctor Kearsley, who had shown indignation at this spectacle. He was hoisted on to the wagon in Hunt's place, and, when he struggled, received a bayonet thrust in the hand. The crowd smashed the windowpanes and frames and the doors of his house, hurled curses at him, and dragged him to the Tavern to be the butt of the drinkers. Bare-headed, bleeding, and with his clothes dishevelled, he kept on denouncing the crowd which mauled him. Finally they tossed him a bowl of punch, which he swallowed at a gulp, so dry was his throat, and the fun was over.

It was better not to make any attempt to help your friends. Otherwise you might lose your prestige, your windowpanes, and your plate, if not more. It was better not to receive any letters, for they were all opened, and, if some ignorant patriot did not understand what they contained, you ran the risk of prison. It was better to keep your mouth shut, for all your conversation was amplified and came back to you in distorted form. You had to be prudent, but still you had to mix with the crowd, which suspected you if you did not.

Around the Franklins and the Baches everything collapsed, except the Revolution. Franklin's old associate in his political enterprises, Joseph Galloway, suspected of royalism, went into hiding on his estate at Trevose, but, even so, did not succeed in getting himself forgotten. Franklin's own son William, the Governor of New Jersey, took sides with the King of England, and the wrath of the populace threatened him, together with his father's curse.

But William did not care about that. An illegitimate son of Franklin's, he owed England what his father himself had not given him — respectability. Governor of New Jersey for the King, he had made up his mind to remain the Royal Governor, even if he had to be repudiated as a son. In vain did Franklin write to him, — gently, firmly, persuasively, imperiously. In vain did Sarah Bache intercede with him. The Revolution had entered into the Franklin family and shattered it.

In the tumult of the Revolution, Benjamin Franklin and William Franklin fought each other to hold William Temple. William had engendered him; Benjamin had brought him up. For the past ten years Benjamin had given him a home. For the past ten weeks William had taken him back into his home. Benjamin had attached himself to him with the greedy affection of an old man, and deserved his affection in return. William had treated him as his son, and received from him the respect due from a son. Between Benjamin and Temple, the old man and the adolescent, there was certainly more love; but between William and Temple there was that more intimate and more profound tie which unites a father and a son whose souls have the same ring. Temple's face turned towards his father.

The old man could not bear it. In vain did he console himself by caressing Benny. In vain did he plough through the snowy, muddy and chaotic roads of the northern colonies in the depths of winter to go and encourage the army of Canada. In vain did he devote his energy to supporting the patriots who were striving for independence at Philadelphia.

It was he, more than anybody else, who swayed the hesitating people of Pennsylvania in favor of accepting this new government, this new fatherland, this new flag which still frightened them. But the mind of this patriot, victor in the national Revolution, could not turn itself away from the revolution which was devastating his family, and in which he was vanquished.

William Franklin had just been arrested. His wife, overwhelmed by the blow, took refuge in tears, which at least isolated her from human society, and Temple scoured the roads to get some help for his father, some letters on his behalf. In Philadelphia, in Market Street, Sarah wept too beside the cradle of little Sarah, who had just died.

Meanwhile, in the streets, the populace acclaimed the Declaration of Independence, the patriot politicians, the troops and Congress. Volleys were fired to celebrate the launching of the frigate *Washington;* and at the corner of Chestnut Street, between Second Street and Third Street, Mr. Fowler, at the sign of the White Horse and Fountain, exhibited "the remarkable creature called a Satyr, of about two feet high, his body resembling a human body in all parts except his feet," which "walked upright and performed various actions to admiration."

[19]

Benjamin Franklin was tired of all this disorder. He had returned from Canada half-dead. He had a bad attack of gout in Philadelphia. He had to fight interminably to induce Congress to vote the Declaration of Independence, and to win over the city of Philadelphia and the Assembly of Pennsylvania, which still did not want independence. He had to struggle all the time, and his strength was getting exhausted. He felt it.

Congress asked him to go to France in order to negotiate an alliance, without which the Revolution could not maintain itself. Although he ran the risk of death if he were captured by an English warship, he accepted the invitation. What was left to him of his life belonged to his country.

But, artful even in his heroism, Doctor Franklin took advantage of it to filch Temple away from his father and his destiny. He wrote to the youth that, if he came back at once, he had an advantageous offer to make him. Intrigued, excited, dazed by the intoxication of the Revolution, and weak by nature, Temple came.

They set off on October 29, 1776, on board the *Reprisal*, Captain Wickes.

With them they took Benjamin Franklin Bache, aged seven. Mrs. Franklin was no longer there to prevent it, Richard Bache never prevented anything, and Sarah Bache resigned herself to keeping her husband and her home and letting her son go.

Benny followed his grandfather out into the storm. When the tempest raged, he cowered against that old man who carried affection to the point of cruelty, and against his cousin, who was never to know love again.

CHAPTER III

IN ROUSSEAU'S FOOTSTEPS

BENNY had promised to be good. As he had been good about his work and his play in the house in Market Street in Philadelphia, so he was good in the cramped, stuffy cabin on board the *Reprisal*, Captain Wickes.

He was good in the storm which for thirty days harassed them and tormented them. He was good in danger, when English ships chased them, with the object of capturing them and hanging them. He was good in battle, when the *Reprisal*, bringing her sixteen cannon into action, seized the *Vine*, laden with spirits, and the *Success*, laden with wine.

He was good when they were disembarked on the beach at Quiberon, in the midst of strange, hirsute people, peasants of Brittany, who frightened him because they looked like brigands, and who in turn took Franklin for the Devil. He was good in the little carriage, which jolted them over the highroads of France, and in the strange, noisy, crowded house which sheltered them in Nantes.

He was good in Versailles, when they showed him the palace of the Kings of France, and in Paris, when, for the first time, he set eyes on the tumultuous life of a great city, with narrow streets, full of coaches, poverty and luxury. He was good in his room in the Hôtel d'Hambourg, in the Rue de l'Université, where they finally came to rest and began a new life together with the New Year.

[21]

Everywhere he was good and obedient; but his big eyes, round with astonishment, gazed at all this as though it were a dream.

He was good when his grandfather took him to M. d'Hourville's boarding school at Passy, and he found himself alone among all the little French boys, noisy and curious, who never got tired of staring at the little "insurgent." He was so good that his grandfather called him "a special good Boy."

He could scarcely be anything but good. He knew neither their games, nor their language, nor their ways. He could do nothing but stare back at them, and run about and live among them, all alone, like an animal of another species among other animals not unfriendly, who did not chase him, but who did not make friends with him either.

He did not start his games again until spring came, when he was sent to M. Lecoeur's boarding school and his grandfather established himself near him on the heights of Passy, at the Hôtel de Valentinois. Here, at least, he merged into the crowd of little French boys, whether he was going to class in his pretty school uniform, or riding on horseback in his fine grey buckskin breeches, or attending his dancing-master's lessons.

Here he found other little "insurgents" like himself, in particular Deane and Cochran, with whom he struck up a friendship. With them he could now romp about, and thanks to them, Professor Lecoeur, with all his respects and regards, sent Doctor Franklin, at the same time as the hair-dresser's, the breeches-maker's and the shoemaker's accounts, a bill for the windowpanes which Monsieur his grandson had broken.

Then, on Sundays, the boys all went together to lunch with the illustrious Doctor. Around the table, laden with stewed-fruit dishes and plates of fruit, they found Americans living in Paris, merchants, ships' captains, diplomats, consuls, spies and traitors, accompanied by their wives, who had come to render homage to the philosopher. They met there also the opulent M. de Chaumont, and the sparkling M. de Beaumarchais. But, instead of looking at them and listening to them, they ran out into the big garden, around the pond, under the quincunxes, and on to the terrace, whence they threw stones into the Seine, along which the *galiote* which plied between Paris and Rouen was slowly drawn by knock-kneed nags.

Afterwards, in the big drawing-room with its plain paneling, Doctor Franklin drew Benny on to those knees of his, so much sought after by pretty ladies, and questioned him about his school. He was proud of his little grandson, who, at the end of the year, had received the great prize for good conduct in the presence of all his fellow pupils. By way of rewarding him, he talked to him about Philadelphia; about his father, Richard Bache, who had just been appointed Postmaster-General of America; and about his mother, who held a prominent place among the patriotic ladies of America, and never got tired of embroidering flags, sewing shirts and knitting socks for General Washington's soldiers.

He told him all about the war and the exploits of the patriots, about the dangers that threatened Philadelphia, occupied by the English, and about the hopes that he must cherish. He inflamed the imagination and the zeal of the boy, whom the majesty of his grandfather, ever surrounded by admiring men, and women both admiring and beautiful, filled with a growing respect.

Benny strove to please him in everything. For his sake he "swotted" over his French, applied himself to his

[23]

drawing-board, and "made leg" to the best advantage with those strong little legs of his, set off by their black silk breeches. He accepted France, and made himself French to please his grandfather — so much so that, in the dream in which he was immersed, America ended by seeming to him the most remote and unreal of imaginary places.

One fine day the Doctor realized the fact and was surprised at it. Benny was a regular little Frenchman; he bowed and walked French fashion; he played French games and was familiar with all those little conventions which make up the mystery of daily life in an old country. It would not have taken much for him to cry, "Long live the King!" and make his sign of the Cross.

The Doctor was shocked at all this. His grandson a French dandy — one of those fellows with red heels! He must lose no time in remedying such a state of things; and, without losing any, Doctor Franklin put himself in the way of making Benny a good Puritan. "I intend him for a Presbyterian as well as a Republican," he said. He sent him off to Geneva.

So here was Benny on the road again, all alone in a post chaise with the noble gentleman Philibert Cramer, a leading member of the Council of the Two Hundred, who was on his way back from Paris after paying a visit to his fashionable and philosophical friends. He was handsome and charming, distinguished and intellectual. One might imagine him the ambassador of a Prince-Bishop, or the lover of an Archduchess. In any case, bookseller though he might be, he was by way of being a lord in his own Republic of Geneva; and it suited him very well to take home with him in his post chaise the grandson of the most famous philosopher who walked the earth. For that matter, he treated Benny less as a child than as the offspring of a great genius.

"Respectable" Gabriel Louis Gallisard de Marignac — such was the title to which he had a right, in his capacity as Master at the College of Geneva — was no less disposed to surround his new boarder with flattering attentions, which would redound to the credit of his establishment. This consisted, as a matter of fact, only in a little, cramped, three-storied house, in the middle of the Rue Verdaine, whose slope in winter, when it was freezing hard, threatened to make you turn a somersault if you were not careful. At the back the house opened on a walled garden, which ended at the hill on which the College was perched.

He had only one servant, the good Mother Airre; but he had a great deal of dignity, and in the town, where he was held in esteem as an ex-officer and respected as a poet, it was said of him that he was a "master superior in his talents, his efforts, and his successes." The second Madame Gallisard de Marignac, *née* Mallet Genoud, was quite sure of the fact, and she made this faith of hers shared by her four children, who filled the house with noise as their father filled it with importance.

He did not fail, in well-turned epistles, to explain to Doctor Franklin all the care which he was taking of his grandson, and he sent him bills in which even the item of purgatives had a pious and imposing air. But he took care, above all, of the boy's soul, and every night when Benny went to bed, after greeting him with a ceremonious "Good night" — he begged him to bear in mind that, before he went to sleep, it was his duty to address his thanksgivings and his petitions to the Lord.

At Monsieur Gabriel Louis de Marignac's, the teaching

of Republicanism had a curiously pompous aspect about it, very appropriate to that Geneva which Jean Jacques Rousseau loved and at which Voltaire mocked. At Madame Philibert Cramer's, everything had a drawing-room air about it. She was a daughter of one of those pretty lordlings of Russia who were so much to the taste of Peter the Great. From this father of hers she had inherited a beauty, an off-handedness, a nobility of mind and an unfitness for life which enabled her to enthrone herself in Geneva like a queen.

She had bequeathed to her son, Louis Gabriel, the same traits, the same charm and the same incapacity to protect himself against harm. This best friend of Benny's was a tall, fair boy, with a pale complexion, enormous light-colored eyes, and slow, caressing movements, who did good by instinct and harm by chance, and subjected all his actions to the serene laws of idleness.

Benny's other friends were not so very different. Everybody made him welcome, and in this small town he was quite a personage. Above all, the leisured and rich foreigners who lived there delighted to entertain this nice, shy boy whose grandfather was such a famous man. Mrs. Serre asked him to tea every Thursday, because she had in America a son, of whom she hoped to obtain news through the Doctor; and her table was well provided with cream-cakes and jam.

Because he was a Whig, the rich Mr. Piggott entertained him at his château of Penthes, just outside Geneva. Here Benny met the Duke of Gloucester, and he was very much surprised that such a proud prince should have an ordinary sheepskin saddle on his horse. But it did not occur to him to be surprised that Mr. Piggott should receive under his hospitable roof both the grandson of the King of England

[26]

and the grandson of Doctor Franklin. Why should it surprise him?

At Madame Arthaud's, at M. Monet's, at Mr. Boisier's,
he was treated in the same way. He was invited to balls
everywhere. People took him to the theater to see "L'Amant
Bourru" and "Les Etrennes." There was no entertainment
at which they did not make a point of having the grandson
of the celebrated Doctor Franklin. M. de Marignac regarded it as his duty to put no obstacle in the way, either
because he thus wanted to defend Geneva's reputation for
hospitality, or because this was his idea of education, or because it gave him a way of obliging his friends and other
people.

Benny also went to the College; and there he received the
same consideration. In the old building, constructed by
Calvin and ornamented by Jean Goujon, nearly five hundred
schoolboys sat crowded together on the hard wooden
benches, and from half-past seven in the morning to seven
o'clock in the evening spent long hours reciting lessons
from Mermolius, pages of Cicero, and passages from the
Old Testament. They wrote endless essays and stupefied
themselves with Greek grammar. But they only came to life
when, by stealth, they sang the "Song of the Escalade,"
which was forbidden to them, highly patriotic though it
was. The College had its principles.

But the College was no longer what it had once been
in the days when every morning, at six o'clock, the pupils
had to present themselves in the icy classrooms. Now the
little Genevese worked around warm stoves, helped in their
tasks by the purring of the fire.

They began to get excited only towards prize-giving
time, for there were many prizes, and the city of Geneva
set great store by them. For prizes, medals were struck,

[27]

which were given to the boys and forever after adorned their families' glass cases. Prizes for good marks, prizes for essays, prizes for piety — there were all sorts of them, and the whole town talked about them.

When spring came to an end, preparations began for the great ceremony, and one fine morning about mid-June a great noise was to be heard. Preceded by drums and a fanfare of trumpets, the College proceeded to church. First came the band — bugles, drums, fifes and violins — followed by the professors in their gowns, walking slowly and with dignity. Behind them hastened the boys, for their legs were shorter and they were excited by the solemnity of the occasion.

With their hair tightly plaited into pigtails which were tucked up again and adorned with bright-colored ribbons, with bouquets of flowers in their hands and their little three-cornered hats on their heads, they descended the narrow streets. The proudest of them, those who were going to receive prizes, wore silver galloons in their hats, and people looked at them as they went by.

At the gate of Saint Peter's church, all the magistrates were waiting, and everybody went into the church with them to the strains of music and the pealing of bells. There were Messieurs the Syndics, and the Magnificent Council, and Messieurs the members of the Council of the Two Hundred, and there was also the Venerable Company of Pastors. When the pupils had been settled in their places and everybody had sat down, the ceremony began.

Monsieur the Moderator offered a prayer.

Monsieur the Rector delivered an address.

Messieurs the Masters pronounced allocutions.

The most distinguished pupil delivered an address in Latin.

Monsieur the Principal read out the names of the prize-winning pupils.

Monsieur the Rector summoned them to him one by one.

Then Monsieur the Rector made a speech to them, encouraging them to persevere in well-doing.

Finally Monsieur the Moderator pronounced a prayer of benediction and thanksgiving; and everybody went off again, fully satisfied with a ceremony from which nothing had been lacking, except perhaps brevity.

Then there was a great banquet for the professors, and a fine tea for the pupils, for the prize-winners had to celebrate their glory. Such was Benny's fortune in 1780, and M. de Marignac made sure that he had a good tea, for which Doctor Franklin sent him his approbation and four pounds. Benny won several prizes more for good marks, and he would have had still more, if it had depended only on Messieurs the Masters and Messieurs the Syndics, only too happy to have chances of praising and rewarding the most docile grandson of the greatest of insurgents.

But Benny was by no means one of those people who attract all prizes to themselves. He was by no means one of those people who grab, but rather one of those people who let things and people, hours and days, slide past them and flow away and escape. Far away from his parents, from whom the ocean separated him, and from his grandfather, who scarcely ever wrote to him, this good but lazy boy, sensitive and shy, surrendered himself to the rhythm of the passing months.

Geneva, where he found himself so free and so flattered, also provided him with opportunities of wandering about by himself, or with his little comrades, along lanes and through thickets, on the trail of a guilty cat, or in pursuit of one of those furtive and ambiguous pleasures which make up the mysterious joy of childhood.

One day Benny went to see the giantess, and admired her arm, which was at thick as a man's body, and as dirty as more than one man's. He decided to beat a hasty retreat, for the pleasure of the sense of sight did not compensate for the suffering of the sense of smell. Another day he marveled at the famous Pinetti, who tore up handkerchiefs and seemed to recreate them out of nothing again by some miraculous art. He also went to see wild animals fighting and other curious spectacles.

But his real delight was his vagabonding in company with Louis Gabriel Cramer and Cooper Johonnot. They made up the finest gang in the world. Johonnot had just arrived from America, since his grandfather, the famous Doctor Cooper, the greatest preacher in Boston, had insisted that he should study in Europe. Long and lank, shrewd and self-assured, Johonnot contributed to simple Benny and careless Gabriel ideas in which they were lacking.

Gabriel had received everything from life, and found it all very pleasant. So he did not put himself out in the least, being sure that everything would continue to come his way. Benny had been jostled about by life, and thrust from one corner of the planet to another without having anything to do but accept the situation with resolute courage. He went on throwing himself becomingly into all the adventures that piled themselves upon him. But Johonnot, a magician, or a mystic, had learned that life was just a matter of knack, and he taught some of the tricks of it to his comrades.

This band of three devoted themselves to great deeds. As good Calvinists, as good Republicans, they had the instinct for justice, and their expeditions were often crusades. There was the summer crusade against the watchdog at the

Château Banquet. Benny had forgotten why the dog ought to be killed, but he knew that it had to be done. So they set out, one armed with a knife, another with a sword, and Benny without anything. Unfortunately the dog had the bad manners to choose Benny as his adversary, and tore his clothes. "The others," said Benny, "arrived, but a bit late," so that this was rather a trial trip than an accomplished expedition.

Then there was the spring crusade against the carnivorous cat which had killed their guinea pig. This time it was a highly moral tale. Johonnot had toothache, and during this time the guinea pigs had young. To take his mind off himself, Johonnot went to tea at Madame Serre's, and the cats seized their chance. One of the young disappeared. Benny was indignant, and Johonnot suggested that they should smoke out a cat, guilty or innocent.

Accordingly on Sunday, March 6, 1783, on the eve of the day when they were dictated a theme of piety at the College about repentance, Johonnot and Benny put to death a cat which, so far as they knew, had nothing to repent. But they had the satisfaction, once the execution was over, of learning from some neighbors that their victim was probably the guilty party. The cat had been seen carrying away the little guinea pig. Benny was filled with a sense of righteousness which proved the good effect on him of Calvinist instruction.

He developed. All his body and mind awakened amid the innocent joys and the sweet flattery of Geneva. For the first time in his life, events had ceased to push him about. For the first time, the present spread around him, secure and calm, without the risk of some new incident turning up at any moment to break it like a glass or dissolve it like a dream. Benny could sit down at his table as he used to do in Philadelphia, and he was able to keep his little diary. He looked out of the window at the snow which spread away into the distance, shining, unsullied, solid and substantial. Down there towards Plainpalais there were fine ice rinks. He took up his pen, and on the virgin sheet, in regular, firm writing, he noted down a decision. "I propose to do nothing but skate during my hours of recreation, and for that reason I mean to forget my diary altogether until next year." So he wrote on December 5, 1782. Accordingly the rest of this month remains in his diary as white as was the ice over which he glided, and as white as his good boy's soul was white in white Geneva.

From the plain of Plainpalais to the slopes of Chantepoulet, from La Coulevrenière to Versonnex, the boys had the run of the town. There they met giants, hunchbacks and Savoyards, a big wolf which destroyed everything in the region of Sècheron, libertines who lay in wait for them; and one day they saw an old woman whose house fell down while she was putting on her shift, so that all the passers-by could contemplate her backside.

They also saw a revolution. On February 10, 1781, the party of the Representatives staged a *coup d'état* at the expense of the Constitutionalists, and they finished it off on April 8, 1782. It was a revolution of very big words, but of very small parties, very little disorder and very little panic. The Representatives declared themselves friends of reform and philosophy, and the Constitutionalists defenders of order and tradition. One might call the Representatives democrats and the Constitutionalists aristocrats; but, as a matter of fact, they were only two small groups in a town closely hemmed in by the mountains and closely watched by its neighbors.

[32]

Monsieur de Marignac, like a wise man who had a sense of his duty and of prudence, took refuge outside the town. Madame Cramer and her whole family, which had Constitutionalist leanings, fled to Sècheron. So, every morning, in order to get to the College, the boys had to take a walk; and henceforth all their tea parties were picnics.

But the revolution brought them other pleasures besides, since France, Switzerland and Piedmont, in order to restore order, sent troops to occupy the town and reëstablish the constitutional authority. The entrance of the troops was a fine sight, especially that of the French, who made their way in through a breach in the walls in the Cornavin district. The Swiss, for their part, had a depressed air about them, for they were uxorious fellows, and the idea of occupying Geneva while their wives were knitting at Lausanne or Glaris filled their hearts with sadness. As for the Piedmontese, they were swarthy and shifty-looking.

Finally the troops spread all over the town, and the Zurich contingent was quartered in the College. There were no more classes; or at least they had to be held in the masters' houses in the Rue Verdaine. This meant holidays, or at worst holiday courses; and henceforth the streets were nothing but a continuous circus.

In the other revolution which he had seen at home, Benny remembered squares crowded and clamorous, mobs in procession, rioting. Here there were only soldiers, reviews, parades and fêtes. It was gayer and more amusing. The boys kept hanging around the troops, in the hope of seeing some scuffle or other. Sometimes a French soldier would quarrel with a Swiss, or a Piedmontese would assail a Frenchman. Once, at the theater, poor M. Martin was pommeled by a French officer on whose foot he trod while he was making his way to his seat; the next day he had the honor of being run through and declared himself satisfied.

The Piedmontese were the most interesting, for they delighted to prick the arms of impolite burghers with the points of their sabers. Their reputation was very bad, and Benny heard many stories about them; but the most curious of all he could not understand, for unfortunately he had interrogated a man who stammered. This annoyed him very much, and he noted it down in his diary.

The finest spectacle of all was the feast of Saint Louis, when the French troops held their review, and then discharged thirty-six pieces of cannon, fired a salvo of three rounds of musketry, and let off Roman fire. The Piedmontese had nothing as fine as this, but they provided a stranger spectacle. They shot one of their own men who had stolen a few cents.

Surrounded by his regiment, the criminal was led forward, with a priest accompanying him. They sat him down on a grass slope and tied him to a stake, while the priest began his homily. It got finer and finer, more eloquent and thrilling; but he kept on edging away from the victim! On a signal from the officer, the squad fired. Then the regiment filed around the body and carried it away. Benny followed it step for step. He had learned how men are shot.

They were certainly far from empty days. A revolution teaches innumerable lessons. Here some French soldiers practised fencing, there Piedmontese played *morra;* and in a lane some Swiss soldiers raped a servant girl. Benny Bache made a note of everything, like a methodical, good boy.

But already he was growing up. Monsieur de Marignac had to have a dozen brand-new shirts made for his adolescent body. Benny was no longer a child, and, if he scarcely realized the fact himself, women were beginning to know it. One fine day there arrived from Philadelphia Mistress Dorcas Montgomery, who knew the Bache family. She hastened to claim acquaintance with Benny, and, when she met him, she could not restrain herself from testifying to her extreme fondness for him.

"Your son is very well," she wrote to Mrs. Bache, who did not appreciate her compliments in the least, "and a very charming boy; and is grown surprisingly. He retains his former likeness very much, save that his features are a little enlarged. His mouth is still that sweet little one. He begins to speak French pretty well. I wish it was in my power to describe to you my feelings and your son's look on our first meeting. His countenance blooming and animated, and I believe his black eyes were inclined to compliment mine, which overflowed upon our first meeting." In short, Mistress Dorcas Montgomery, who was a good forty and had a responsive heart, burst into floods of tears at the sight of Benny's smile.

However good you may be, you cannot very well ignore the fact that you are a fine young man, admired by ladies and influential people, blessed in the streets because of your grandfather, and fêted everywhere because of the fame of the people to whom you belong. People came and asked Benny to write to Doctor Franklin for some of the medals which he was getting struck in honor of the freedom of America. Benny wrote to him on his own account for books to read, for money to give a tea party, for thirty cents a week pocket money instead of ten, so that he could amuse himself better on Sundays.

M. de Marignac, who was keen about encouraging the industries of Geneva, and also about seeing his pupil live up

[35]

to the rank which belonged to him, suggested that he should get his grandfather to give him a fine gold watch, which Benny obediently requested; but the Doctor firmly refused it.

Benny consoled himself about it, for he was a good boy and a docile scholar. Accordingly he had learned a little Greek, some Latin, a good deal of theology, swimming, an odd orthography in which French was mixed up with English, some rudiments of drawing, and a little science. But, above all, among these good people who did not jostle him and left things around him alone, he had learned to live quietly, simply, cheerfully.

Emerging from his only too lengthy dream, he had learned at Geneva the hardness of the earth, the softness of the sun, and the vivifying freshness of the winter wind that came down from the mountains. He was still good, but he was beginning to be different from other people. More reserved, prouder, purer and shyer, he was also more courageous and more straightforward. So many eyes had been fixed on him that now he knew the boundaries which separated him from the rest of the world and the strength which he possessed in himself.

Whenever he could remember it, he was still obedient, whether his grandfather solemnly adjured him to date his letters or to write to his parents regularly, or urged him to preserve a republican simplicity of life or to go to the dentist's. But he started forgetting his duties in favor of his desires; for desires were awakening in him.

In the calm of Geneva, they came to birth. In contact with the real, hard earth, Benny began to be a real individual, — and a lonely one. Together with the happiness of being alive came the sorrow of being alone. He was depressed. He was restless.

[36]

He wrote to his grandfather:

"You are going to London, I hear, my dear Grandpapa. As I should have a very great desire of knowing those countries, and being extremely fond of voyaging, and above all other reasons being full of impatience to see you, I ask of you as a particular favor to permit me to go with you."

Summer came, peace came; and around Doctor Franklin, who did not go to London, rose the tide of old age. He could scarcely move, and, like all prisoners, he felt lonely. Benny's appeal touched him. He decided to recall the boy from Geneva, now that he must be a good Calvinist and a good Republican.

So ended the Genevese education of Benny Bache.

Book Two

THE EDUCATION OF A RADICAL

A PHILOSOPHICAL APPRENTICE

THE great Doctor Franklin's grandson! Around Benny at Geneva everybody had murmured these words. They had encompassed him with a halo of glory, they had rocked him to sleep; they had affected the attitude of everybody with whom he came in contact and the color of his whole life.

Wherever he went, he felt that his grandfather was with him to protect him, to watch over him as a father watches, as God watches. The longer the days went on, and the more Benny realized how far away he was from his grandfather, the more Franklin's majesty struck him as imposing, the more the sense of his power filled him with pride, and the more he missed his affection.

When, on July 19, 1783, after leaving the banks of the Seine, passing the monastery of the White Friars, and climbing the slopes of Passy, his carriage drove into the courtyard of the Hôtel de Valentinois, Benny could not wait any longer. He dashed into the house and flung himself into his grandfather's arms.

The old man was surprised. He remembered a shy, reserved child. He saw coming into his room a youth, slim but already strong, with the manners of a young gentleman and the yearning for affection of a heart even now rich in experience. Benjamin Franklin was touched. Temple had accustomed him to a rather frigid off-handedness, in

[41]

which affection seemed a form of politeness, and politeness a weapon of defence. Benny did not dream of standing on the defensive or of being simply polite; and at the same time he was gentle, charming and deferential.

Then the heart of the valiant old man swelled with love and longing, just as his mind swelled with wisdom and philanthropy. He had just achieved the finest victory of his life, by imposing on England, which was reluctant to accept it, on France, which was hesitant, and on the United States, which raised difficulties, an equitable and epoch-making peace. He was the center of admiration. Towards him flowed the eulogies of the whole world, and beside him the most charming women in the world, those Frenchwomen of Versailles and Paris, Auteuil and Passy, crowned him with a wreath of compliment and flattery.

The sight of Benny awakened other dreams of pride in him. He decided to make the young man his master-piece.

Poor lad! They had already taught him reading, writing and the Episcopalian catechism in Philadelphia. At Passy he had received lessons in dancing, riding, deportment, and French. In Geneva they had lavished good Calvinist precept and example on him, and taught him Greek, Latin, drawing, the French of Switzerland, and virtue. The insatiable Franklin decided on the spot that, in order to "finish" him, Benny should be sent to England to learn the English language, English ways, and the English idea of liberty.

After that, Benny would lack nothing, and, following in his grandfather's footsteps at one stride, and in imitation of his cousin, he would undoubtedly become a high official of the United States, a diplomat. This idea filled the Doctor with a glow of joy. It delighted him to dream about it. He even talked about it.

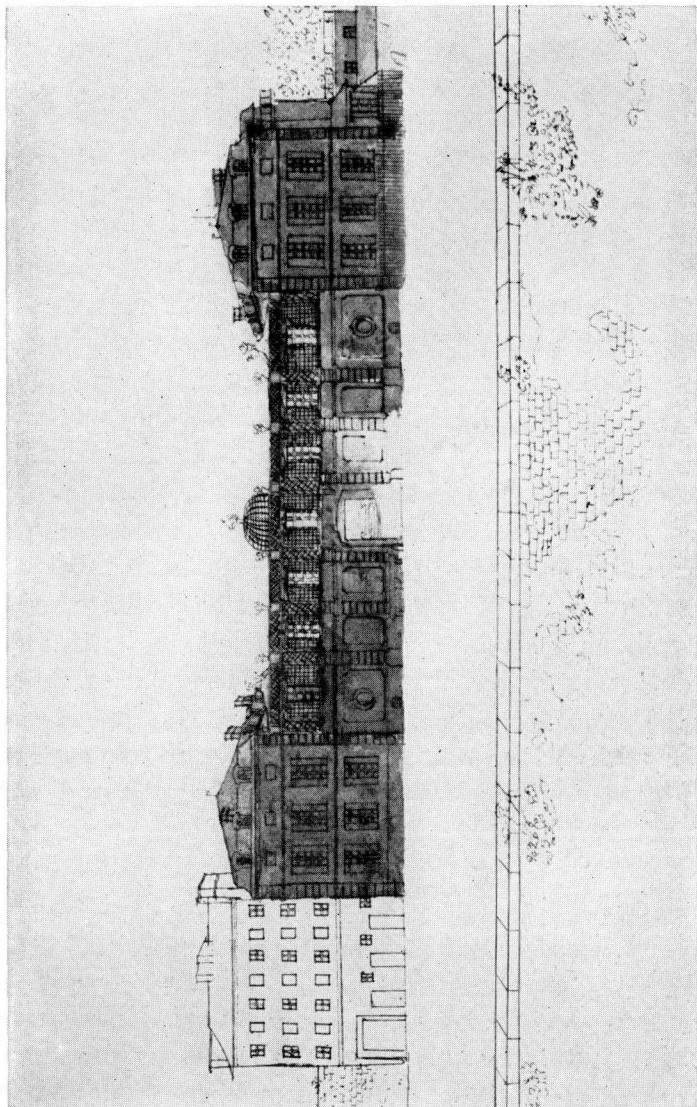

A VIEW OF THE HOUSE OF FRANKLIN IN PASSY

But it made Benny cry. He did not so much mind being a diplomat, or anything else, if they insisted; but he simply refused to be a masterpiece of education. He wanted to stay in this home which he had found again. They showed him portraits of his mother and his father, whom he could no longer recognize. They told him of his little brother William, a baby when he left America, and now, so they said, a very wide-awake young gentleman, who in no way resembled the idea which Benny had formed about him. They talked to him about his little sister Elizabeth, and about his brother Louis and his other sister Deborah, whom he had never seen.

Temple showed him letters, pictures, papers, told him stories and explained things to him enough to make him realize all that he had lost. He did not whine; but his wretchedness was so obvious that it made everybody pity him.

Temple was not one of those people who are easily given to pity, at least for other people; but he was beginning to be sorry for himself. For the past seven years he had been living with his grandfather in the capacity of secretary, confidant, factotum, and *alter ego*. He was fed up with glory, and sometimes he even let it be seen that he was weary of the old man's wisdom, and that his grandfather's warm affection palled on him a little.

Benny arrived as a gift from Heaven. He was docile and simple-minded. He was by no means suffering from a surfeit of sentimentalism; he was not saturated with sagacity and disgusted with devotion. All this was fresh meat to him; and he ought to have a good appetite for it.

Doctor Franklin might have ignored Benny's unhappiness; but he had lost the habit of being able to make up his mind for himself, and he bowed before Temple's stern will. The business which piled up around him, the documents which lay in disorder on his desk and on every table in the house, the confused activity which centered upon him, and in whose midst he reigned serene and majestic, but a little dumbfounded, had ended by handing him over to the elegant and conceited, ready and decided young man who was his son's son. The sullen hostility which Franklin sensed in Temple's attitude made the old man's affection for him more anxious, more disposed to pacify him and give way to him.

Benny's tears and a few curt sentences of Temple's settled the matter.

Then there began for Benny a life of enchantment.

Rising at six o'clock in the morning, and even earlier in summer, he disputed with the sun the pleasure of awakening his canaries, his dear canaries. He filled their little bath with fresh water and gave them seed and cake. He admired their seriousness when they were broody and waxed indignant over their ferocious frivolity when they broke their eggs almost as soon as they were laid. They were the great joy, and the great tragedy, of that quiet, furtive life of his, — that life which children hide from their parents, but which fills the emptiness of their indolent existence and colors those big eyes of theirs, that look at the world without seeing it and people it with their own fantastic mirages.

With them alone did he share his room; for now, at his grandfather's, he had his own room and his books and his servants. He was no longer a shifting shadow in a world immense and strange; he had a home and people and things that were his very own. He arranged his belongings in his drawers — his knives and his bits of string, the canaries' nest and his skates for the winter, lettuce seed and drawing-thread, sulphur, camphor, plaster of Paris, garter buckles, pins, shuttlecocks and even worms for fishing, for which he paid the gardener twelve cents.

Then he went out into the garden, always full of something new and thrilling. With his little friend Alexander he played at battledore and shuttlecock, or shot with a bow; and, when an arrow stuck in a high branch, they had to climb the tree to get it. Sometimes they used a ladder, but that did not prevent them from missing their footing and tumbling down, at the risk of breaking their necks and tearing their coats and trousers, and being highly delighted over it.

Everything that happened in the garden meant something. One day Benny discovered a mourning sword, a little bent, lying among the spearwort — belonging, no doubt, to some libertine who had been paying a visit to one of the chambermaids by night. Another day a friend of Monsieur de Chaumont's fell in the dusk into the ditch which surrounded the park. He ought to have broken his neck, but he did not, although he turned three somersaults, and Benny could never understand what had saved him. Maybe he was drunk.

One morning, under the trees, they found an eaglet which was fluttering clumsily. The boys gave it a pigeon to eat, the gardeners made a cage of broken trellis for it, and the philosophers said that it was a present from Jupiter to his colleague, the other god of thunder, Franklin. The poets put it into verse, which the papers published.

But the garden was finest of all in winter, when it froze hard, the snow covered the ground, and the ponds were frozen. Then Benny, armed with a broom of dry twigs, carefully brushed the ice. He put his bedroom in order, shut up his books, locked up his diary at the back of a drawer, and then he skated as long as he liked — two hours, three hours, all day long.

With the thaw came the boredom of spring, but with the warmth came its pleasures. The whole village was a garden where everybody felt at home. They paid visits and gossiped, the houses were full of people, through open windows came the sound of music, and laughter rang out from the gardens. Everybody planted and cultivated according to his fancy. Roses climbed along the terraces, and on the slopes the grapes ripened.

The Seine became warm, and Benny ceased to think about anything but swimming. He did not care about the rascals who came and stole one's clothes, or about the clumsy fellows who got themselves drowned in an eddy. He was a young insurgent, supple and strong, who had swum in the Delaware at the age of six and in the Lake of Geneva at the age of twelve, and he was not in the least afraid of the Seine, despite its current and its traffic.

He piled his clothes on his head, and then, with steady strokes, cradled by the water which caressed his body, he swam across the river. Sometimes some loose change fell into the stream, and Benny duly noted in his diary: "lost while bathing, one livre ten sous." Other times he met the *galiote* and had to dive to avoid it, or perhaps it washed the clothes off his head into the water. But what did that matter? At nightfall the half-naked boy on his way home met nobody but indifferent strangers, or friends who smiled at him.

Everything was a delight — the rain, the snow and the frost that changed the look of the countryside, the long sunny days that threw the fields and the roads open to anything that the heart of man could desire. If it was a torrid afternoon, Benny went off and fished in a quiet backwater, shaded by the willows, remote from noisy boys and the vexation of *galiotes*. When the cool of evening fell, he went for a long walk, and cutting across the fields, light of foot, raced Temple's cabriolet home.

Everything was a delight; and everything would have been sheer bliss if he had had companions of his own age. But at Passy he no longer found either Deane, who was mentioned only in a whisper since his father's treason, or Cochran, who had gone back to America. He had lost Johonnot, who had also sailed for home; but Doctor Franklin did not regret it, for Johonnot's vivid imagination and his flights of fancy made the philosopher distrust him. Louis Gabriel Cramer was celebrating his first communion at Geneva before going to serve the King of France at the military academy at Colmar. Robert Montgomery, together with the sentimental Mistress Dorcas Montgomery, was on the point of starting home to Philadelphia.

Sometimes they brought a French boy to play with him. His name was Boisroger, and he was at school at Passy. But there is no intimacy between children unless they have secrets to share, and Boisroger was too well behaved at table. Alexander suited Benny better. He was the son of a friend of Franklin's and lived with them. Alexander swam, fished, shot with bow and arrows and played the fool as a boy ought to do.

Benny was very fond of him. He sympathized with him when he had a stomach ache. He forgave him for opening the door of the canaries' cage. Fortunately the canaries had more sense than Alexander. They made a voyage of exploration around the room, but they did not fly out of the window, although it was open. Alexander and Benny and the canaries understood one another. Unhappily, in the fall

Alexander went to England; and Benny was left alone with the philosopher and the canaries.

There was Temple, of course. Temple was ten years older than Benny, and during these ten years he had seen a lot of things and people — especially ladies. He was handsome and dressed well. He wore red heels and was always changing his fine shirt frill. He had a smart cabriolet and a thoroughbred horse. His dog Boulet was well brushed, and his lackey had a spruce air about him.

Temple was kind-hearted enough. He liked to take Benny with him to drink tea with elderly ladies to whom he had nothing particular to say, and rewarded him for his company by bringing him to Vauxhall in the winter, to see the Royal Troupe of Dancers, or even to the theater. He showed him the Saint Germain Fair and the illuminations for the birth of the Dauphin and those which celebrated the peace.

He had not much more sense than Benny. One fine day, when Madame Le Veillard had entrusted them with two bottles of syrup of vinegar for the Doctor's kitchen, they contrived to break one of them, which made a mess of the carriage and their clothes. There was nothing of the mentor about Temple. All he could teach Benny was to laugh at the American ladies of Paris, their big feet and their unpolished manners, and to joke about Mrs. Montgomery's addiction to tears and Miss Adams' pedantic ways. But Benny remained respectful.

Temple might also have taught him how to please the fair sex. He was not backward himself, either in intrigues or in successes. In August, 1783, Sir James Nicolson one fine day discovered in his wife's wardrobe a number of letters from Temple and other sentimental souvenirs. On the other hand, he could not find a certain familiar miniature of hers, and finally she burst into tears and confessed that Temple had "stolen" it from her. Sir James, almost as deficient mentally as matrimonially, filled Paris and Passy with his protestations. He complained bitterly to Temple, demanding immediate restitution of the "stolen" property, and even carried his complaints to Doctor Franklin. With a flourish, Temple retorted that he would always be glad to exchange one portrait for another.

He was at the moment in pursuit of something better than any picture. He was after the dowry of Mlle. Brillon de Jouy, daughter of the rich M. Brillon de Jouy, receiver-general of consignments to the royal council. Her dowry was to his taste, and so was the girl herself. He had had some good drinking bouts with her father, which ought to have prepared the ground. Her mother, charming, weak and affectionate, was too fond of the Doctor to refuse him anything. As for the girl, Temple knew how to get around her heart. What woman could resist him?

To make assurance doubly sure, he had taken his close friends, the Chevalier de Saint Olympe and the Chevalier de Beauharnois, and the *abbés* Chalut and Arnoux, into his confidence. He had accomplices on the spot, Donatien Le Ray de Chaumont and Louis Le Veillard, who acted as spies and scouts for him. With their support, with his grandfather's glory, and with his own charm and address, he felt sure of winning. But he was wrong.

When the marriage plan was broached to Madame Brillon, she burst into floods of ready tears and kissed her dear Papa Franklin over and over again. Then she consulted her lawyer, and, in a letter equally emotional, she refused her daughter's hand.

That day Benny's canaries had laid two eggs. This consoled him for the sorrow which reigned in the house. To console himself, Temple had Blanchette Caillot, young and tender, white and pretty, who gave him assignations at twilight and sent him missives moist with the tears that welled from her heart. It was a heart all too responsive, which lured her body into charming sin, with the result that Temple became a father and poor Blanchette wept harder than ever.

Temple did not weep. He knew how to dodge, and, as Blanchette was married, nothing could be easier. He went driving in his cabriolet, taking Benny with him, and talked to him to distract himself, and for the pleasure of instructing somebody else. He was quite ready to take Benny's education in hand. But the boy was too bashful to lend himself to women's ways.

Only his grandfather could educate him and bring him on in the world. The garden at Passy, at this time, was the Mecca of philosophy and philandering. All the great ones of the earth, potent princes, sophisticated savants, archimandrites, nuncios, reigning beauties, generals covered with glory and financiers laden with gold, besieged Doctor Franklin's drawing-room. Benny, even though he lurked at the door or hid behind the old man's armchair, could not escape all this fawning on his fame, all this affectionate flattery. It embarrassed him, even though it enchanted him. M. Le Veillard took him to dinner one evening at the Duc de La Rochefoucauld's. "There were a lot of dukes and duchesses," he said, "which abashed me." Still, he got used to all this.

In September, Prince Henry of Prussia came to see his grandfather, with the Duke of Dorset. Benny was in the next room. He was playing; and, despite the servants who urged him to go and look at one of the great people of the

[50]

world, he went on playing. He cared nothing about great people, and, besides, his hands were dirty.

Some indiscreet person told the prince that there was a grandson of Doctor Franklin's in the next room, who was too shy to present himself to such a great prince. "All right," cried the prince, "I'll go and see him myself," and so he did. Benny was tongue-tied, and he could hardly answer the questions which the prince asked him, very courteously, about France and Switzerland. Still, he noticed that the prince "was very small, plain of face, very simply dressed, and had only one pin to attach his frill to his shirt." Temple's lessons were bearing fruit.

As a rule, he was less critical, and contented himself with running away or taking refuge with the more human of these great personages. Among these fine ladies, sages and dandies there was always somebody with the temperament of shepherd or shepherdess, some rustic soul who loved Nature; and Benny could always get on with anybody like that. He wrote in his diary in the summer of 1784: "I went to lunch in Passy with my grandfather at M. d'Hardancourt's, and to tea at Monsieur d'Ailly's; I amused myself there by watering the strawberries with some other gentlemen and ladies who were with him."

He got on best of all with his grandfather. Of course, he had his masters and professors, and they taught him dancing, fencing, and Latin in accordance with the fashion of the time; but he took more interest in drawing, in penmanship in the English style, and in science, for he knew that his grandfather had chosen these subjects for him. Above all, he applied himself to feeling in the same way as Doctor Franklin, and thinking along the same lines as he did.

He accompanied him to lectures in physics at the Musée de Paris. He sat beside his chair during the little concerts which the Doctor's lady friends improvised to enliven the long hours at Passy. Sometimes it was Madame Helvétius who brought her "little stars", as she called her daughters, and his "opera" as Franklin called them; or else her rival in affection, Madame Brillon, came to play the piano, while Father Pagin or the famous violinist Vioti accompanied her. There were also Morellet's niece, and Mademoiselle Paradis, blind since the age of two.

They played Gluck; they played Haydn. Madame Brillon played her "March of the Insurgents", composed for Franklin in honor of the United States, and finally, to please the old man, she played "The Little Birds" or some simple, tuneful Scots air. Franklin nodded his head, said that he preferred simplicity in everything, including music, and drafted a dissertation to prove the superiority of Scots airs; and Benny wrote in his diary: "I did not like the music, because they only played those fine airs so mixed up that you can make nothing out of them."

He also shared his grandfather's enthusiasms; and he dreamed about balloons.

They were so fine, the balloons of that time! — big globes of colored paper, decorated with the royal "LL" or the arms of France. Adorned with festoons and garlands, they ascended with the pompous, naïve majesty of the hopes of the period. Sometimes they carried aloft in their rope or wicker baskets a sheep or a fowl, offered as a sacrifice to science by admiring, scared men. At other times, aëronauts themselves took the risk of climbing up into the sky, where they were to be seen disappearing, while they waved their plumed hats and their multicolored streamers in the wind.

Doctor Franklin became an enthusiast all at once, and Benny was fascinated. The Doctor started observing bal-

[52]

loons wherever there were balloons. When he could not go himself, he sent Temple or Benny. He got them to write reports, descriptions, summaries for him; and he drew up learned considerations for learned societies. He discussed the inventions of the brothers Montgolfier, and Charles' improvements; the attempts by Pilatres de Rozier and the fine achievement of Jeffries, who crossed the English Channel with Blanchard, though they had to strip themselves stark naked to lighten their balloon, and then had to spend twenty-four hours in a tree top, waiting for help and a couple of pairs of trousers.

Benny listened in enchantment. He got up before dawn to observe the experiments of the Duc de Chartres. He manipulated a telescope so as to lose nothing of the movements of the balloon, light and clumsy at one and the same time. One night he sat up late when he heard that the Duc de Crillon, the Spanish Ambassador, was sending up a balloon in honor of the birth of two *Infantes*. He was richly rewarded. About one o'clock in the morning, quite close to Franklin's house, there emerged from the trees of the Bois de Boulogne a big, brilliant ball, adorned with a gorgeous lantern. Benign, bewitched, it climbed above the bare branches and, swaying gently in the very still night, soared up into the sky to join the other stars, which the cold of winter seemed to have frozen.

Benny, not stopping at mere admiration, made a balloon for himself with gold-beater's skin and "inflammable air". It was a friendly, polite balloon. For several days it bobbed against the ceiling of his room, which it refused to leave, under the shining eyes of Benny, the philosophical observation of Doctor Franklin, and the startled stare of the canaries.

But it was no joking matter. Doctor Franklin, who some-

[53]

times had difficulty about believing in God, believed in balloons at once. It would not have taken much to make him contemplate a journey to the moon. Half in jest, half in earnest, he sometimes talked about such a journey; but it was in all seriousness that he demonstrated how balloons were henceforth going to prevent war. What state, indeed, would be able to defend its frontiers against five thousand balloons, well armed and provisioned? Balloons, as weapons of war, would impose peace on princes by terror, and shed enlightenment on peoples.

If some sceptic jeered at balloons, Doctor Franklin, an expert in scepticism himself, knew how to put him in his place. "What is the use of this new invention?" such a rude person might ask. "What is the use of a new-born child?" retorted the sage.

But, above all, he was interested in the control of balloons, and he encouraged Benny to construct kites. With Alexander or with Williams, Benny went to the carpenter's. He bought hickory staves and a hoop. Then he adjusted, and glued, and whittled until he had made a fine big kite. He ran full speed along the slopes above the Seine to launch his apparatus on the wings of the wind. On the banks the hoodlums of Vaugirard and the neighboring villages watched him, fearfully and suspiciously; and, on the highroad, fine ladies stopped their carriages to see better. He had to keep off the inquisitive and the acquisitive, run his hardest to defend his kite when it fell down, watch out for the masts of the *galiote*, plunge into the river and swim across if the wind carried the kite over.

Benny was crazy about it. He, too, made up a minor philosophy for himself. His successes filled him with pride; but bad luck did not dampen his courage. Had not his grandfather tamed the lightning with a kite?

[54]

A PHILOSOPHICAL APPRENTICE

How fine it was to be alive at his age, when wisdom came so easily and so pleasantly! Sometimes Doctor Franklin sighed and told Benny how he regretted that he was not as young as Benny was, for the years to come would see so many great discoveries, so many changes, that it was hard for a mind as curious as his own to have to miss them. Meanwhile he found his heart's delight in philosophical hopes and dreams, in intellectual conversation and in philanthropic teaching. He molded Benny's mind with an eye to those days of the future, which were going to be so brilliant that one had only too little time to prepare himself for the assured happiness of humanity and the blinding triumph of enlightenment.

Everything was enlightened at Passy, and even the trees contributed to the wisdom of men. It was a fine sight when Doctor Franklin's garden itself coöperated with the great man's mind to unmask the charlatanry of Monsieur Mesmer, and the boys could not contain themselves for joy. In Paris, Monsieur Deslon, a disciple of M. Mesmer's, had the whole town and Court running after him. He electrified duchesses and cured chimney-sweeps. Around his magic tub financiers and marchionesses joined hands, and before his door, around the tree which in his charity he had charged with electricity, shoe-shiners and lady's maids formed a chain to get a cure, or at least a shock.

Only at Versailles the Queen, only at Passy Doctor Franklin, remained incredulous; but these two great personages induced the Academy of Science to set up a tribunal to judge Monsieur Deslon. The tribunal assembled at Doctor Franklin's, where the magnetiser had been invited to come and perform; and here is what Benny saw on Saturday, May 22, 1784 — here it is in his own words:

[55]

"M. Deslon made several passes with his wand against a tree. Then they brought out, with his eyes bandaged, a young man whom M. Deslon had brought with him (and who had been cured of a paralysis, which affected half his body, in the space of three months by means of animal magnetism). They made him hold on to several trees for two minutes. At the three first trees which he clasped in this way he felt, so he said, a shock which increased from tree to tree; finally, at the fourth, he clung to the tree and made no reply when he was questioned. Then he fell down and they carried him on to the grass, where he went through some strange contortions." But the poor fellow had mistaken the tree. Deslon hadn't touched the tree which had given him his fit.

The Doctor came to the conclusion that Deslon was a charlatan and that the electricity set in motion by him had nothing magnetic about it. The scientific jury backed him up in a fine report, which was not shown to the ladies. The Doctor confided to Temple: "Some feel that consequences may be drawn from it by infidels to weaken our faith in the miracles of the New Testament." But Temple sneered: "You fix the prophets all right, Grandfather! What would be left of Jeremiah, if this is how you treat M. Deslon?"; and Franklin nodded his head, for he never contradicted Temple.

He had given up preaching morality to him; but he preached it to Benny. During the winter evenings, Benny read to him after supper until nine o'clock at night. When he was tired, or when the Doctor felt so disposed, Benny stopped reading, and then Franklin would tell the attentive boy some anecdote or aphorism, always to the point, always witty. He preached virtue to him, but by no means in the manner of Geneva. "If criminals knew all the advantages of virtue," he said to Benny, "they would all be dishonest enough to turn honest."

Then he preached economy to him. Once in Philadelphia, he told him, a Quaker had accosted him one Sunday when he was wearing a white vest.

"My friend, thou art wearing a vest which is not thine own; or at least thou hast not paid what it must cost thee."

"I beg your pardon, I have paid the tailor's account in full."

"That is the least part of what it will cost thee. I see plainly that, when thou didst buy it, thou didst not think of the laundryman."

Benny, delighted to feel himself so wise at such small cost, filled his little diary with his grandfather's fine words and stored in his mind all the lessons of his wisdom.

He was too good and too obedient to measure everything that his grandfather said to him. He could see the audacity of certain of his quips well enough. When Franklin, bringing a saying of Poor Richard's up-to-date, declared that "the King's cheese is half wasted in parings; but no matter, it is made of the people's milk," Benny had no difficulty in understanding him. Again, when the Doctor rejoiced over the multiplication of sects and religions, on the ground that competition is a good thing in any line of business and improves the quality of the merchandise, there was nothing mysterious about that either.

But to such downright remarks as these Franklin preferred those "kind of underhand jokes" whose veiled boldness charmed his fine lady admirers and made his clerical friends laugh. When he suggested to the Papal Nuncio that he should get the Pope to ordain two American Episcopalian clergymen who refused to go to London to be ordained, and insinuated that the Pope had a striking opportunity here of demonstrating his philanthropy, he charmed the good Madame Helvétius, but Benny endorsed what he said without being very clear about what he meant.

No small boy could possibly understand everything that went on under Doctor Franklin's roof at the Hôtel de Valentinois, and in the coach house where he had his printing press. Grown-ups themselves were at a loss there, and only the most knowing ladies could understand the Doctor's silences and smiles. There were so many people always coming and going, so many people writing, so many people begging for favors.

The vulgar public saw nothing in all this; but initiated friends were full of admiration, — and sometimes of consternation. During this summer of 1784, when Benny read aloud to him, Franklin did the most daring thing that he had ever done to date: he inaugurated the French Revolution.

He had a young friend, with a bluff, bland, bloated face, who had just come out of prison, had just changed his wife, and for these reasons needed money. He also had a thirst for glory. Franklin promised him both if he would write what he told him and boldly sign the first open attack on the hereditary principle; and Monsieur le Comte de Mirabeau agreed, though with some trepidation.

Then Doctor Franklin handed him an English manuscript. It was a diatribe against the Society of the Cincinnati, a military order which had just been established in the United States among former officers, under the presidency of General Washington. In order to perpetuate the memory of their great deeds and their comradeship in arms for ever, these officers of the War of Independence had founded this institution and had made membership of it hereditary. Though the society had the most pacific objects and no very great influence, one hundred per cent Americans waxed indignant about it. Protests were raised in all directions.

Franklin heard about this in January, 1784. He immediately drafted a pamphlet, which he got Morellet to translate. Then he acquired the services of Mirabeau and sent him to London to polish his work at his leisure — keeping a wary eye on Madame de Nehra at the same time. It was not until July that he let him come back for a reading of the pamphlet, to which Franklin added a few sarcastic touches of his own. Finally the finished product was printed in London quietly and quickly, and broadcast throughout France towards the fall.

In the newspapers and in the drawing-rooms it made a great stir. "M. de Mirabeau is attacking the Monarchy," people said; "M. de Mirabeau is attacking the nobility." Doctor Franklin nodded his head. "M. de Mirabeau is attacking Washington," said M. Grimm, rather shocked. Doctor Franklin kept on nodding his head, while M. de Mirabeau raised his arms to Heaven. "What could I do? Franklin wanted me to do it." The docile Victor de Mirabeau had obeyed him, just as Benny obeyed him.

Everybody was carried away by the patient, dominating strength which the Doctor had in him. Fine ladies, philosophers, priests, financiers and adolescents — they were all in his hands, just like that electricity which he alone knew how to handle.

To all of them he was a god, and he might have believed that he was one himself if America had let him. But America did nothing of the kind.

From America, by every mail, bad news reached the Doctor; and Temple who was close to him, Benny who was close to him, could see his hands tremble and his eyes look despondent whenever he opened a letter from overseas.

In the United States Congress, Adams had denounced him as a traitor who had sold himself to France, and Mr. Lee of Virginia kept on pursuing him with his hatred. There was a majority in Congress only too ready to make him expiate his popularity in Europe. If the King of France had permitted it, Franklin would long since have been recalled.

As they could not strike him in person, they avenged themselves on his relatives. Richard Bache had been deprived of his office as Postmaster-General, from which he was dismissed like any lackey. William Temple Franklin might beg Congress for a diplomatic post, and the Doctor might set forth his merits and overwhelm his best friends in Congress with cordial, beseeching and eloquent letters: Temple was refused any post whatever. He even lost the one which he had held throughout the war, and an officer, a friend of Washington, Colonel David Humphreys, was appointed secretary to the Paris Embassy.

It was in vain that the old Doctor writhed. This last blow was too much for him. That, to clear himself, he should have to ask his collaborators, American diplomats who were his juniors, for certificates of his loyalty — this he could accept; for he was used to democracy's mean deals. That people should be jealous of him, and in a hurry to see him making room — for this he could console himself; for he had had his time, and he wanted a rest. But to the fact that they should rage against his grandson he could not resign himself; for he remembered that he had taken Temple away from William in order to make a good American of him, and that he had robbed the youth of his father in order to give him to the United States.

He could feel anger and embitterment rising in Temple's

heart. The young man's overtures for ingratiating himself with Mr. Adams and Mr. Jay, coming to an understanding with Mr. Lee, and detaching himself from his grandfather, were scarcely tactful. His anxiety to see his father again was manifest. The intimacy which had linked Doctor Franklin with his grandson had meant nothing to Temple but a career — henceforth a career without an issue, which was simply a burden to him. He was exasperated with his impertinent servants and his tearful lady friends, and he could not stand his grandfather any longer. He set off for London.

Franklin was left alone with his unwarming glory, and with Benny. He was too wise to complain, too human not to suffer, and still too keenly alive not to try and go on living, despite everything, to try and live down everything. Temple had turned away from him. Already the old man could no longer see his clear-cut, hard profile except through a mist — the mist of his own tears of absence, of separation. On the other hand, close beside him, turned towards him, Benny's young face, impressionable and keen, was like a mirror of his last hopes, a reflection of his first desires.

Benny was now sixteen. He was tall and strong, but he had remained slight and preserved the grace of adolescence. When he ran, swam or fenced, his movements were quick and virile; but with his grandfather, with children and with women he had the gentleness of a girl. His black eyes looked straight in front of him fearlessly and confidently. Sometimes they shone with eager enthusiasm, but as a rule they were veiled and seemed rather to glide over people than to concentrate on them.

From his errant childhood he had kept the habit of being a dreamer in the very heart of action, enjoying the sweetness of solitude in the midst of the most animated company. Few things seemed to touch him or affect him. He was accessible only to the tenderest of emotions. His heart expanded only to those ideas which were at once the most general and the most generous. He was incapable of loving people unless he respected them. Before his eyes Benjamin Franklin shone like a god.

The old man wanted to return him the compliment and make an angel out of him, or at least a kind of modern hero. He would not spoil him as he had spoiled Temple. He would not hand him over to the flattery of women and courtiers. He would by no means let him intoxicate himself with that worldly incense which ruined young Americans forever when they lived in Paris. He would give him the habit of hard work, to which he had himself once owed his return to the paths of virtue, his making of a fortune, and his winning of glory and peace of mind.

In order to round off Benny's philosophical apprenticeship, he decided to make a printer out of him. At the outset, from November, 1784 to March, 1785, he gave him as his master a printer and type founder, M. Emery, who came to Passy every day. He supervised their work himself; it revived in him delightful memories of his own adventurous, hard childhood.

From London his good friend Mrs. Hewson, a widow and a philosopher, still young but already settled down, came to keep him company with her three children, — William, Thomas and Eliza. Whereas the preceding winter had been long and hard, covering the ground with snow from Christmas to the end of March, that of 1784-1785 was mild and rainy, though just as protracted. In the Hôtel de Valentinois, in the heart of deserted Passy, amid closed houses, empty streets and leafless gardens, Doctor Franklin and his little family led a patriarchal life. They had breakfast together early. They parted to go and work. They dined together and read around the fire, while the children played cards. In the evening, while the wind whistled outside, Mrs. Hewson made tea in the English way, and the Doctor drank it in little sips and told tales of long ago.

In the spring Benny, whose progress had been rapid, was sent to Monsieur Didot the elder, the best printer in France and in the world, to learn the delicate art of engraving and perfect himself in all the details of his craft. He no longer lived at Passy, but he went back there on Saturdays and holidays.

On such occasions he visited Paris with Mrs. Hewson. On Good Friday he took her to see the concourse of courtesans, who were in the habit of parading in the Bois de Boulogne on that day in memory of the old hermitage at Longchamps. They went to the Invalides, where Benny was equally impressed by the shining marble chapels and the kitchen with its enormous cooking pots. They also went to Notre Dame, to the Foundling Hospital, where fifteen thousand of these little unfortunates were crowded, and to the King's review, at which he admired the uniforms of the Swiss Guards and those of the French Guards, and the ladies of the Court in their carriages.

Then he went back to M. Didot's, where for the whole week, mingling with the workmen, he toiled at his bench, armed with an engraving tool and a mallet.

At the end of the week, Temple, now back from London, came in his smart cabriolet to pick him up, and, when he had got the dirt off himself, took him to the theater to see "Georges Dandin" or to the Marquis de La Fayette's to dine with a duchess or two. On April 27, 1785, in Madame Le Roy's box, he saw "The Barber of Séville" played and found that the cast was excellent. But he was still more attracted by the fine spectacle which was staged in the

Place Louis XV on the night of the fête given in honor of the churching of the Queen.

An immense, gay crowd, gathered to celebrate the good news and admire the illuminations, packed the square. The façades of the buildings turned red and green under the light of Bengal fire, while other fireworks flung into the air their multicolored splendors, finer and more fantastic than ever because of the massive, heavy shadows cast by the great buildings around. Benny was struck dumb with delight when at the end, past midnight, after the firework finale, a rain of fire, incandescent and luminous, covered the whole square with its glory.

He loved such great spectacles as this, and he loved his work. He loved a pretty, gilded drawing-room full of fashionably dressed women, and a smoky workshop in which men labored, intent on their work. He loved the stir of the crowd in a great city, and the silence which spread at nightfall over a peaceful room in which a wood fire crackled. He loved the variety of life and its diversity. He believed in the happiness of mankind and in their wisdom. He had confidence in their straightforwardness and their steadfastness, and in the justice of the Supreme Being.

His grandfather had once been a workingman, with a frenzy for work, who sacrificed everything to make himself master of the tools of his trade, and then used them to conquer the world. Benny was no workingman, nor was he frenzied about work. His work was a kind of game, good for the body, good for the mind, in which he found pleasure, but to which he did not devote himself any more than to the other games which life offered. He derived his happiness, not from what he did, or what he wanted to do, but from what he was.

[64]

Whatever Benjamin Franklin might have attempted, France had turned Temple Franklin and Benny Bache into two men of quality. Incidentally, and unintentionally, Franklin had made a libertine out of Temple, whereas he had made a philosopher out of Benny Bache. Now the job was done. Nobody could help it — not even that wise old man.

For that matter, the old France was finished too. Faced with the growing deficit which threatened to swallow up the Kingdom, Vergennes, the last great Minister of the French monarchy, was working himself to death.

Doctor Franklin's mission was ended as well. On May 4, 1785, he finally received from Congress the long-feared, long-desired permission to return to the United States.

Another sage, another philosopher, Thomas Jefferson of Virginia, the draftsman of the Declaration of Independence, was to replace him as Minister of the youngest and most rustic of Republics to the oldest and most urbane of Monarchies.

A sudden sense of joy carried the heart of Doctor Franklin by storm. He was going home. He would be able to die in peace, with his own people around him. But this return of his was, in itself, an exile. Alas! How was he henceforth to know peace anywhere on earth — he who called himself a "cosmopolitan," and who had, in fact, become one to such an extent that, wherever he might be, he was always parted from most of his friends? His roving mind, his loving heart, had roamed the world so widely that only the width of the world itself could now provide him with hearth and home.

In Paris he had not felt this so much; for Paris was the heart of the world, and there you met everybody, sooner or later. In Philadelphia he would be like a child stuck in

[65]

a corner in disgrace. This would hurt him all the more in proportion as he had accustomed himself to the language of Paris, made up of half-words, of implied meanings, of sudden, bold association of ideas, of emotionalism sharpened by thought, of wisdom softened by feeling, of audacity always sobered by scepticism, purged by experience.

Where could he find in the future any such delight? Who could bestow upon him the incomparable flattery, the popularity which France had lavished upon him? Did they not warn him under their breath that he would be hissed on his arrival in America, denounced by the politicians and repudiated by the populace? Jefferson was so much afraid of his getting such a reception that he multiplied his letters to high personages overseas, telling them that Franklin ought to be well treated out of consideration for France. After nine years of peril, of daily struggle, Franklin, who had left America to defend her against her enemies, was on his way back to defend himself against his own compatriots.

"Ah!" he said to Madame Helvétius, "we are leaving France, the country that I love the most; and I am leaving my dear Helvétia here. She may be happy here. I am not so sure of being happy in America; but I must go there all the same."

Temple, too, made ready to return to this country, his own country, where he had spent just enough time to see his father ill-treated, arrested, and thrown into prison; this country of his which he had served long enough to gain clear proof of the fact that republics were ungrateful, as the philosophers said. For that matter, he did not waste too much time thinking about it. He had many farewells to make, he was in a fever; and he had found that thinking does not get you anywhere.

As for Benny, he had no time to think. His grandfather

[66]

who could not move, and his cousin who could not be bothered about moving, left it to him to do the packing. There were a hundred and twenty-eight cases to be packed. For a whole month Benny drove nails in, and saw to nails being driven in, without having any time at all to do anything else.

When the one hundred and twenty-eight packing cases were ready, on June 30, 1785, they were loaded on to a barge, and the Franklin household set off in a coach. Everybody wept, and so did Benny.

But, as they passed through Yvetot, he noticed "that all the women are lacking in hair on their foreheads, because of a certain kind of bonnet they wear which pulls it back and makes it fall out"; and he entered the fact in his diary. Then, when they put to sea, he saw a dolphin and made a sketch of it.

He was not seasick, he had left France, and he was sixteen.

CHAPTER II

THE SWEETNESS OF A HOME

THE city of brotherly love, Philadelphia, received Doctor Franklin and his grandsons, when they disembarked on September 13, 1785, with shouts of joy, ovations and processions, — in short, with an outburst of brotherly love.

As this was not what they expected, they were at first moved to tears. Then they looked around them.

Benny had plenty to look at — his father, who had aged a little and got much fatter; his mother, who seemed as strong as ever and handsomer than ever with her crown of white hair; William, who was quite the little gentleman, and his two little sisters and his two little brothers whom he had never seen before, Elizabeth and Deborah, Louis and Richard. As he kissed them, Benny gave himself up to those feelings which any decently born person must feel in such circumstances, but which, as he said himself, only writers can describe. He, after all, was still only a schoolboy. With that reflection ends the diary which he kept in French.

He looked at his grandfather too. Doctor Franklin moved among the crowd like a god. Women, children and men, old, adolescent and adult, leading citizens and urchins, rich and poor filled the streets and escorted him home with blessings and cheers. It was the sound of popularity, indistinct as the sea, intoxicating as wine.

All day long, all evening long, while they settled down

[68]

again, while they picked up the too long broken threads of familiar ties, while they recalled the names of servants and the position of the furniture and the lie of the rooms, and while Temple's Angora cats, restless and curious, roamed around the house, old friends and new friends, intimates and strangers, thronged around the Doctor.

The first official visitor whom he received was Richard Henry Lee, President of the Congress of the United States, his dearest, his most faithful, his most patient enemy, who came, in his own name and in the name of Congress, to express to him his high regard for him and the joy which his fortunate arrival gave him. They embraced with tears.

Then appeared a delegation from the Assembly of Pennsylvania, who came to tell him that his return delighted them, that his glory would endure throughout the generations, and that they wished him the best of health. He replied to them that he was touched by their good wishes, that his glory was due to them, and that he was well content if he had satisfied them.

Next the American Philosophical Society presented itself, old savants and famous doctors, who notified him in a body how proud they were to welcome him on his arrival, how proud to reëlect him their President, and how proud to reflect honor on philosophy in the person of a man who, "distinguished by his deep Investigations and many valuable Improvements in it, is known to be equally distinguished for his Philanthropy, Patriotism, and liberal Attachments to the Rights of human nature." To them he replied that the Society did him too much honor, that he congratulated them on their "laudable Endeavors for the Promotion of Useful Knowledge among us", and that he rejoiced to be their President.

[69]

Finally the Provost, the Vice-Provost, and the professors of the University of Pennsylvania, wearing their caps and gowns, advanced to felicitate him on his happy return, on his labors and his virtues, and on the admirable work which he had accomplished in founding the university where they taught and "exalting and refining the genius of America by the Propagation of useful Learning, and for qualifying many of her Sons to make that illustrious Figure, which has commanded the esteem and admiration of the most polished nations of Europe." To them he replied that it was very good of them to compliment him in this way, that they did well to instruct the young, for it was very necessary, and that they might indeed rejoice that they had trained virtuous men, for all else was vanity.

At last he could sit down. He was tired, and he was in a hurry to dictate letters to Benny for his friends in France, to tell them what a welcome he had received and how much he missed them.

He added that he had immediately been elected a member of the City Council by the people, president of the City Council by the city councillors, member of the Assembly of Pennsylvania by the electors, and president of the Assembly and of the Supreme Executive Council of Pennsylvania by the members of the Assembly and the Supreme Executive Council of Pennsylvania. He confessed that he had had the "weakness" to accept these appointments, for these marks of popular confidence and national gratitude had touched his heart.

He settled down in glory. But it was a glory with spikes on it.

Doctor Jeremy Belknap of Boston, an eminent man of learning and a well-informed person, wrote to his crony

Manasseh Cutler, a benevolent but shrewd clergyman, that Franklin's "accepting the office is a sure mark of senility; but would it not be a capital subject for a historical painting — the Doctor placed at the head of the Council board in his bathing slipper!"

In fact, the honor which was done to the Doctor was very much like asking a tired traveler to sit down and have a rest on a nest of hornets.

He was popular. Nothing could prevent him from ranking with Washington as one of the most famous men of America. From Philadelphia to Pekin his name was known. Before him Benny had seen the most pompous of the mighty and the shyest of the humble bow down. But he had also seen the politicians turn aside, and he had felt their complicated intrigues around his grandfather. He could still feel them, and, when he listened to his father and mother talking, he understood why.

The Doctor had been too long away. His keen, bold mind soared too high above the brains of the politicians, absorbed in day-to-day affairs and suspicious of anything outside their range. In the immense disorder of 1785, when America, convalescing after eight years of war and fifteen years of revolution, was not yet on the road to recovery, but seemed to be abandoning herself to chronic disorder; at a time when whoever governed her had nothing to gain and everything to lose, they were only too ready to offer him the chance of compromising himself.

Franklin's intimates trembled for him. He knew it himself. He said it himself. "A Man in high Place has so many Occasions, which he cannot avoid, of being disobliging, if he does his Duty; and those he disobliges have so much more Resentment, than those he obliges have Gratitude, that it often happens when he is strongly attack'd he is weakly defended. You will, therefore, not wonder if you should hear that I do not finish my political Career with the same Eclat that I began it."

Still, he was willing to be fooled and to suffer. How could he avoid it, when he had outlived the pleasures of the senses, and when he had enriched his heart with innumerable ways of suffering?

Richard Bache and Sarah Bache and their children surrounded him with affection. William and Louis and Richard, Elizabeth and Deborah, came and clambered over his knees. Each of them in their own way gave him their love; but they all had need of him. He was their great man. He knew himself for their slave.

Sarah basked in his glory; but she could not do without it. Richard, as constant in his commercial failure as in his conjugal fidelity, needed his money. He had to educate William and Louis and Richard, and Elizabeth as well; and Deborah clamored for jam.

In the too small house Benjamin Franklin felt stifled. He opened his window to the noise outside, the traffic of the street.

Like him, Benny roamed from room to room, among these little brothers and these little sisters of his who did not speak the same language as himself, who did not salute or eat in the same way. He envied the Angora cats, lithe and brazen, who went where they liked and whom everybody petted, even when they raided the larder, even when they corrupted the lady cats of the neighborhood. He went and kissed his mother; but in the evening, when she said to Richard, "Don't forget your nightcap, Richard, when you go to bed; it's cold to-night," he remembered M. de Marignac, who bade him, before he went to sleep, think of the Supreme Being and Eternal Father.

Soon, however, he set off for the University, where he was to finish his studies.

Temple had not waited at all. He had set off at once towards freedom, towards men who were a power in the land. He had taken the stage-coach for New York and paid a visit to Congress, which was then in session there. He presented his credentials and those of his grandfather to Mr. Jay, Secretary of State. He wanted to see whether the beauties of New York were an improvement on those of Philadelphia, and whether they would remind him of his passionate nights in Europe.

He also wanted to find out whether there was still anything to be made out of his grandfather's glory. With his cold courtesy and his fine figure, presenting his excellent letters of introduction and paying his friendly calls, he made his rounds. Everybody received him with great politeness, and everybody nodded his head, and everybody put him off with promises and with a smile, which Temple knew only too well, for it was his own smile.

When he went back to his lodging, this time, Temple no longer strutted in front of his mirror. Instead, with his elbows on the table, he opened Blanchette's last letter, took out the lock of golden hair and the little medallion which she sent him, and he, usually so indifferent, wrote to her on the instant, begging her to send him news of their son posthaste.

Then he wrote to his father, now a gentleman of leisure on the other side of the ocean, who had generously handed over all his estates in America to him. He wrote to his friends, the great lords of Versailles and the little masters of Passy. He cracked jokes with them.

But he did not feel like laughing any longer when he got back to the house in Philadelphia. It seemed to him like a

[73]

prison, with his little cousins as warders and his grandfather as chief jailer. He could not stand it.

Benjamin Franklin suffered too much himself to be able to stand it either. His old prophet's heart trembled before the hard, set face of the young man, full of reproach. His old tribune's courage drove him to act, to bear any burden rather than his bitterness. On Temple he settled a farm and an estate. For the Baches and for himself he went in for building. He added a wing to the house, he constructed two outhouses on the street, he planned a garden, he made a passage between the back of the house and Market Street. He interviewed painters and masons, glaziers and carpenters, gardeners and navvies, plasterers and slaters. He discussed details with them and kept his mind off himself by tiring himself out.

So he kept pain and boredom at bay. He forgot how the tide of death was rising in him, sometimes steadily, sometimes in surges. It was but lately that he said: "I leave others still in the field, but, having finished my day's task, I am going home *to go to bed.*" But he could not yet sleep in his bed. She whom he awaited had not yet arrived. She was by no means ready for him, and, rather than the implacable, searing slowness of these hours of waiting for her, he preferred the frivolous distraction of work. He tried to take it seriously. "I seem," he wrote, "to have intruded myself into the company of posterity, when I ought to be abed and asleep."

But his mind and heart had never known how to sleep, and the passing years, far from making them drowsy, had deprived them still more of any laziness, any talent for repose. Now they were, so to speak, stripped and eager to be up and doing.

[74]

To keep them quiet, while he awaited Death and all her soothing, he made use of politics.

Politics, in the Pennsylvania of 1785, was of such a kind as to enchant a mind as subtle as that of Doctor Franklin and drive any other man to despair.

Two parties strove for power: the Constitutionalists, who wanted to maintain the Constitution of 1776, and the Republicans, who wanted a new Constitution. The Constitutionalists were Democrats — philosophers with bold ideas, Westerners with rough manners and equalitarian instincts, Irishmen and town artisans who were looked down upon by comfortable burghers and shopkeepers. The Republicans were wealthy merchants, big farmers and solid middle-class people.

The Constitutionalists declared themselves very well satisfied with the Constitution which had set up a single Chamber and a "Supreme Executive Council" consisting of several members, charged with governing the State in common. The Republicans regarded this régime as monstrous, since it was remote from the English tradition of a bicameral Parliament and a sole Executive. Everybody was agreed that the Constitution of Pennsylvania made the government weak and amorphous. The Constitutionalists drew from this fact the conclusion that it was the best possible form of Constitution, and the Republicans that it was the worst possible form; for the former wanted to be governed as little as possible, and the latter as much as possible.

It may be added that the Constitutionalists, living for the most part far away from the seat of authority, had every reason against strengthening the hands of a government in which they could play little part; whereas the Republicans, concentrated in the capital, or near it, wanted to see a

[75]

strong government which they could turn to their own advantage.

Ever since the Constitution had been established, the struggle had raged around it. It was in line with the convictions of Franklin, who believed in the essential goodness of the people, and who had consorted with the French physiocrats, opposed to two Chambers. His son-in-law, Richard Bache, looked at it with a less kindly eye; for he was in business, and people told him that it was bad for trade. Without being very sure about it, he thought it was. But Richard lived by business and did not bother much about ideas. Franklin lived by philosophy, and what interested him was ideas. He even went so far as to be suspicious of business, ever since he had mixed in high society in Europe.

So he was the man for the Constitutionalists. They threw themselves upon him. At the time when he arrived, they had just won an electoral victory, and they proposed to take advantage of his return to establish their authority, which they felt was precarious. Franklin seemed to them a gift from Heaven. As a matter of fact, he was. Quietly, without taking sides, unostentatiously and without advertisement, he worked for them. He succeeded in baffling all the efforts of the Republicans and defending the Constitution.

If age had made action more tiring and more difficult for him, it had increased in him the talent for delay, which in parliamentary politics is the supreme form of wisdom and shrewdness; for it diffuses expectancy and hope over everything — and it is only in such periods that institutions are perfect and the governed find it easy to tolerate them.

Helped by his years, his reputation for wisdom and his

[76]

CARICATURE ENTITLED "ZION BESIEGED"

poor health, Franklin carried on a conservative policy, to the benefit of the Constitutionalists. But it became daily more difficult to stem the rising tide. With the return of peace, business improved again, and the merchants loudly demanded stricter maintenance of order and a more active government. They were organized, and their influence kept on growing. Over against them, the Constitutionalists split into factions and wasted their efforts.

The Irish had, indeed, founded an organization of "Sons of Saint Patrick"; but, however great a saint he might be, and however efficacious he might have shown himself against the snakes, Saint Patrick still had very little influence in Philadelphia, where there were more substantial Quakers than snakes. The Irish, isolated, poor and held in no great respect, could achieve nothing.

They proposed to form another society on a wider basis — the "Adopted Sons of Pennsylvania." The idea was a good one; but it provoked keen opposition on the part of the Anglo-Saxons who were cocks of the walk, and whose powerful associations, the "Sons of Saint George" and the "Sons of Saint Andrew," had also just been reorganized. Saint Andrew and Saint George formed an alliance against Saint Patrick — even in his Pennsylvanian disguise.

Colonel Oswald, patriot, journalist, Whig and Anglo-Saxon, declared in his newspaper, the *Freeman's Journal*, which at this time was the most fashionable and the most brilliant paper in Philadelphia, and also the noisiest, that these Adopted Sons of Pennsylvania were "such Arabs, such horrible vipers, such gorillas of ingratitude, and so detested by the whole of Pennsylvania, that all Americans ought to treat them with the supreme disgust which is all that they deserve."

The terms of this article shocked one of the leaders of the

[77]

Adopted Sons of Pennsylvania, the publisher Matthew
Carey. To cleanse the honor of the association, he chal-
lenged Colonel Oswald to a duel. The colonel did him the
honor of putting a bullet into his hip, Mr. Carey limped for
the rest of his life, and that was the end of the Adopted
Sons.

The Constitutionalist Party itself was swept by a tidal
wave which convulsed the whole nation.

The American Revolution was over. The Americans had
driven out the English and expelled their friends, and they
now had a fine, big country all to themselves. All they had
to do was to make use of it. But the mass of Americans,
who had made the Revolution, not in the least as a matter
of philosophy, or to set an example to the world, or out of
hatred of the English, but purely and simply in order to
feel themselves at home and to govern themselves as they
liked without having to ask permission for everything from
a government three thousand miles away—these Americans,
who had made a nice little revolution to keep their land and
enjoy it, now found to their astonishment that they had let
loose a storm in their country which refused to come to an
end.

To stir the masses, it had been necessary, from 1765 to
1778, for an elite — big merchants of Massachusetts,
lawyers of New England, aristocrats of Virginia — to
preach revolution to them. It had been necessary for Englishmen, such as Tom Paine, imported in 1775, to excite
and intoxicate them with a belated enthusiasm, while other
Englishmen who came later, such as Charles Lee and
Oswald, and French idealists like the Marquis de La
Fayette, set them the example of patriotic zeal. Thanks
to them, despite many difficulties, reverses and delays, the

Revolution had succeeded. The one and a half million Americans, who had never sent more than thirty thousand soldiers to the army, and who had neglected to pay the war taxes, had applauded its success.

Now they were highly annoyed to find that all the rabble whom they had required to do the revolutionary job, tar and feather the English, whoop after officials, chase Loyalists and serve in the army, all that lousy mob who had drunk deep draughts of the revolutionary intoxicant still seemed to believe in it. In 1786 a revolt of small fry, farmers and debtors who wanted to avoid paying their debts, upset Massachusetts and startled the country. It captured public attention, which was already tired of seeing Congress marking time and the States squabbling among themselves like ailing, tearful and badly brought-up children.

Spontaneously an alliance was formed among the veterans of the Revolution, organized in the Society of the Cincinnati, who did not want to have fought for nothing; the merchants, who were anxious about their business; the rich farmers, who wanted to export; and the former Loyalists who had remained in the United States or returned after the peace. They had a General Staff in the persons of the politicians of the East, where business interests were dominant; those of the Center where monarchist ideas had remained strong; and those of the people of the South who had economic ambitions or an instinct for order — Jay, Hamilton, Madison, Robert Morris.

The majority in the South remained aloof from these new aspirations and hostile to them. The South was an agricultural region, which cared little about a strong government, and it distrusted the people of the North. In the country as a whole, moreover, men of bold, philosophical

and restless minds were not disposed to let a forceful authority be constituted.

If they were to succeed, the "Federalists", as the nation-
alists were called, needed Washington, to carry the South
with him or at least neutralize its hostility by his prestige,
and Franklin, who alone could keep the radicals quiet.

Washington was unenthusiastic. He was cultivating his
land and concerning himself with Mrs. Washington, cata-
loguing his books and repairing his house. Politics made him
tired, and power meant nothing to him. He had no son to
succeed him, and nine years of war had taught him that
commanding is the worst way of obeying. He had not
enough imagination to become King, and he had too much
sense to become Prime Minister. He preferred hunting and
growing pumpkins.

He had to be removed from Mount Vernon and brought
to Philadelphia almost by force to make him preside over
the Constitutional Convention, assembled thanks to the
patient efforts of the efficient middle-class nucleus. There,
under the vigilant eyes of his lieutenants, he behaved himself well, though he often went fishing and hunting and to
see the pigs of the neighborhood; for this question of the
porcine species lay very near his heart.

His wisdom and his dignity, and his marvelous skill in
keeping his mouth shut and letting what was useful be
done, while holding himself aloof from what was harm-
ful, put him in the front rank, the more so as he was
indispensable.

So everything was arranged with the South.

There remained the problem of the radical elements.
Luckily Paine, the noisiest of the radicals, was in Europe.
Jefferson, the most adroit of the philosophers, was in France,
as Minister to the Court of Versailles. Franklin alone was

an embarrassment; but he was eighty years of age, he liked to play politics, he valued his popularity, and he delighted in the interplay of ideas.

For four months, and for five hours a day, he had his fill of them. Other people talked, and he talked; he was always in the breach. He was eloquent, subtle, and idealistic. He proposed that Federal officials should not be paid, for the good of their virtue. He favored a single Chamber and a plural Executive, as in Pennsylvania. He invented and suggested an artful apparatus for balancing the votes of the States and making their value vary in accordance with the question in debate. In short, he played on the Convention as though it were a chessboard.

They let him have his say, and even sometimes his way, since he had an imposing presence and plenty of good fellowship about him. For the rest, he was not much of a nuisance, for his eloquence was not of the kind which sways an assembly; his words carried more weight in a limited circle.

He made some fine, clever speeches, bearing the stamp of the purest doctrine; but he might have stayed in his bed and got his granddaughters, Elizabeth and Deborah, to deliver them for him, for all the good they did him. He was not granted the pleasure of persuading.

He had another pleasure left to enjoy — that of giving way. For any keen and active mind, which despises anger, abhors inertia, and likes to be admired, the only revenge in defeat is to give way gracefully, and so prove that you are superior to your opinions and master of your temper. Franklin gave himself this pleasure; and, as he was a great philosopher and a master of the art of writing, he did it with extreme refinement and derived a great deal of satisfaction from it — without realizing that he was thus

[81]

destroying whatever was still left to him of political influence.

He thought himself face to face with adversaries like himself, and he appealed to their feelings and their judgment, sure of winning in the long run, for among men the higher wisdom always triumphs. But he was, in fact, himself a man faced with a machine; and, while he was thinking about wisdom, they were thinking about force.

Franklin rallied to the new Constitution ostentatiously in the name of national unity, while at the same time he hinted that he did not like it and that he was afraid of a monarchy. But in the din of battle, nobody listened either to his declarations or to his reservations. He alone might have provided the anti-Federalist Party with ideas; he kept them to himself. He alone might have constituted a rallying center for them; he rallied to Washington. He alone might have stood for a certain order of things; he accepted the new order. He discoursed about wisdom and philanthropy while other people talked in terms of force and power.

In eighteen months the whole country was conquered by the Federalists, thanks to the methodical labors of the Chambers of Commerce, the Cincinnati, the landowners and the Washingtonian General Staff. Washington was hailed as the great federator, Franklin as the great conciliator.

But it was the federal epoch which was beginning, and the epoch of conciliation was ended. Washington was invited to go to New York, there to become President of the United States. Franklin had to quit the Government of Pennsylvania, where his party collapsed.

He went back to his library. Nothing was left to him but his library. All his other kingdoms, the salons of France

[82]

and those of England, where he had throned it as a prophet; the far-off chancelleries of Europe, where he had reigned as master; the American assemblies, where he had laid down the law; and the associations and the lodges and the federations and the conventions, where his proposals had carried the crowd — all this was ended. He would never see them again. Others reigned in his stead.

There was left to him his library. It was big and bright, with two windows that faced south and two windows that faced north. It was warm and comfortable, with its fine, large hearth that commanded it in the middle. It was impressive, strange and philosophical, with its walls covered with bookshelves filled with books, the prints and plans which littered its tables, and its bizarre paraphernalia: the snake with two heads, caught in the Schuylkill and preserved in a large phial, which Franklin in his indiscreet moments compared with the Constitutional Convention; the long, artificial arm and hand for taking down and putting up books on high shelves which were out of reach; the Doctor's great armchair, with rockers and a large fan over it, with which he kept off the flies, while he sat reading, with only a slight motion of his foot; the rolling press for making copies of letters, an invention of his own; and, above all, the mysterious glass machine for exhibiting the circulation of the blood in the arteries and veins of the human body, with its glistening red fluid, which terrified and tantalized the children.

As he stroked his two-headed snake with one hand, and with the other opened the immense book, with its fine engravings, which Linnæus had given him, Doctor Franklin, in the twilight, looked like some benevolent sorcerer, capable of releasing the obscure forces of the earth and letting loose destructive dragons upon the world, but who had

[83]

chosen instead to make friends with them, tame them and play with them.

In this last kingdom of his he received his friends. In this room, and in his lecture hall underneath it, he assembled the members of the American Philosophical Society, and the members of the Society for Political Research which he had just founded. To them he bequeathed his system of thought, trimmed as it was with anecdotes, reticences, reservations and fine shades, but suddenly illuminated by some general idea or transfigured by some startling flight of audacity.

He told them the story of those Ministers whom he had known in England, who read the annals of their country not in order to avoid the follies of the past, but to adopt and imitate those they relished most. He explained to them how he could have bought the liberty of America for one-hundredth of the money which the War of Independence had cost, and he discoursed on the folly of wars, which were murderous, useless, and degrading.

He related to them the life story of that Pythagorean Quaker, Benjamin Lay, whom he had known in his youth in Philadelphia, and for whom he had printed a book against slavery. In order to indoctrinate the people of Philadelphia, and purify himself, Benjamin Lay had ended, one fine day, by giving away all his belongings to them in Market Street. They had taken everything and then turned around and laughed at Lay, who went off half-naked and at a loss.

Nevertheless, said the Doctor, it was he who was in the right. Luxury was the curse of nations. It lowered individuals and made slaves of them. Benjamin Lay was right. A man ought not to tolerate being the slave of the things he thought he possessed, and he ought not to admit that other

[84]

men, like himself, should be pulled down to the level of these things.

The Doctor looked around him. He saw his friends smiling and nodding their heads. His stories were good and delighted them. They admired his ideas. His theories charmed them. How novel and original they were! But his friends' souls were already stocked. There was no longer any room in them for anything outside of the simple, commonplace desires to eat, drink and sleep, to do their duty and to be respected. So nothing could now trouble the quietude of their lives, lulled by a gentle, monotonous purring.

He alone preserved within him an insatiable need for life, enlightenment and faith, which neither defeat nor victory, neither discovery nor error, nor conversion, nor even the long wear-and-tear of life or the sweet shadow of death, which calms and numbs, availed to overcloud.

Beside him, like him, a youth strove in solitude.

CHAPTER III

THE LAST SAYINGS OF "POOR RICHARD"

BENNY BACHE was not happy. He was feeling his way. They had taught him many things, and all these things were alien to him. They had taught him the fine manners of Europe, but now he was embarrassed by them, or at least they embarrassed his friends in Philadelphia. They had given him the strict virtues of Geneva, but everything and everybody demonstrated to him that these virtues had no place in the Philadelphia, rich and grasping, in which he lived. They had taught him French, but nobody spoke it here or took any pleasure in hearing it spoken.

It was a foreign language in America, and he, who thought in French, realised that he was thinking like a foreigner. From March, 1787, he started to think in English; but for him English was a foreign language, and his thoughts, when he formulated them, seemed to him to have a foreign ring about them. He had said to his mother with a laugh, at the time of his return, that he was an Anglo-Frenchman. He did not say so any more, for he was no longer able to make a joke of it.

At the University they taught him Moral Philosophy, as it was understood by the Reverend Doctor Magaw; Ethics, together with the Nature of God; the Laws of Nature, Natural Philosophy — what we now call Physics — in addition to Magnetism, Mechanics, Hydrostatics, and As-

[86]

tronomy. They taught him Belles-Lettres according to the good M. Rollin, Logic according to the English philosophers, Universal History according to the French historians, and the Theory of Contracts according to American common law.

All this he wrote down obediently in his notebooks, in whose margins he sketched a few designs by way of keeping boredom at bay. All this he drove patiently into his head, mixing it up with daydreams to make it more tolerable.

But, at the end of lectures, he was in a hurry to get away from the classroom. Quickly, with his books under his arm, he went along Fourth Street, crossed Market Street, and elbowed his way through the crowded market. Then he found himself on his own ground, in the court which bore their own name, which led to their own mansion, and at the end of which, framed in great elms, he could see the red-brick front of their house and Doctor Franklin's windows.

His little brothers were playing in the garden. They were having a fine row with some of the young scamps of the neighborhood. "Shut up, you scapegraces!" Benny cried, as he passed them; for he knew that his grandfather was working, and that he could hear the racket through his open windows. But the boys simply shrugged their shoulders, without even looking at him. What did they care about this Frenchified gentleman? For their part, they were free Americans, who proposed to play just how they liked; and, if anybody interfered with them, they would climb over the wall into the next garden, and their mother could shout after them, for all the good it would do her.

Benny went up to his grandfather's room. There, he knew, there was always a corner for him. Often the old man dictated letters to him, or the story of his life. For a few months he had had as his secretary Benny's cousin Josiah Flagg, a nice boy, whom his apprenticeship to a shoemaker had scarcely prepared for such work, but who made a fair hand at it and imagined that nobody would notice his failings. He did not realize that the Doctor noticed everything. At the mere sight of Benny, his grandfather always knew how he was feeling, and whether it was better to make him work or to tell him stories, to instil maxims into him or to ask him what was on his mind.

To make him laugh, the old man would tell the young man about a wag who entered a tavern. "He desired the waiter to give him a penny'th of Bread. Having received it, he told the waiter he had altered his mind and would, instead, take a penny'th of Beer. The Man brought it and the wag drank it, and was turning about in order to walk out. 'But what, Sir, you have not paid me for your Beer!' 'How, did not I give you Bread for it?' 'Well then, Sir, you have not paid me for your Bread!' 'How, you dog, you — did I eat your Bread? Sure, I returned it to you.' The waiter was fully confirmed the man reasoned just, and was also clear he was a penny'th out of pocket."

Or he would tell him the story of the good housewife who had accepted a bad three penny piece in the market, and whom her husband scolded for it. "I'll be able to get rid of it," she told him, though he was doubtful about it; and in fact, some days later, when she was buying twopence worth of butter, she slid her three penny piece in between the twopence which she put into the butter-merchant's hand.

Above all, the old man loved to tell him stories about doctors, for he knew them inside out, and he was too ill to wish them much good. Among all these stories, the one he liked best was that of the French doctor who had to deal with an epidemic of putrid fever in one of the islands of the West Indies, and finally found himself left without any medicine. In despair, thinking all his patients doomed to death, the poor man invoked all the saints in Paradise. What were his surprise and his delight to see his wish fulfilled! All his patients got well — now that he could not treat them any longer. . . .

Benny laughed. Benny took out his notebook and jotted down his grandfather's stories. Benny, with his big, black eyes softened by his mirth, made deeper by his attention, moist by his affection, followed every one of the old man's gestures. Sometimes he too started telling stories.

He told his grandfather about the ridiculous duel between Mr. House and Mr. Fisher, which had excited all Philadelphia. "What a silly business it was!" so the young man said. House had insulted Fisher. Fisher, if he wanted satisfaction, had only to insult House. He could even, if he wanted to do the thing handsomely, insult him five times over. But to come to blows, to sword thrusts — what insanity, what lack of a sense of proportion!

The old man assured him that he was quite right, that any violence, any war, was ridiculous, useless and silly. He could himself, if only they had let him, have bought from the French, at very small expense, all that territory in Canada over which French and English had spilled so much blood. It would not have cost the tenth part of what the war had cost. He would himself, if only they had been ready to listen to him and take his advice, have had no difficulty in buying the whole English Parliament and saving all the lives that had been wasted in the Revolution.

War was inhuman and war was foolish. It was always more costly than a little commercial transaction would be,

[89]

and armies were devouring monsters which had to be fed, housed, warmed, paid and armed, and which were, for all traffickers and crooks, marvellous instruments for trafficking and crookery. If only princes would learn a little arithmetic, they would realize all this.

When Benny laughed, the old man would add, "How lucky you young men are to be living nowadays and to have learned arithmetic! Humanity is so fine, and it is going to be so great in the next few centuries. The happiness of mankind is bound to go on increasing, for philosophy, morality, politics and even daily life are undergoing marvelous improvements. People have invented and manufactured so many utensils and so many useful instruments, and, as things are going now, so many new discoveries will be made in the years to come, that I cannot help regretting that it was given to me to live nowadays, rather than two or three centuries hence."

He taught Benny that he must love the present moment, and the people, and have faith in them, and not burden them with elaborate institutions, and not encourage them too much to aim at wealth and luxury, the source of all vices, all jealousies, and all excesses. He jeered a little at parliaments where men chattered, and governments where they strutted, and constitutions which they complicated, and institutions which they had to explain. He wanted everything in politics to be simple, spontaneous, close to the people, always subject to their will and their initiative. For he believed less in immutable principles than in eternal sentiments. He had less faith in the cleverness of the human mind than in the rectitude of human hearts. He refused to admit that politics was very different from morality, or morality from wisdom.

Benny listened while the old man told him: "One must

[90]

be virtuous because such is the greatest wisdom; one must be wise because such is the greatest cleverness; one must be clever because such is our interest. Work, Benny, work night and day for the happiness that you will get out of it. Be wise and be virtuous, so as to deceive your enemies and never to be deceived yourself. Never will you find anything better than virtue. Benny, do not seek to be rich; seek to be happy, and you will be the happier the simpler you are, the less things you possess, and the fewer the people on whom you depend. Depend only on yourself, learn to make use of yourself, and be master of yourself through wisdom and virtue. Get to know the 'art of life', Benny, and practice it. Avoid all the vices which torture us even more than they harm our neighbors. Do not be avaricious, for that is a bad thing and does evil. Do not give way to anger, for that leads to mischief. Do not be sour of disposition, for that is dirty. That's a vice, Benny — ill humor is dirtiness of soul. Smile, so that the world may smile upon you."

The boy smiled and admired the wisdom of his grandfather. In his notebook he wrote: "The object of every man is his happiness. A sober life means happiness." He exalted the just man, he exalted the wise man, he exalted him who learns how to preserve health in his mind and heart; and he thought of his grandfather. He learned to hate idleness. He exerted himself to conquer pain and make the best of it. "He who has not endured suffering cannot enjoy the same pleasure as he who, after having suffered, finds the end of his pain," he said to himself; and he looked at his grandfather — so stout-hearted, so serene, so bursting with joy just after the most searing sufferings of his merciless malady.

To please him, he exalted that orderliness which the old man had always cherished and pursued with more zeal

even than happiness, and he persuaded himself that orderliness is an increment of wealth, and cleanliness an aug-
mentation of health. He made himself a rule of life in three
articles. "Be temperate. . . . Keep things in order, and
your mind will be clear. Whatever you undertake, do it
well."

One day he was shown a little notebook, well margined,
well paged, well written — the notebook of the virtues
which Franklin at the age of twenty, had drawn up for
himself in order to devote himself, every week in the year,
to the acquisition of one of the important virtues — the
young man was delighted with it. He hastened to buy a
similar little notebook, to margin it, to page it, and to
write down in it the names of the finest virtues, in a noble,
well-rounded hand which promised well. It promised too
well; the notebook remained empty. But Benny's heart
was always full of zeal and inflamed with admiration for
his grandfather.

He could not see why his grandfather should have
labored over his virtues so much, and why he, for all his
good will, neglected them so much. He could not possibly
see it. He could not imagine that, to win these virtues of
his, his grandfather, when he was a youth, had been obliged
to work hard and had done so with joy, as one might do in
the excitement of a game; whereas he, Benny, poor good
boy that he was, surrounded by all the virtues and cradled
in them, could scarcely find in virtue the same keen, acute,
novel kind of pleasure.

He was far from having sinned enough to know satiety of
evil and gluttony for good. To him goodness, purity, affection and generosity were not conquests to be achieved, but
impulses which his own heart bade him follow. He exhorted
himself. He said to himself: "Work! Nature ought to be

our main guide in all our actions. Nature ought to be our guide, since she created us." And he decided to follow the voice of Nature in everything — to eat what he liked, dance as he liked, and love where he liked.

Then Benjamin Franklin shook his head and talked to him about God. "Benny," he said, "there is a God, a very great God, a very good God. There is a God Who made the world and Who guides all men, as He guides all things. There is a God Who reigns in the hearts of men, and Who will reward them some day, for the soul of man is immortal, and God is eternal; and God is just, and God is good."

Then he said to him, half in a whisper, "Benny, there is a very great God, a very good God, of Whom all men have always spoken, and of Whom they will always speak, if they are not monsters; and, of all the men who have spoken of Him, without doubt Jesus Christ is He Who has spoken the best. But what He said has been repeated so often, and the priests have put on such airs about it, that they have made many things involved. Benny, it is for you to choose your own religion; but mark you that my grandfather was a dissenter from the Church of England, and so was my father, and so am I. You must always love God, even if you do not love priests. You must always pray, even if you do not know the name of God; for God has many names, and it matters little what one you choose for Him."

Lower still he murmured, "Benny, God is very great, God is very powerful, and the Universe which He made is immense, and in the Universe there are many worlds, and every world has its own principle, and you will never know all the principles that exist in the Universe. But, Benny, the soul is immortal, and perhaps it will know much more than we know in this life; for there is another life, Benny, maybe many other lives. Who knows, Benny, who knows?"

The voice of the old man died away in the falling night, shot through with the red rays of the setting sun, laden with the disparate, distant noises of the town. With his hand on the boy's shoulder, the old man dreamed.

The boy wrote eagerly. "I believe that there is a God," he said, "who made this world and everybody who lives in it, as well as the plants and all the bodies which belong to this system and revolve around the sun, and also the inhabitants of these planets; for I believe firmly that they are peopled — as firmly as one can believe anything without seeing it. All the other stars which come under the denomination of fixed stars are so many suns, centers of as many systems created by other supreme powers, or which may have had the same cause, some of better construction, others not so good, as ours. But, once set in motion, [they] govern themselves, having the principle of motion in themselves, namely specific gravity, and not needing, like so many worlds, to have a force always renewed to keep them in motion.

"I am of this belief also," he continued, "that there is no need for new souls to be created to animate the new bodies that come into this world, but that these bodies are filled by the souls of dead men at the same time as the body is formed. That the Supreme Worker who made us, when a man's soul leaves his body, rectifies what requires to be rectified before permitting this soul to be used again, having perceived by the way in which the man has conducted himself in life what he lacks. If he was rough and given to anger, He softens his character, and if something else, He makes other changes suitable to render him better; in other words more apt to be happy in the next journey which he undertakes."

Satisfied with his work, Benny concluded: "So far as

the Christian faith is concerned, there may have been a man named Jesus Christ who was in possession of much learning and ambition, but I could never believe that he was the son of the Supreme Being. I believe that his miracles were deceptions, sleights of hand to acquire power or reputation. But, at the same time, I am sure that the religions which all men profess to believe all have a good object, namely to retain in their duty those who do not fear men, who are really to be feared, but are weak enough to be ruled by an imaginary Hell and by rewards in another life which are also quite unreal, and for whom the happiness which they might enjoy by being virtuous is not enough to make them love virtue."

Then, proud of his performance, he laid down his pen. He was still more proud when, on going through his grandfather's papers as he was arranging old files of the beginning of the century, he found the declaration of faith which Franklin had drawn up at the age of twenty. What a miracle! In 1727, at the age of twenty, Benjamin Franklin, and in 1786, at the age of eighteen, Benjamin Franklin Bache thought the same and invoked the same God in similar terms. How could it have happened?

Then the boy interrogated the old man, gently and at length. "Your creed is so fine," he said to him, "it is expressed with such beauty, and it coincides so well with my own thoughts. Grandfather, how can this be so, since I never knew what you thought?" Franklin smiled, for during the past ten years he had watched day by day over that mind feeling its way and walking with halting steps towards the light which he showed him.

Now he could give him that light.

"Be very strong, Benny," he said, "be very independent, and be very pious."

[95]

But it is less easy to give enlightenment than desire for enlightenment.

Sometimes Benny shook his shoulder, and his grandfather's hand fell back on to the table. Sometimes Benny said to him, "No, I do not think the same as you do. You say that God rules over the world. That is not my opinion. He has created men, He has put them into the world, and He can take them out of it again. For the rest, He does not concern Himself about us. And why should He — when virtue is happiness, and happiness a form of skill?"

Then the old man was disturbed. "Benny, take care! Respect Providence; revere its verdicts. Look at the impious and the libertine. They forget the presence of God, and they sink into unhappiness. Virtue is not only a matter of skill. It is also a matter of obedience, courage and perseverance.

"Benny, consider Temple and try and profit by his sad example. You know that I gave him an estate, Franklin Park on the Ancocas, so that he might live and work there; and you know that he turned it into a farm and installed a farmer there, so that he could go off and play cards and dance with the girls of Philadelphia and New York. You know that he was not even able to keep his farmer in order, that he quarreled with him, and that so he is left, incapable of making a profit out of his land, incapable of living there, incapable of finding another occupation, and still wanting to seem a Gentleman. A Gentleman! The unhappy boy forgets that every Gentleman has to pay for the honor of being one, and he will soon have nothing left with which to pay for it. He is diving swiftly to ruin, and he alone will be the cause of his ruin.

"Let Temple's fate be a lesson to you, Benny, and, while there is still time, come to your senses, turn away from these balls and pleasures that attract you, take up your work again and devote yourself only to it; for you cannot be both a Printer and a Gentleman, and you have not the fortune to be able to play the Gentleman. Do not divide your time between business and society, or you will never become rich. And make haste, for to-morrow it will be too late."

But the youth jibbed against the hand of the old man, who wanted to guide him by frightening him and enlighten him by flattering him. "I work better," he said, "when I have had a good time. I am quite ready to work as hard as you say, but let me amuse myself for a couple of hours a week. I do not hold by wealth any more than you do; I am in no more of a hurry to make a fortune. My only object on earth is that virtue about which you have told me, that virtue which is happiness; and my pleasures which you condemn are my happiness. So they are the legitimate object of my life."

"These pleasures are vain mirages," cried the old man; "they are not real joys, they are deceits."

"They are very good," Benny rejoined, "inasmuch as they suit me. You cannot say that they are false pleasures, when they are mine and I know them myself. I also know my own nature and I know that I need pleasure. Do you not think that the pleasure of good company is one of the least foolish of pleasures?"

What did Doctor Franklin think, and what did the experience of his life show him? Benny did not find it out then, and never did he have the chance of discovering it. Never was it given to him to tear away the halo of glory which hallowed his grandfather and realize why these simple, innocent pleasures of Benny's frightened him so much, whereas perhaps other pleasures, about which they

[97]

had not spoken, and which were less decent, might have left him less moved.

Doctor Franklin said nothing; for he was thinking about those turbid, ardent days of his youth, when other pleasures, which some people called vices, served as a spur to plunge him into work and urge him on towards glory, whereas such honest, middle-class and social pleasures as Benny's might have kept him back among the common herd of idlers, at the mercy of all the eddies of life. The old man could not explain this to the boy. It was a conception of wisdom which the sage, out of respect for wisdom, had to keep to himself.

It was an idea of virtue which enhanced his indifference to good and evil, and which shone with all the more luster in proportion as it disconcerted the human mind. Doctor Franklin was very familiar with it, for it was his own essential mainspring, and he relied upon it for his justification before the Supreme Being. But before men, even before his grandson, he never spoke about it. His contempt for perfection, his glorification of utility, which was the shield of his soul, remained a mystery to those nearest to him.

Benny, sentimental and Genevese, could not have made head or tail of such a lesson. The Doctor gently took the young man in hand again, as one guides a child. He let his mind rear and prance, but, step by step, he led his body and his will where he wanted them to go.

On Market Street, at the entrance to Franklin Court, he had two fine houses built, smaller than his own, but solid and substantial. On the ground floor of one, along the street, extended a big room intended to serve as a workshop for type founding; and beside it, in the passage which led to the main building, another room was destined for binding. Above was installed the printing house, with a variety of fonts such as was to be seen in no other establishment in America, ranging from the tiniest nonpareil to the largest type, like that which is used in advertisements. In the attic were piled up any number of curious and scientific instruments, which made the place a regular museum: electrical material, physical and even astronomical apparatus.

Franklin took Benny by the hand. He led him, with his slow, heavy steps, leaning on him in such a way that the young man could not get away from him, across the garden to the door of the new building. Then he opened it and said to him, "Look, all this is for you; this is your workshop, this is your business, this is where you belong."

There was no answer to that; and the boy traveler, the boy exile, the boy harried by revolutions and overwhelmed by his grandfather's glory, was henceforth a prisoner within these walls, because they constituted his refuge, something that was his own.

He kissed his grandfather on the brow, and firmly, enthusiastically, he declared to himself: "My main object on earth shall be to make myself esteemed as virtuous, to make myself regarded as learned, and so to be of service to my country and to humanity. Ambition is, I believe, my strongest passion."

In his own mind he had made the sacrifice. Henceforth he was the worker that his grandfather wanted him to be. He wanted to be one himself.

CHAPTER IV

THE TWILIGHT OF A GREAT GLORY

IT was by no means so easy to succeed in becoming a real worker.

From all sides life fawned upon him. Whatever he might do, at the University he was the cherished grandson of the great Doctor Franklin. Whenever there was any ceremony, he was thrust to the fore. At every opportunity he was treated with special consideration. When he came to the end of his studies, on the occasion of Commencement, he was asked to make a speech, and, before his assembled comrades, despite all his correct good boy's modesty, he had to make one, in which he pronounced a eulogy of education, a eulogy of parents, a eulogy of the public who was good enough to lend him such an attentive ear, and a eulogy of morality, which was the safeguard of the human race. He tried to praise other people; they insisted on praising him. Everybody sang his praises to his heart's discontent.

He was glad to escape from all these compliments and get out of such an oppressive atmosphere. He shook the dust of college off his feet and was delighted to get back home.

But he could not stay there. Philadelphia, showering invitations upon him, kept on offering herself to him. How could anybody resist her, when the whole town, still intoxicated by the Revolution, was a perpetual parade, a brilliant, baroque fair?

[100]

The streets were filthy and foul, all dust and mud. Since the town privileges had been abrogated, nobody cared about street cleaning any more. Anybody who chose threw his garbage into the middle of the road, housewives sawed their wood outside their doors, dogs wandered about at their own sweet will, and everywhere were displayed the signs of taverns, pool rooms, and dives where you could play cards.

To tidy things up a bit, it was decided that criminals and prisoners should clean the streets. In gangs of a dozen, they were to be seen in their degrading uniforms, with handcuffs on their wrists and chains on their feet, dragging their heavy iron balls around with them. They cleared the gutters, swept up the dust, sprayed the sidewalks, repaired the street lamps; but, whenever a passer-by did not watch out, he got a cloud of dust in his face, or a splash of mud on his clothes, or he found his foot suddenly crushed by an iron ball thrown with clever carelessness.

The convicts had lost none of their artistry. Hampered as they were by their handcuffs, they could snatch your purse or your tobacco pouch with consummate skill. One fine day the prisoners in the Chestnut Street jail decided to make a break for freedom. They were in too much of a hurry about it and they were caught. The next year, in October, they were luckier; thirty-three of them made their escape and were not recaptured. They made life in the neighborhood of Philadelphia very exciting that winter.

Life in town was no less amusing. During the sessions of the Constitutional Convention it was nothing but a sequence of dinners, meetings, military parades and civil processions. General Washington was fêted. His birthday was celebrated and so was that of Doctor Franklin. Tammany honored May Day; the Freemasons in fine procession, with their little aprons on their bellies, solemnized Saint John's Day in summer; the Sons of Saint George kept the feast of their patron, the Society of Saint Andrew that of theirs, and everybody drank and sang and rang bells and fired off salvos on the Fourth of July.

High society was scarcely less gay. In winter the "Assembly" met every Thursday evening at the City Tavern and there was dancing from seven o'clock until midnight. The younger set paid two pounds sterling a year for membership and, under the chaperonage of their elected "managers", they danced gracefully, elegantly, indeed majestically. Not everybody who wanted to could get into the Assembly. You had to move in good society and show a clean record. If you drank too much or got quarrelsome, you were expelled. If you made a mistake about a figure in the cotillon or the country dance, you became the laughingstock of the town.

But, if you knew how to behave yourself, you could enjoy the most attractive company there — that of Miss Arietta Budden, Miss Caldwell, the pretty Misses Hamilton, the charming Polly Shippen, and all the belles of the place. With them you could dance rhythmically and perform the clever, complicated evolutions of quadrilles and minuets. With them you could drink punch or coffee, when it was cold, and wine, beer and lemonade, when it was hot, while they nibbled biscuits and devoured their rivals with their eyes.

With them, too, you could whisper. "Benny," Budden asked him, "what are you going to do? Miss Caldwell wants to squeeze Arietta at the Vaughan sale."

"I'll bid her up; I'll bid her up good and high," Benny replied gallantly.

Benny went to balls, Benny went to "routs." The girls of Philadelphia could not ignore his eyes, which were good to

[102]

gaze into, or his legs, which were good to dance with. In
November, 1786, he had taken up dancing again. In January, 1787, he started going out into society. He liked it
and it liked him. He liked the girls especially, because they
liked him for his genteel, polished manners which smacked
of Europe, for his friendly simplicity which recalled his
grandfather, and for his youth, which was himself.

Young men liked him because he was straightforward,
unaffected, and good-hearted, and because they thought he
was rich. Mothers of families brooded over him affection-
ately. Fathers shook his hand cordially, and in the street old
gentlemen, as they saw Doctor Franklin's grandson going
by, polite and busy, declared. "That boy's a hustler. He'll
go far."

All this pleased him but it also disturbed him. He felt
that there was a misunderstanding about him. They imagined that he was rich. He was nothing of the kind and
there was a good chance that he never would be. They
regarded him as the favorite grandson of the famous Doctor
Franklin and drew the conclusion that he was going to be
a gentleman, whereas the Doctor's ambition was to make a
working man of him.

While Franklin, by his precept, urged him to become a
craftsman, he obliged him, by his glory, to act the lordling.
While he preached simplicity, industry, frugality and love
of the people to him, his three houses, his sedan chair, his
titles and his fame gave him the rank of a nobleman. When
he thought about this, Benny felt wretched and ashamed.
But what could he do about it?

He went back to his workshop. He arranged the fonts of
type, assembled them and completed them, made a careful
inventory of them. When summer came, he went, on behalf
of his grandfather, to hand some fonts over to printers who

[103]

were in the market for them — Childs in New York, Carey in Philadelphia. So it was that, in 1787, he traveled to New York to deliver to Childs's printing house the fonts which Franklin proposed to sell him.

But, here again, Benny could not escape from his destiny. The fonts which he handed over to Childs were mutilated, incomplete, and badly arranged, for they had been packed and unpacked too often since Passy; anyhow, even if they had not been, Childs would not have been satisfied with them. He was that kind of man. Benny's mission, therefore, was neither a pleasure nor a success, from the business point of view.

But how entertaining it was, thanks to his cousins, the Baches, the sons of the important merchant Theophylact Bache! They took him to see two Newfoundland ships which were then being fitted out for codfishing, and took him rabbit shooting on Long Island, picknicking in the country with girls, and to lunch at Mr. Jay's country house and at Mr. Bleecker's fine town house.

Benny went home delighted, but downcast. How could they hope to make a business man out of him, if everything always ended in picnics?

He gave up type founding. There was too much competition and he had not enough customers. He had no adequate assistance and his grandfather was too old to help him and instruct him to the extent he required. He went in for printing instead. It was with some pride, and a good deal of emotion, that Benjamin Franklin could say, "I am too old to follow printing again myself, but, loving the business, I have brought up my grandson Benjamin to it, and have built and furnished a printing house for him, which he now manages under my eye."

The old man and the young man started publishing.

[104]

They issued books for children, charmingly and fastidiously printed, full of little verses, old saws and pretty illustrations. Under the auspices of the University of Pennsylvania, they published a Latin Grammar and a collection of Latin texts, and they prepared a Greek Grammar. Doctor Franklin talked to everybody about them and Benny went the rounds of the colleges to offer his wares.

But the children of America at that time were not very much interested in books. The colleges were small and pedantic. No professor had much confidence except in books which he had written himself, or at least which he knew already. The friendliest of them told Benny that they would advise their pupils to buy his publications. The frankest of them added that this advice would probably serve no purpose, since their pupils did what they liked and had books enough already.

The more peevish of them asked him whether he thought it logical to print and sell Latin and Greek books, when his grandfather was publishing everywhere vehement condemnations of all classical studies. Professor Nisbet, of Carlisle College, after remarking to him that he had found fifty mistakes in his book without reading it, told him that his efforts to sell books about Latin were in vain, if a swarm of ignorant and illiterate scribblers went on attacking that noble language and flattering American laziness. He was referring to a certain article in the *American Museum*, which was attributed to Doctor Franklin's pen. Pretending that he did not know this, Nisbet added, "I have never seen so many absurdities intermingled with so many falsehoods, and I am bound to think that the author is a Methodist, since that sect seems to be his ideal."

Benny could not put up with this insult. He retorted that the article in question was extremely good, extremely judicious and wise on all points, and that he had himself no admiration for classical education or for Latin, though the language had its uses, since it had once been the universal language. In any case, all that was a matter of the past, and he had made up his mind to publish no more Latin books, classical grammars or Greek collections.

He had confounded Doctor Nisbet and avenged his grandfather; but his publications were dead. When he thought about it, he could not imagine how it had happened.

To please his grandfather he had turned type founder. But immediately his grandfather had strayed into such complicated imbroglios with such few customers as addressed themselves to them that they had all found themselves out of their depth and lost any desire to do business.

To please his grandfather, he had turned printer, and he had published a classical collection. But the ideas and the writings of his grandfather turned against him and prevented him from selling his books.

The glory of his grandfather appeared to open all doors to him when he needed friends and to close all doors to him when he needed customers.

His grandfather seemed to be in a great hurry to give him a trade and make him work; but his grandfather could not resign himself to setting him up properly, letting him take his chance for himself, and making a regular printer out of him. The whole thing was nothing but a toy, a pretence and an affectation.

The sense of solitude which Benny had experienced before grew denser around him. Now it was no longer merely strangers who were strange to him, but his nearest and dearest themselves, and the dearest and nearest of all of them, his grandfather, was also separated from him by the most mysterious of all barriers. Cloaked in his glory, he slipped out of Benny's embrace; either because eternity raised him above mere mortals, or death detached him from those whom he loved the most.

Benny was desolate. No friend on earth, nothing but the chill of loneliness, when he had so great a need of warmth and affection!

Only his notebook consoled him. But what cold comfort for a sensitive heart, for an eager heart, for a soul on fire! No other confidant but virgin paper, when he was ready to sacrifice his whole life to the public interest, and when he wanted to shout his zeal and his philanthropy from the housetops! Alas! there was nothing he could do. His philosophy told him that only self-interest guides men, and that you should never rely upon their generosity; while his experience had shown him how dangerous the best of them may be, how disappointing the wisest of them may be, and how cruel the closest of them may be; for among them, whatever people may say, their interests never coincide, their dreams of happiness never agree, and all their most gushing confidences are merely monologues behind the scenes, or else deceits.

Oh, if only he could find a woman's heart! To become great, Benny said to himself, a great man needs nothing but himself, money, and a woman's heart. A woman's heart would mean no stranger, but a woman who became your friend, who became your wife, who became a part of yourself. She would have no other interest on earth but yours and you would have no interest which was not hers. There was the support he needed; there was the principle of unity.

Unfortunately, it is not always easy to find a woman's heart, even if you know many women. Among the girls of

Philadelphia Benny groped awkwardly to see whether, in the course of a quadrille, as he held a pretty hand fleetingly, he might catch a heart.

He joked with Arietta Budden, he played with Miss Caldwell, he was a great friend of Anne Hamilton's, and handsome Polly Shippen treated him nicely. He also consorted with the other two Hamilton girls, who were rich and graceful, and Miss Bond, who gave such fine parties, and Miss Dickinson, who was wealthy, and Miss Cadwalader, and Miss Allen and Miss Martin. He danced with them; he played cards with them in the evening, while their parents drank tea. In summer he went on picnics. In winter he went to the theater, to Rickett's circus, to the museum kept by Doctor Simitière, and to concerts. He made careful notes on all these girls' characters and their clothes. He liked all of them; but he did not love any of them.

He loved Miss Margaret Markoe.

He loved her; and he was very much in awe of her. Perhaps otherwise he would not have loved her; for he was in the habit of loving what he admired and he could not love if he did not admire. She was fine and proud, and some people found her cold, but to Benny she was noble and she represented everything that was decent and stable in life.

She was the daughter of a planter of St. Croix. They had large plantations down there, which produced plenty of rum and plenty of debts. Her grandfather Hartmann, who was still living on his estates, was regarded as one of the wealthiest planters. Her uncle, Abraham Markoe, was one of the richest merchants of Philadelphia, and his house on Second Street was admired by all the passers-by. Her mother, after Francis Markoe's death, had married Doctor

Kuhn, who was often to be seen at Franklin's and who belonged to the élite of the doctors of the town.

She had two brothers, Peter, gay and giddy young spark, and Francis, who seemed sedate, and a sister, Elizabeth, whom the family thought clever. But, while child-bearing and then affection seemed to have effaced her mother, and the other children's characters were still undeveloped, Margaret stood out as the only member of the family who was a strong positive personality.

The moment he set eyes on her, Benny became entranced. In that oppressive, indeterminate atmosphere of Philadelphia, she stood out ethereal and real. She, too, came from somewhere else, and her smile, when she did smile, was better than a promise, it was in itself a kind of happiness. When she sang "Caro mio," she brought back to Benny all the charm of Europe, all the sweetest dreams of his childhood. Often, on behalf of everybody, he asked her to sing "Caro mio," for himself; and she sang it.

She did not talk to him much, and he hardly talked to her at all. But they were often together; and when the spring came, the sudden, overpowering spring of Pennsylvania, when the pain of loneliness came, when he began to feel himself aloof from his grandfather, he needed love so much that one fine evening "Caro mio" ruined all his philosophy, and, at the risk of becoming the laughingstock of the town, at the risk of being looked upon as a fool, he told her, as they sat on the sofa in the little drawing-room, that he loved her. He was overwhelmed by what he had done, — enraptured and aghast.

She did not answer him but she smiled at him. She was so very well brought up that he could not tell at first whether this smile of hers was a laugh or a sigh; and he started writing her feverish letters. With his candle beside him, he would make a draft of his letter, then sketch it out, then make a rough copy. Then he would write it out neatly, he would correct it, he would copy it, he would begin it all over again; and, by the time he finally got it off, he had emptied his inkpot, broken his pen, stayed awake all night, and wept buckets of tears.

He knew that she was proud and pure. He did not ask for a reply. Let her merely deign to cut out of his letter the line in which he said: "I love you" and send it back to him without writing anything herself; and he would understand and celebrate his happiness. Or let her burn his letter and send him back the ashes; and he would understand and weep in silence.

But he got nothing. She just smiled; and, when she whispered into his ear, they were not burning words, but sober sentences, straightforward and sensible, which contained neither refusal, nor reproach, nor promise: remarks about his youth, about the course of life, about the folly of girls who married before they were twenty-three, about the duty you owed to a widowed mother, an ailing mother, a loving mother, a mother who depended on you. She deprived him of opportunity for either intoxication or despair — or, at least, she would have deprived anybody else. But Benny was too rich in contradictory sentiments not to be able to derive, from all this worldly wisdom of hers, infinite resources of melancholy, of dreaming, of desire and of hope.

He multiplied his impassioned letters. He had seen her blush when she looked at a young man; and, before he went to bed, he sent her a flamboyant picture of this supposed rival of his, this rascal, this libertine, this debauchee, this cynic, this coxcomb! Then, the next day, he hastened to make excuses for saying all this. He reproached himself for loving her so much, for shedding so many tears over her.

She did not avoid him; but he kept on pursuing her so ardently that she always seemed to him to be in flight. His fear turned to panic when he heard that Margaret and her mother were going back to St. Croix for the next six months. Then nothing would satisfy Benny but that he should become engaged to her. He talked about it to his father; and, as Richard Bache was in a jovial humor at the moment, and as Miss Markoe was believed to be rich, his good father simply slapped him soundly on the back, without saying anything.

He talked about it to his mother; and she, remembering how she had adventurously married for love, became rather sentimental. He talked about it to his grandfather; and he became very sentimental, for he was an old man, and he loved emotion, and he had always loved girls.

Benny's secret swelled his heart and also filled the whole house. He thought about it day and night and the others talked about it all the time. Only Margaret remained undisturbed. She neither refused herself nor surrendered herself. She neither hid the matter from her parents nor permitted Benny to approach them about it. She denied him no hope and vouchsafed him no promise. She was proud; she was fine. Benny, obsessed with her nobility, could not help finding himself every day more unworthy of her and finding her every day more worthy of any sacrifice.

He was merely young and she was merely worldly wise. He loved her in the way of a man whom philosophy had intoxicated rather than educated; she loved him like a woman whom the world has trained rather than instructed. He talked nonsense to persuade her and she turned herself into ice to hold him.

He invoked all the highest principles to induce her to become engaged to him. Did not Nature demand that people

[111]

should marry young, in order to attain unity, unity of hearts, unity of life and interests, without which marriage was a mockery? But she had never thought about the morality of self-interest and she believed that a woman was less of a fool at twenty-three than she was at twenty.

Then Benny resorted to his final argument, his most tragic and his finest argument. Not to get married now, at least not to become engaged now, meant depriving his grandfather of his only remaining joy on earth — that of seeing the eldest of his grandsons happy and, in turn, the head of a family; for the old man must soon die.

To this argument he did not think that there could be any reply. Nor, indeed, was there any reply. Margaret made no answer; but, with one last smile, on November 8, 1789, she set off for St. Croix.

Benny would have gone mad if he had not been mad already. He plunged into literature. As she had given him permission to write to her, but forbidden him to be passionate in his letters, he gave himself up to debauches of eloquence, of learning, of ponderousness, of philosophy, and of gossip. Everything went into his letters, from the theories of Hume about happiness and those of La Rochefoucauld about egotism to accounts of the feathers on the hats of the ladies of Philadelphia. He told her anecdotes of the Doctor's, sure that she would appreciate them as much as he did, and he expounded to her his theories about the education of women. He demonstrated to her the danger of wearing corsets, the vanity of human beliefs, and the utility of brushing one's teeth.

He depicted for her the big quarrel between the young men and girls of Philadelphia, when the latter, at an Assembly, had decided to dance a cotillon by themselves, and the former had retorted by dancing another cotillon by themselves. He informed her about the great feud which divided high society into partisans of the cotillon and partisans of the quadrille. As a philosopher, he remained neutral. As a lover, he soared above such petty disputes.

But, above all, he begged her to write to him in return, to send him news of her, a little affection, if that was possible, or at least some hope. He told her about the conflict in his own family. Richard Bache, good-hearted as ever, but now better informed, had decided not to let his son marry a girl without money; for people said that Miss Markoe would not have any. Mrs. Bache, touched and softened by her son's love affair, as any mother who is loving and understanding, ought to be, was nevertheless obedient to the will of her husband, as any good mother of a family always should be when the interests of the family were concerned.

Finally his grandfather, dreamy and melancholy, could not imagine that Benny was any different from himself, or Margaret any different from Deborah Reed, his one time fiancée. In 1722 Deborah Reed and Benjamin Franklin had been in love. Then Benjamin had set off for England, after they had sworn eternal love and fidelity. But, before he came back, Deborah had got married and he had done even worse. That was how life and love went, the old man told the young man; and the young man shuddered and hastened to write a letter of ten pages.

All those anxious days when he could neither work nor rest! All those feverish nights when he could neither sleep nor amuse himself! Benny shrank to a phantom pursuing dreams.

Everything around him added to his fever. America seemed to have emerged from a stupor and suddenly found herself a nation. With bells ringing, cannon roaring, and muskets firing, and speeches and sermons inciting him, General Washington proceeded to New York, there to become the first President of the United States.

Towards New York, the federal capital, from every point of the Union, flocked all those who wanted jobs, all those who were eager to make money, all those who had complaints to lodge, and all those who had nothing better to do. Temple Franklin and Richard Bache were among their number. With their portmanteaus bursting with letters from the Doctor, they set off for New York: Temple to obtain that diplomatic post which had been on his mind for the past ten years and for which he had intrigued on every possible occasion; Richard to have justice done to him and recover the office of Postmaster-General from which he had been so shabbily ousted in 1781.

The learned Doctor himself, on the threshold of death though he was, dispatched all his accounts to New York, in the hope of obtaining the money that was owed to him. The Franklin family hastened to render homage to the Federal Government, to the creating of which they, more than any other family in the United States, had contributed, and invited the Government to do them some small service in return.

The family was full of expectation. General Washington was so agreeable, and their neighbor, Robert Morris, was so big-hearted, so cordial, so influential.

Robert Morris gave Temple a very good reception. He welcomed Bache with the greatest cordiality. General Washington was very affable with Mr. Richard Bache and very polite to Temple. Jay and Carroll and Jefferson opened the letters of the illustrious old man with every mark of emotion. They expressed their profound admiration for a mind whose light shone with equal luster in all periods and at all the ages of his life. They paid the greatest compliments to his son-in-law and his grandson. They went so far as to ask them for some little, friendly services in Philadelphia, where Congress and the Government proposed to establish themselves. In this way they demonstrated their confidence in them and their amity towards them. This was the only testimonial that they gave them.

Richard Bache also had the pleasure of boon companionship with some of the good Tory merchants of New York, friends of his brother's, and, out of this journey of his, he extracted at least a few copious drinking bouts. Temple also had the pleasure of fluttering around Congress, where they were debating the difficult question of the title which should be given to the President: "Excellency", "Majesty", or "Your Grace." He saw some passable enough women, some brilliant enough balls, some pompous enough ceremonies. But did all this suffice? He scarcely thought so.

As for Doctor Franklin, he got nothing but his own glory. He was rather tired of it.

There was nothing in New York which the Federal Government wanted to bestow on the Franklin family.

When Richard Bache came home, he was moody; when Temple came home, he showed himself sulky. They were disgruntled with Washington because he would not give them anything. They were soured on Franklin because he had not been able to get them anything. Richard Bache still had at least his own family and his own good humor; but Temple had neither.

That long, cold winter was a melancholy one in Market Street. Doctor Franklin, whose health was better, was able to taste all the bitterness of being a fallen politician. He could read regret and disappointment in the eyes of those who surrounded him. Only in Benny could he rediscover the sweet delight of love, with all its madness and all its sanity.

He gave Benny his final lessons and at the same time he avenged his family. Before he left this vile earth, he launched one last anathema, sarcastic and dogmatic, against Negro slavery, and against those who encouraged and maintained that slavery. Anybody reading between the lines could not fail to realize that the slave owners whom he thus denounced were those fine Virginia gentlemen, those gentlemen with their coaches-and-six and their postilions, who governed the United States. He who had ears to hear, let him hear. But there were not in the United States, at the moment, many ears open to hearing. There were, above all, mouths open for begging; and the two things went badly together.

Franklin and Benny were very much aloof, very much alone in the library in Franklin Court. The Doctor went on drafting the story of his life. He went on arranging his papers, which he had never succeeded in arranging. Benny poured his heart into his letters; and, on the topmost branches of the trees, springtime, sheer and green, started to bud. The light of evening lay longer on the roofs, tinged with rainbow hues, and on the river with its bluer sheen.

It was then that the Doctor died. Nothing foreshadowed his death, and nothing, it seemed, doomed him to die. He had been better for the past two months, the weather was mild, the doctors were more hopeful, and Benny was beginning to look forward to Margaret's return. He counted the days. He was sure that his grandfather would help him to persuade his parents, to persuade Doctor Kuhn, to per-

CARICATURE MADE IN 1790 OR 1791, SHOWING ROBERT MORRIS CARRYING
CONGRESS FROM NEW YORK TO PHILADELPHIA

suade Mrs. Kuhn, and that he might even murmur some good advice into Margaret's own ears. He believed that his grandfather would set him up in business.

But it was then that the Doctor died. About the 10th of April he began to suffer severely. He found difficulty in breathing. Nevertheless, he went on working; but sometimes he would take Benny's strong and cool hands in his own feverish hands, and hold them for a long time, — eyes closed.

He ate scarcely anything. He forebore from talking or complaining. He never mentioned death; but they could tell that he longed for it. Benny knew it.

On the morning of the seventeenth he refused to eat anything; nor did he want to do anything. He never stirred again. He took the young man's hands in his, and, without paying any attention to anybody else, he spent long hours in happy dreaming. The rest of the day passed slowly.

About eleven o'clock at night, Benny and Temple, who were at his bedside, noticed that he was breathing faster and that his pulse was failing. Benny ran for his father; and Richard Bache, half-asleep, with his eyes puffy and his wits wandering, approached the bed where Doctor Franklin lay, still alive.

The old man sighed, — a gentle, deep sigh. He breathed a few moments longer, and then everything was over for him — struggle, and waiting, and sickness, and the pain of going on living.

Doctor Franklin had a fine funeral, the finest that had ever been seen in Philadelphia. All the city companies took part in it, all creeds figured in it, and his dearest enemies waxed eloquent over it.

In France the National Assembly, and the city of Paris,

and La Fayette, and the printers, and all the patriots and all the most charming women went into mourning. There were funeral orations in his honor all through the land. Mirabeau, the Duc de La Rochefoucauld, Abbé Fauchet, and many another, prayed, wept and glorified the hero.

The National Assembly transmitted its condolences to Washington. Washington transmitted them to the country. But, in his message, he forgot to mention Franklin.

Everybody wept as the occasion required. Only Benny wept as one weeps when life does not seem worth living any longer.

He kept on writing to Margaret. He knew now that he was going to marry her. He knew that they were going to live together. But that did not matter so much any more.

He had lost his grandfather and his youth. He had lost a great deal. Perhaps he had lost everything.

Nothing remained to him but to serve his country.

Book Three

THE FORGOTTEN MEN

CHAPTER I

GENTEEL PHILADELPHIA

In 1790, while France was being consumed in the flames of liberty, while the fire was spreading to all Europe, Benjamin Franklin Bache and the United States were setting up house.

Benjamin Franklin was dead; George Washington was President of the United States. One era was ended; another was starting. The thousand-year-old power of the French monarchy was foundering in verbiage, ideology and blood. The young glory of America was taking root in the New World and planting the first of modern democracies amongst the last virgin forest.

Quitting New York, which was not central enough, the Federal Government installed itself in Philadelphia. Thither it brought its Congressmen and its Senators, and the officials, who followed Congress, and their wives, who followed their husbands. Thither it brought the Ministers and their staffs, and the foreign diplomats and their households, and the ambitious persons who followed the Ministers and the diplomats. Thither it brought the newspaper men, who keep company with all authority here below, and the inquisitive people who always follow journalists.

Thither, above all, it brought General Washington, in his fine coach-and-six, with his tricked-out postilions and his imposing bodyguard, and that majestic presence of his which struck people dumb in the street when he passed, and that incomparable renown of his which filled the United States with faith and pride.

There it caused plenty of stir, which tickled the crowd and also Benny Bache, because he was young, like the crowd of Philadelphia; but which at the same time jarred the crowd of Philadelphia, for it had a Quaker soul, and also grieved Benny Bache, because he had just lost his grandfather and for him life was quite empty.

He had lost his grandfather! The library was a void! They were clearing the house of its furniture. They had to lay aside the sedan, never to be used again. They had to remove the armchair with its adjustable back, and the artificial arm used for taking books from the top shelves, and the Doctor's thick folios and his electrical instruments. They had to bundle up all his papers, which Temple was to take to England and get them published there. They had to strip his room, where other people were henceforth to live. They had to make a clean sweep; for he was dead.

Three hundred officials and dignitaries and members of Congress were arriving in Philadelphia by stage-coach, diligence, carriage or on horseback; but the Franklin family was leaving Philadelphia, now that the soul of Franklin had departed from it. While Benny's father settled in the country to get away from the tumult of the city, which tired him, and to enjoy at leisure the income which Franklin had left him; and while Temple, sighing with relief, at last could pack his portmanteaus and return to his dear Europe, Benny Bache stayed there all alone.

He was alone indeed, since Margaret was taking care of her dying mother, and his parents were in great haste to be gone, and all his childhood was dead with his grandfather. He was all alone, and of his past little remained to

CARICATURE MADE IN 1790 OR 1791 APROPOS OF THE REMOVAL OF
CONGRESS FROM NEW YORK TO PHILADELPHIA

him but what he needed, what he expected of the days to come. His grandfather had left him no money; but he had left him some papers and a printing house, an encouragement to live his life, a faith in the future.

Geneva scarcely survived in him except as a yearning for devotion, moral purity, and self-sacrifice. Of his French education he retained nothing but an instinct for refinement, intensity of feeling, and eagerness of mind. Out of all the dogmas, out of all the beliefs, which he had received, learned, kept and discarded, he preserved only that faith in the future, in the spontaneous energy of the people and of Nature, whom his grandfather adored in such simple and such mysterious formulæ, which he had himself learned to venerate at his side, and which remained the sole worship of his soul.

Around him, America still believed in God the Father and in George Washington. Preachers lauded the Father of his Country and orators extolled him. The crowd shouted in his honor and fine ladies donned their best for him. On his birthday they gave balls, and the soldiers paraded, and the pastors mingled his praises with those of the Eternal. In the taverns they clinked glasses to the General and at all the banquets he was the first toast.

He was the glory of America, and the symbol of her moral unity. His noble, rather ponderous presence filled the country with a sense of satisfaction and serenity. It was shared by the merchants, the farmers, the veterans, the housewives, the urchins in the streets, the trappers on the frontier, the soldiers on guard in the forests, the genteel and decorous ladies in drawing-rooms, the students in the colleges, and even the emigrant who landed on this soil which was to be his own, once he had learned how to belong to it.

There was no national sentiment whatever in the United States in 1790–1792 which did not spring from Washington and flow back to him. Every mortal thing in the United States was matter of national sentiment during these years — the fine weather which gave fine harvests, and the fine buildings which they were making ready for the Government, and the fine trades which people drove, and the fine speeches which they made. This wave of patriotism and love for Washington washed over everything in Philadelphia. It surrounded Benny Bache, it seeped into him; but Benny could not help feeling, deep down in him, the death of his grandfather and his loneliness.

Benny wanted to live, he wanted to get married, he wanted to work, he wanted to serve; and he groped his way. He fitted up the printing house which his grandfather had left him and proposed to go into business as printer-publisher-bookseller-journalist in that Philadelphia of Franklin.

But, when he put out his hands to feel his way, when he looked around him, when he asked questions, Benny could no longer find the Philadelphia of Benjamin Franklin, or the America of Benjamin Franklin. He found the America of George Washington and the Philadelphia of George Washington.

It was no longer the Philadelphia of William Penn, about which his grandfather and other old people had told him: that little settlement crouching on the threshold of the virgin forest, where Indian wigwams neighbored the rough log huts of the thick-set Swedes and the humble cabins, made out of the trunks of eight great trees, in which William Penn had housed his companions. It was no longer that quaint, rustic hamlet, with its narrow streets

[124]

full of verdure, where the wild beasts of the forest still came prowling by night, and the mysterious noises of the deep woods surged in after dusk, when the voices of men were silent.

It was no longer that pious, naïve small town, in which stood just one brick house, Laetitia's house, built by Penn and named by him in honor of his daughter, which looked so imposing with its six windows, its projecting porch, and its slate roof, and at the sight of which tattooed Indians stopped to gape when they passed it. It was far different from that Philadelphia of William Penn, whose quiet streets bore no other names than those of trees and flowers, — chestnut, lime, mulberry, sassafras, — and whose only people were a few wary Redskins, a few stolid Swedes, and the peaceful Quakers in their wide-brimmed hats.

It was dead and buried, and with it, swallowed up by time and prosperity, had passed the Philadelphia of Benjamin Franklin: the fine, snug little town with its houses of brick, of wood, and of stone, and its Town Hall-Market-Courthouse, where, pell-mell, bacon and vegetables were sold, the members of the town council elected, causes pleaded; that genteel little city where everybody knew everybody else and everybody said "Thee"; where, bareheaded, the philosopher-printer-grocer-savant-politician sold goose quills, lampblack, Bibles and Telemachus; where the belfry of Christ Church loomed high above the foliage, those fine bells that tolled the hours and announced midnight; where the night watchman, with his monotonous, plaintive, pious note, which had soothed and sanctified the good ladies of Philadelphia for generations, startled them all one night by crying, "Past twelve o'clock — and Cornwallis taken!"

All this was very far away. It was gone for ever, that

Germanic and Quaker Philadelphia where Franklin had sold his first almanacs, and introduced the first public library in America and the first lightning conductors in the world; where Benjamin Lay was to be seen in the public street giving all his possessions away to the poor; where Whitefield had made tears flow in streams and spread religious zeal to such good purpose that psalms sounded from every house, and where one summer evening, the crowd assembled opposite the balcony of the City Hall, while he was preaching, was seized with a great trembling of terror and burst into heart-rending sobs.

There were still, here and there, houses belonging to those days. There were still old folk who could tell about those days, those things, those people. But Philadelphia was now a fine capital city of sixty thousand inhabitants. Its paved streets had sidewalks, protected against the traffic by stout curbstones, and these were streets straight and regular now that almost all the Lombardy poplars and all the elms that once adorned the city had been felled; so that now one could see, all in a line, imposing houses of two or three stories solidly built of that beautiful brick peculiar to Philadelphia, with white paint setting off their fronts and window frames, or more sumptuous mansions of five or six stories, whose basements, steps and door jambs were decked out in an elegant white-veined marble, that was very noble to look upon.

Strangers admired, above all, the monuments grouped in the center of the city, around an esplanade planted with trees, which was boarded by Fifth Street and Sixth Street, Hazel Street and Walnut Street. On Hazel Street, on the Sixth Street side, Rickett's circus and the New Theater faced one another, and then a whole range of imposing edifices opened to one's view: along Hazel Street

[126]

were the Law Courts, where Congress sat, the Capitol of the State of Pennsylvania, the City Hall of Philadelphia; while on Fifth Street, hard by the City Hall, one could admire on the one side the severe building where the American Philosophical Society met and where Peale's Museum was installed, and on the other side the Public Library, one of the handsomest in the world, with its freestone moldings, cornices and fasciæ, and its fine flat roof in the Italian style, with a stone balustrade and five ornamental urns on each side. A grand double flight of steps, adorned with a statute of Doctor Franklin, carved by the Italian Cerrachi, and paid for in good dollars by Mr. Bingham, rounded off a really elegant edifice.

But connoisseurs appreciated no less the Prison, which stood on the other side of the esplanade, on Walnut Street, and whose stone arcades were considered to be the finest in the world, in their own way. This was the prison for criminals. The debtors had another one near it, not so fine, but still in very good taste; and the city prided itself on these two institutions, which Monsieur le Duc de Liancourt came all the way from Europe to admire.

There could be no mistake about it: the Philadelphia of George Washington was a great city and foreigners compared it with London.

When you made your way through its clamorous streets, where coaches, carriages and cavaliers jostled one another, where a fine fountain stood for every forty roofs, and where six hundred and sixty-two double-branched lamps shed their rays by night, you did not know which way to look or what language to speak. Around Fifth Street and the Liberties, the northern suburb of the city, you would hear scarcely anything but German. Southwards, around Saint Mary's of the Irish, everybody had a singsong accent. But in the center of the city some people jabbered in French and others in Italian, and the oysterman, with his vague, but vociferous cry, made himself master of ceremony of the deafening din all day long.

At ten o'clock at night he stilled his voice, and over the city at rest the night watchman seemed to reign. He was back on the job every night like a reminder of the past, and in his melancholy tone he called the hours and told the state of the weather, and with the end of his stick he rattled on the shutters of burghers who wanted to get up early and take one of the twenty-five diligences which set off at four o'clock in the morning for Baltimore and Annapolis, Burlington and New York, Lancaster and Carlisle.

You felt that you were alive; you kept on the go. Rich and poor, white and Negroes, men and women, old and young — everybody in Philadelphia had every opportunity he could want for entertaining or amusing himself, edifying or instructing himself. Out of the thirty-three churches — Presbyterian, Catholic, Baptist, Methodist, German Lutheran and Swiss Lutheran, Unitarian, Calvinist, Moravian and Episcopalian, not to speak of the two synagogues, the five Quaker meeting-houses, and the African temple, reserved for the Negroes — you really had plenty of choice. You could pray any way you liked.

Or, if you did not like to, you need not pray; for at Rickett's circus and at Lailson's you could see fine feats of horsemanship and daring tight-wire dancers. At the two theaters, for a quarter, you could admire Shakespeare, Sheridan, or a harlequinade. Lowbrows on the cheap contented themselves with Harlequin. Highbrows went to the concert or to Peale's Museum. There they could contemplate Chinese fans six feet high, stuffed birds of paradise, the skins of rattlesnakes and giant boa constrictors, toucans, Pennsylvania bats, Redskin tomahawks and wampums, a fine show of scalps, very curious petrifactions, violet crabs from the Carribees, a beautiful American faun, the noddy, a bird remarkable for its falling into a deep sleep the minute it alights on a vessel, and the "kitcat-length" portrait, among others, of the Marquis de La Fayette, in his most resplendent uniform.

Sentimental people preferred to go to the Sign of the Grape on Third Street, between Market Street and Ark Street, to see the waxwork show of William Geisse, who there presented Washington in all his glory, the Royal Family of England in their robes of state, the Bishop of New York, the Duchesse d'Orléans, a beautiful "Nun at Confession" and a friar in his proper dress receiving the nun's confession, English bishops and admirals, a damsel presenting the head of the Baptist to Herodias, wife of Herod, on a charger, King Cyrus, an Indian chief painted and dressed in his war habit, holding his bow and a real scalp, and, above all, when you peeped through a curtain, the charming, the perfect, the incomparable "Sleeping Beauty", masterpiece of its kind — and all this for a quarter!

To tell the truth, the crowd liked the taverns above everything. There were more than sixty of them, and there you could drink anything you liked — all the beverages of Europe, all the brews of the West Indies and the liquors of America, cider, beer, Madeira and Canary wine; wines of France and Spain, brandy, rum, tafia, gin, whisky, punch, juleps, the wine of Virginia, maple-sugar drinks, and ash-bark beer.

The young fashionables went to Oeller's, where they had installed a vast ice house and where you could enjoy sherbet and cold punch in the height of summer. Ladies frequented Richardet's shop, where they served ices made by a pastry cook from Cap Français. But business men and speculators flocked to the City Tavern, where every hour the names of the ships approaching Philadelphia were given out; for the merchants had organized a coastguard service which kept them informed all day long.

As soon as they disembarked, travelers betook themselves to the City Tavern. There they found all the information they could want, a warm welcome, a passable bed, and a few bedbugs. But they did not mind about these. Better a few bedbugs than the rudimentary comfort of the American provincial inns, where, lying on straw none too clean, or on a communal bedstead, eight or ten travelers, all under the same covering, slept side by side, without taking off their cloaks or even their boots.

Here met the trappers, come from the West to sell the skins of wild beasts which they had killed in the virgin forest; the German farmers, bringing cauliflowers to market; French marquises fleeing from the guillotine; the ship's captain home from a long voyage, with China silk; the itinerant preacher just arrived from some corner of New England; the glib and self-important Congressman, and the dentist just landed from England to draw teeth and sell emetics.

Everybody met here. It was like being still out in the street. Warm-hearted, good-humored, hospitable — it was the American street, with all its cheerfulness, its good fellowship, and its chances, around whose corner, at any moment, you might meet fortune or power, and where you were bound to find a pal. It was the sole shelter, the sole welcome, in a city of closed shutters, which seemed to treat Congress to mean looks, scrutinize any stranger suspiciously, and open its doors only to receive a customer, discuss a business deal, or snatch at Fortune as she flew.

Behind their porticos, with their classic ornamentation, or their flights of steps in the Dutch style, the houses of Philadelphia looked surly. Twice a week, on Wednesdays and Saturdays, barefooted servants emerged from them to wash the door and the sidewalk. It was up to the passers-by to watch out. In winter they ran the risk of slipping on the water which froze on the sidewalk; in summer they got themselves all bespattered. Nobody cared if they did. It was very rarely that they were invited inside.

The city had grown too fast and everybody was too busy. There was little enough time to scrub the hall, the parlor and the kitchen. There was still less in which to make yourself at home. A few pieces of walnut furniture, a few chairs painted green, stocked your house. You had neither leisure nor means to entertain. You had your living to make and you had no time to waste.

Only the rich people were addicted to entertaining. They cultivated one another's acquaintance.

With the coming of Congress and the National Government, Philadelphia became the center of American high society. Important officials and substantial merchants mixed together constantly. They formed a society; they constituted a party. They had their section commanders and their leaders, such as the banker Robert Morris, "Robert Coffer", who had obtained for Philadelphia the honor of becoming the capital; Thomas Willing, the president of the United States Bank; and Abraham Markoe, who had built such a fine house for himself.

But the most famous and the most prominent, the most influential and the most important of all was Mr. William

[131]

Bingham, for he had an immense fortune which grew every day through his speculations in real estate; he played a leading rôle, which he owed rather to his position as Senator and friend of Mr. Hamilton's than to his own intellectual gifts; and he enjoyed great social prestige, which he owed to his wife, the prettiest woman in Philadelphia, the most adroit of hostesses and the most discreet and best informed of coquettes.

He owed much also to his architect, who had built an imposing mansion for him, and to his cabinetmaker, who had provided him with superbly genteel furniture. For his drawing-room Seddon's of London had sold him armchairs of the newest taste, with backs in the form of a lyre, and festoons of crimson and yellow silk. The curtains of the room were a festoon to match, and the carpet one of Moore's most expensive patterns. The room was papered in the French taste, with great classical and architectural designs after the style of the Vatican in Rome.

Around Mrs. Bingham's table, graced with fine china and crested silver, thronged all the fashionable world, bankers and ministers, defenders of the régime on which they were speculating; foreign diplomats, eager to ingratiate themselves with the American aristocracy; refugees from Europe, downcast and hard up, trying to hide their poverty behind a well-pressed shirt frill, and their melancholy behind a well-turned, well-aimed joke. There were to be seen Robert Morris and his wife, M. le Vicomte de Noailles and Omer Talon, representing the Regent of France; Hammond, the English Minister, and Bond, Consul of Great Britain; Colonel Hamilton, Secretary of the Treasury, General Knox, Secretary of War — and Mrs. Knox, whose toilettes made the ladies rage and the gentlemen smile.

"Madam Knox was worth going to see," said one of them.

"She was really a treat; figure to yourself a fancy dress, purple body, long white sleeves, gold muslin train and coat; handkerchief inside, drawn tucker childlike outside, that not an atom of the shape would be hid; purple satin turban, pink tiffany band, ornamented with beads stuck on the very top of a high cushion, and you have the Goddess of War in *statu quo*. How do you like her?"

CHAPTER II

A PARALLEL OF TWO GREAT MEN

MADAM KNOX left plenty of people so dizzy that they did not like her and they shunned her. They also shunned Mrs. Bingham's drawing-room, too aristocratic for their liking. Benny thought as much, and many a burgher of Philadelphia found the forms of her house not suited to his manners. You cannot so easily implant luxury and splendor and airs and graces among shrewd and cultured Quakers who call you "Thee." While generals and ministers, bankers and planters flocked to Mrs. Bingham, the Quakers kept away from her.

In their black coats and their somber vests they went to dine at Stenton. Doctor Logan lived there, with his wife Deborah. He was a descendant of the Logan in whom William Penn placed his fullest confidence, and she was a descendant of Norris, one of the first colonists of Pennsylvania. On the road to Reading, they had a great estate, with a manor house shaded by great trees and surrounded by vast outhouses, in which the servants lived and which also gave shelter to books, art objects and physical instruments; for Doctor Logan was a man of learning.

Just as Mr. Bingham had speculated always and everywhere, in war and in peace, in the West Indies, where he represented Congress, in France, where he had traveled, and in Philadelphia, where he had set up house; just as he had made money everywhere, but spent it there, so Doctor

[134]

Logan had studied everywhere, physics in England, medicine at Edinburgh, philosophy in France and throughout Europe; so he had gleaned fine learning and useful science everywhere, but he had come back to Philadelphia to practice farming and philanthropy there.

He had been elected to the Assembly of Pennsylvania, and had settled down at Stenton, where his table was free to everybody who went there — the poor, the rich, or the middle class; Federalists, Democrats, or neutrals; men young, middle-aged or old; Quakers, Episcopalians or Lutherans, — anybody as long as he was virtuous and well-mannered. Jefferson resorted there, and there you might see the Minister of France, Doctor Hutchinson, Doctor Shippen and Doctor Rush, the great astronomer Rittenhouse, the savants of the American Philosophical Society, fiery Charles Biddle, sly General Mifflin, Governor of the State, and his subtle secretary Alexander Dallas — in short, all the finest minds of the neighborhood, who were not afraid of facing a little dust in summer, a little mud in winter, to cover the few miles which separated Philadelphia from Stenton.

In Philadelphia, in Mrs. Bingham's fine purple drawing-room, the glory of President Washington shed its rays, his name was on every lip, and people sometimes laughed at old Franklin. Under the great trees at Stenton, the General was revered, with mild, enlightened friendliness, because he had served men well; but the memory of the great Franklin was venerated, because he had loved mankind. People did not talk about power and glory, but about wisdom and benefaction, under the great trees at Stenton.

Mr. Jefferson discoursed there. He told anecdotes, over which everybody breathed charmed sighs, and talked about

[135]

his travels, to the great delight of the company. Then sometimes, when there were not too many people, he raised his voice and denounced the political and philosophical "heresies" which he could see spreading in Philadelphia, and everybody was thunderstruck; for Stenton was by no means, like Mrs. Bingham's drawing-room, the headquarters of a great party from which watchwords and orders were issued, but rather an oratory, where devotees of the same worship went into retreat together.

Sometimes Mr. Jefferson talked about that devil of a colleague of his, Alexander Hamilton.

Like almost all devils, Alexander Hamilton was charming and popular with the ladies. He had married a young and lovely one, noble and proud, General Schuyler's daughter, on whom he lavished his love and who returned it a hundred-fold. He was a model husband, and his little infidelities towards his wife were scarcely more than a way of fanning the fire of her passion for him, and confirming and refining the regard which he had for her.

He was also a fine figure of a husband, in the flower of his age and strength, with that well-shaped head of his, held a little high, his full, mobile lips, his chin that thrust forward a little, and his dark blue eyes which sometimes turned almost black. His fair complexion and his reddish hair, which he wore brushed back and powdered, added still more to his air of robust youth and engaging energy.

You felt that he was a gentleman, but far from being the last of a line — a brilliant beginning, on the contrary; and your feeling was right, since nobody knew much about his father, whereas everybody had heard about his mother, a charming and vivacious Frenchwoman who had loved not wisely but too well.

Alexander, therefore, was born of a burst of affection

rather than of due deliberation. He was given the name of Hamilton more or less at random, and his mother had transmitted to him, together with the yearning to be a nobleman, an irremediable incapacity ever to become one. This was why he loved nobility, just as a woman adores the lover whom she awaits and whom she can never meet.

A love child, he remained faithful to his parentage, and so did it to him; and this thrust him into adventures to which his sense of original sin, obsessing and burdensome, contributed some fever and much murkiness. He needed extraordinary qualities to shed luster on his life and the fact that he always succeeded in doing so proves that Alexander Hamilton was a great man.

Women felt it, men knew it. Women delighted in it, men made the best of it; and, since he was not their equal, since he would never admit that he was their inferior, and they would never have admitted that he was their superior, fate obliged him to be always their leader.

He became one betimes, and he soon reached a point where he had scarcely any respect left for his fellow countrymen. He was too noble to wish them any harm and too honest to think that they were much good. He was too proud to hold anything in esteem other than monarchy and aristocracy, the supreme exaltation of the individual; but he was too farsighted to try and impose this ideal of his on men by any means other than the exploitation of their lowest passion, their love of lucre, their greed, their gluttony, the only motives that have power over them — enough, at least, to make them like order, which otherwise they would hate.

From a spirit of chivalry and zest for life, he fought against the English in the War of Independence. Then he offered the crown to Washington, whom he admired; and, after Washington's refusal of it, he worked, as delegate to the Constitutional Convention, as organizer of the Federalist Party, and as Secretary of the Treasury, to establish in America a plutocracy, out of which perhaps, in the long run, might emerge, as a flower grows out of manure, an aristocracy and an authority worthy of the name.

To him this meant more than the mob, indistinct, drifting, sluggish and incapable of raising itself — though towards it, for that matter, he felt more pity than anger, for he had a warm heart and a positive mind. It was never against facts, against reality, that he got into a rage, but against pretences, against unreality.

So, with a little gold and plenty of mud, he aimed at building the future greatness of the United States, of which his genius had been the animating spirit. Washington served him as his shield, and Jefferson as his driving bolt.

He labored patiently at this great task of his. For its sake he had the crushing war debts of the old Congress and the States taken over by the Federal Government. For its sake he had them funded at a very high rate, unexpectedly high, and he did nothing to discourage speculators, — quite the contrary; he aspired to strength, not justice. For its sake he had the Bank of the United States created, and carefully framed his taxes, his budget, in such a way that everybody's ambitions and desires were felt to be linked with the fate and the permanence of the National Government.

For its sake he went to his office every morning.

He got there early. In the anteroom his usher, clad in gray linen, barefooted, more like a soldier off duty than a civil servant, was awaiting him and stood up when he arrived. From the wall he took down a key hanging on a nail and Mr. Alexander Hamilton entered his office. A cane-seated chair, a big deal table covered with a green cloth, planks standing on trestles and laden with files and papers, in a corner an earthen pot and some pewter tankards on a tray, — this was all there was in the office of this Spartan, engaged in building Babylon.

He loved effort, hard work and danger. He loved his long, hard task, and his clear mind loved to pierce the opacity of figures. His keen intellect devoted itself by choice to the most resistant material; he made himself master of it and in this way gave himself more of a sense of triumph.

He loved all this struggle; but he hated Thomas Jefferson.

He could forgive the crowd for being base, a thief for his theft, a fool for his folly, a poor man for his poverty; but how could he forgive a great man for being a liar?

Mr. Hamilton did not know Mr. Jefferson well; but he could appraise him. When he saw him coming back from France in his fine suit of embroidered silk, with silk stockings, a big shirt frill, and a topaz ring on his finger, he contemplated him with curiosity. When he saw him again, a few weeks later, clad all in black and carelessly groomed, talking in the street with some Congressmen from the West, he formed an opinion; and this opinion became a conviction, and then an obsession, when he had listened to him for a few months at Cabinet meetings.

It appeared to Mr. Hamilton that Mr. Jefferson never opened his mouth except to emit a piece of philosophy — in other words, dissimulate the facts under a deceptive phraseology. It appeared to him that Mr. Jefferson preferred to tell people what they were thinking, rather than what he was thinking; and that he could usually do it.

Mr. Jefferson called this tolerance, philosophy and politeness. Mr. Hamilton called it lying.

Finally, it appeared to Mr. Hamilton that the most disconcerting quality about Mr. Jefferson's falsehoods resided in their clairvoyance. The veil which Mr. Jefferson cast over his own mind never prevented him from seeing clearly everything that was in his interlocutor's mind. On the contrary, indeed, it helped him to see it — to see only the other man, only the other man's thoughts.

If Mr. Hamilton hated anybody's not seeing life in general as a concrete, definite thing, he found it quite unendurable that anybody should see into his own life too clearly, and that anybody should know about the conflict that he suffered in his own mind between the very high esteem in which he held man and the contempt which he had for men, between what he wanted and what he was doing.

He was grieved by his own consciousness of the divergence between his aristocrat's aspirations and his rôle as Secretary of the Treasury in a new-born republic. It humiliated him, but, through action, he managed to forget it; through the exercise of authority he consoled himself. Only Mr. Jefferson always reminded him about it, and every one of Mr. Jefferson's proceedings bore the mark of his tactless comprehension. It revived in Hamilton his own most intimate humiliation.

Hamilton hated being humiliated. He hated the clairvoyance of this cozener.

Mr. Jefferson hated the brutal, crude way in which Mr. Hamilton contemplated the world. He was a great mind, this Mr. Jefferson, and he was a great man. His tall, rather clumsy build, his light-colored eyes with their changing, turbid reflections, his straight nose with its strong nostrils and its square tip, his delicate, mobile mouth, his fine, massive head, with its solidity accentuated by the sandy hair brushed back carelessly — everything about him gave the impression of great, hidden strength.

His courtly manners, kindly but cool; his fine mansion, bursting with elegant objects which he had brought back with him from France, and with rare books which he had picked up everywhere; his conversation, full of anecdotes, of feeling, of ideas, of silences, and sometimes shot through with a brusque brutality — all this demonstrated in him both the wisdom of the philosopher who has learned how to enjoy the varied spectacle of life, and the soul of a great man created to rule.

Born in a manor house in Virginia, surrounded by an environment of opulence, he had known power from his youth, and never was he forced to seek it, never did he have to strive against the pettiness of existence. His lot had cultivated his inborn taste for beauty, harmony and magnificence in life. Almost alone in those still rustic colonies, he had been sensitive to fine forms; his love for the people was an aspect of his taste for all the beauties of the world, all creative, fecund forces, all the spectacles of Nature and art.

Of course, he could see the rougher side of things and people; but he preferred, as a *grand seigneur* and as an artist, to appreciate the brilliance of their color and the nobility of their contour. A fine revolt, like the one in Massachusetts in 1785, left him interested rather than indignant. As part of a setting, the red color of human blood struck him as decorative, and the tumultuous movements of crowds had for him something of grandeur, like the waves of the sea.

[141]

He loved the country and its fields, pictures and fine wines, long talks and light women. He loved the ordering of a great monument and the perfection of carved furniture. He liked to understand people and he liked to be liked. To him it was no delight to command, not even any satisfaction; it was simply a habit.

He did not feel the need of any nobility, since there was one already; he belonged to it and it would always be there. But he did feel the need of a people, a warm, ardent, living people, to animate and fill that too vast landscape. He brooded over it, just as he thought over his architectural plans or his agricultural projects. The idea charmed him, and it did not frighten him; for he always kept a sense of the superiority of his own mind and of the ineluctable sovereignty of wisdom.

He had returned from France with the hope of creating the American people. He knew very well that there was not in America, apart from Franklin, any mind to match his own. Now Franklin was gone, and Jefferson remained alone, the only man capable of counselling his old friend Washington, always so responsive to the urgings of the men around him and so judicious in the execution of ideas which were not his own.

Jefferson, the sole connecting link between the great old man and the great popular forces, would therefore have the power, as Secretary of State and Washington's intimate counsellor, to realize his great dream of a New World, fine in its form, harmonious and vast, popular and philosophical, rural and pacific. With very little government and plenty of persuasion, plenty of intelligence and enthusiasm, he aimed at making America a republic of farmer-philosophers guided by wise men.

France had nurtured him in these ideas, and the French

Revolution, at its outset, stimulated his zeal. He returned to New York full of hope. When he saw Robert Morris and Alexander Hamilton engaged in turning his beloved farmers into speculators and transforming his rural America into a vast commercial enterprise, he was indignant. When he found Washington concerned, above all, not to treat the country as a good father of a family treats his children, but to organize a corps of obedient officials, like any sergeant major, and when he felt himself, Thomas Jefferson, to be merely one of these officials, his philosophical soul turned bitter, and his aristocratic instinct led him to revolt.

He donned black and took the field. But unfortunately he hated blows; he was not made to deliver them and he would rather not receive them. So he devoted himself to a spiritual crusade, and he attacked the Spirit of Evil, Hamilton, who seemed to him the incarnate mind and the living soul of the adverse party.

He put the more zeal into it, inasmuch as Hamilton annoyed him personally. With his frigid gentility, his piercing and cynical mind, Hamilton made everything that Jefferson said look chimerical, and everything that Jefferson was look spurious. Jefferson wanted to be, and meant to be, a great philosopher guiding men; he was a minister under the eye of an imperious chief, whom he tried to double-cross. Jefferson was furious with Hamilton, who made him feel, in all its crudity, this contrast between his attitude and his rôle. He did not like to be taken for a charlatan. He loathed being detected in charlatanry.

Thomas Jefferson and Alexander Hamilton thought that they hated each other. They believed in their mutual enmity. Perhaps it was really intimacy.

Out of all America, they were the two minds which under-

[143]

stood each other best — perhaps the only two which could get on together. Reciprocally they knew each other's real desires, each other's real disappointments. Their lives were a kind of dialogue amid mute and benumbed spectators. They played, between the two of them, a game in which nobody else had any part.

They were a marvellous stimulant to each other; and their quarrel interested them so much that they almost forgot to remember that they were in agreement on the essential points. They were both Anglo-Saxons and aristocrats, determined to establish the greatness of America and to make her Constitution respected. But this secret understanding of theirs about their aims, this intimacy which drew them together, this irresistible esteem which interested them in each other, made them only the more intolerant of their differences.

Their hatred was made up of comprehension, of solicitude, and of a reciprocal fascination. It was a hatred of election, which united them for ever.

Around them few people understood it. Least of all did General Washington. He wanted to create a fine, strong America, closely united. To this end he required peace and collaboration among all the finest minds of the country. He had no use for discord or for needless complications. Judiciously he begged Hamilton and Jefferson to find some way of "merging" and kneading their brains and their activities in a kind of common dough.

But the mere idea filled them with horror. They listened to the General with deference; then they replied to him with indignation, and they left. It was like a schoolmaster playing at hide-and-seek with mutinous pupils.

[144]

CHAPTER III

BENNY BACHE AND EQUAL LIBERTY

In Philadelphia, full of rumors and quarrels as it was, their discussion, so long as they carried it on in undertones, was not overheard; but, when they raised their voices people lent ear and soon their dispute, which made a fine scandal, stimulated the divisions and rivalries which reigned in the city.

Mrs. Bache had foreseen it. Soon after the arrival of Congress in Philadelphia she had said to her son, "Take care, Benny; there is going to be plenty of squabbling here, plenty of coteries. All this fine unity is going to end in schism. Take care on which side of the line you find yourself."

Benny had taken care. He wanted to be on the right side. He needed to be, for the sake of his future, his career, and the little home which he hoped to create. He did not imagine, for that matter, that he would find it difficult. He was at home here. He was popular. The girls in high society sought after him, and familiarly, because of the song that he loved, and of the way in which they loved him, they called him "Caro Bene."

Young men liked him. He was sincere and a good comrade. He had no difficulty whatever about gaining admission to the "Assembly", the city's fashionable dance club, and he was even elected "manager", whereas admission was refused to young men without polish. Shopkeepers were excluded, even though they were sometimes great men such as M. Moreau de Saint-Méry, bookseller and formerly president of the electors of the Commune of Paris, and there were open sneers at the lower class rabble which amused itself by organizing a rival "Assembly", democratic and popular.

In Philadelphia there had to be balls for everybody. On Saturdays the Negroes themselves went dancing, and on Sundays they hired carriages to go and drink and gambol at the resorts along the Schuylkill, at Grey's Gardens or at the taverns on the Lancaster road, where they served you, as well as stronger liquors, tea, coffee, syllabubs and cakes. It was all quite in order. On both sides of the line you had a right to dance — so long as you did not jump over the line.

Benny was on the right side of the line; but still he had to make a living. Such is the main anxiety of every man; but it was so, above all, in the case of a young man in love, whose betrothed had just lost her mother and was left none too well off. Benny took steps to put into serious practice the trade which his grandfather had taught him and to carry on his tradition. He decided to start a bookshop and publish a Gazette. Forthwith he addressed himself to the man who, together with Mr. Hamilton, pulled the strings, and who was, besides, an old friend of Franklin's, — Robert Morris, the banker.

He went and asked him for support from the Government and the patronage of the Ministries — the only means for a young journalist of making sure of a revenue. Robert Morris was good-natured and he treated the young man politely. He replied to him in a detailed letter, in which he told him that, early as he might think his application to be, others had been before him in staking out claims to a share of the public printing business. Mr. Morris added:

Some of your friends here are rather sorry for your intention of Printing a News Paper. There are already too many of them published in Philadelphia, and in these days of Scurrility it is difficult for a press of such Reputation as you would choose yours to be to maintain the Character of Freedom and Impartiality, connected with Purity. They seem to entertain the opinion that you might be more Honorably and more lucratively employed by the Printing of Books, but of this you are the best judge, and I have only mentioned the substance of a conversation that arose upon my producing the prospectus of your intended News Paper.

It was a piece of advice there could be no mistaking. It was perhaps to be read as a threat.

Benny had to watch his step. The Federalist group, which had organized itself at the outset to inveigle the country, adrift as it was, to accept a new and stronger Constitution, had ended by forming itself into a party, with the object of enforcing this Constitution and turning it to account.

It had its General Staff, Mr. Morris, Mr. Hamilton, Mr. Jay, Mr. King, Mr. Ames, Mr. Bingham, politicians and financiers, who maintained contact between the Senators and Congressmen on the one hand and the rank-and-file of the party on the other, and who gave it its watchwords. Its electoral strength consisted of the Chambers of Commerce, where *nouveaux riches* and former Loyalist merchants, who had come back after the war, joined hands to maintain the strong government of General Washington and Mr. Hamilton, and the Cincinnati, who were retired officers of the American Army, proud of their achievement and their leader, and eager to see order established in the country.

It had its strongholds, New England, where trade was undergoing an immense development, and the State of New York, dominated by a group of big merchants. It had its doctrine: peace, order, prosperity, commerce and understanding with England, in order to secure facilities for maritime trade. Was not England the best customer and supplier of the United States, the nation with whose habits and methods America was most familiar? Were not the English also the people for whom a clever aristocracy, wealthy and adroit, had succeeded in founding and maintaining their hegemony?

The Federalist Party had its newspaper, the *Gazette of the United States*, edited by a very honest, very patriotic and very zealous man, Mr. Fenno, to which the Government gave the Congressional printing business and the Federalist General Staff a subsidy. Mr. Fenno had not much imagination and was always grateful for the suggestions which were conveyed to him by men of parts and people in authority. His *Gazette* was a serious paper, not to say weighty.

Nothing was lacking to the Federalist Party. It had a palladium, General Washington, who, without belonging to any party, surrounded himself with Federalist leaders, never refused to listen to them, and even sought their advice at critical moments. His discreet, but consistent approbation of it surrounded the Federalist Party with a kind of halo.

It had its bugbears: Mr. Jefferson, who did not seem ready to subscribe to the supreme law of the public interest and who was suspected of ideology; Mr. Madison, who was too much obsessed by theoretical justice; the people of the West, who were ill-mannered; the immigrants, who formed a noisy rabble in the towns; the South, which did not appreciate the value of trade to the Federation; and France, who permitted herself a revolution when America had no desire for one.

It had its *bête noire*: Benjamin Franklin.

Robert Morris held it against Franklin that he had defended the old, too democratic Constitution of Pennsylvania. Jay, Adams and the Lees held against Franklin the rôle which he had played in France and the close Franco-American coöperation which he had succeeded in establishing. It was hinted that he had made more profit out of it than America had. The business men recalled certain speeches and pamphlets in which Franklin praised agriculture at their expense. The clergy had not forgotten Franklin's religious daring and the Cincinnati had not overlooked his hostility to them. When he wrote his book on American History, the first manual intended for "right-thinking" Federalist youth, the pastor Jedediah Morse, one of the spiritual and literary lights of the party, simply left Franklin out altogether in his description of the American Revolution.

So it was that Benny Bache, with his prospectus under his arm, hurried all in vain from one ministerial office to another, from the Senate to the House of Representatives, from the Treasury to the War Department, from Mr. Bingham's mansion to Mr. Morris's house. There was no place for him among the Federalists.

Then he presented himself to Mr. Jefferson. Mr. Jefferson had much affection and esteem for him. Mr. Jefferson professed a respectful and pious worship of the memory of Franklin the patriarch. He received Benny in friendly fashion. He gave him the best of advice. Could not Benny publish a weekly edition without any padding or adver-

tisements, so that it might be a paper of general distribu-
tion through the States, and address itself to philosophical
minds everywhere? He even had the kindness to send him,
from time to time, copies of the *Leyden Gazette* to facilitate
his task. He excused himself for these officious hints, which
proceeded, he said, "from a wish to serve him & from a desire of seeing a purely republican vehicle of news established
between the seat of government and all its parts."

Then, a little later, Mr. Jefferson took into his office
Mr. Freneau, the poet, and helped him to publish a paper,
the *National Gazette*.

It was a hard blow for Benny.

Mr. Jefferson, with all his great attachment to the
memory of Franklin, remained, above all, concerned about
his own independence, and to Benny, the representative of
an illustrious tradition, he preferred Freneau, whom he
had under his own hand and whom he could manœuver as
he chose. Besides, Jefferson was a Virginian and Freneau
had connections with the South. This was why Benny,
banned by the Federalists, was turned down by the great
patron of the Democrats.

At this time there was yet no Democratic Party, properly speaking, and the groups hostile to the Federalists were
scattered and divided. The South, which objected to the
supremacy of the North and the business men, could not
constitute a party, for nowhere in the South was there any
solid and coherent General Staff, such as the Federalists
possessed in Boston and New York. The West, as a whole
dissatisfied with the new turn of events, might protest, but
it could not act; it was too far away. In the North the opposition was scattered and impotent.

Only Philadelphia offered a secure and compact rallying
point. Pennsylvania had elected as its Governor General

Mifflin, an old soldier of the War of Independence. He may have had more boldness than brains, and more bluff than boldness; but this election was significant, for Mifflin was not very fond of General Washington, who had been his superior officer. Mifflin still could not understand why Washington had been preferred to himself and he had made up his mind to maintain the rights and prerogatives of the State of Pennsylvania against him.

He had chosen as secretary a young lawyer, recently arrived from the West Indies, Alexander Dallas, who came of an illustrious Scotch family and combined a very exact legal mind with a very perspicacious political sense. Dallas had passed many an hour, during the last years of Franklin's life, at the old man's bedside, and had imbibed his doctrines.

Mifflin's bland bluff and Dallas's methodical mind made them a formidable pair of adversaries. The Federalists shrugged their shoulders, for Mifflin was not genteel and Dallas was an immigrant. But already Dallas was watching the arrival of ships and drawing up a register of recent immigrants, future electors, and the Federalists would have done better not to laugh at him.

Dallas and Mifflin lacked money; but there were other people who had it. Among the Irish immigrants there was no love for the English, little liking for Hamilton, and much distrust of the Federalists. The Irish were not all poor. Some Irish merchants had made their fortunes. Mr. John Swanwick had even succeeded in becoming Morris's partner. Mr. John Swanwick was quite a little man, who wrote little poems, wore big cravats, and had a fat strong box.

General Mifflin and Mr. Dallas knew him well. All the Democrats of Pennsylvania knew him well too. For Mr.

Swanwick had his faults. He was a dandy, he had a weakness for poetry, he worshipped the ladies, and he delighted to deliver unctuous discourses in academies for young gentlefolk. But everybody agreed in conceding Mr. Swanwick two qualities. He was devoted to his ideas; and he knew that money was the sinews of war, also of politics. For more than six years Mr. Swanwick was the great treasurer of the Democrats of Pennsylvania. The Federalists did not forgive him for it and they claimed that he curried favor with the Democrats and the ladies because he could not do better for himself. So true is it that politics leads even the best brought-up people astray from any decency.

The same reproach could scarcely be levied against what was the great hotbed of opposition to Federalism from 1790 to 1798, — the American Philosophical Society. Here you had scholars of the utmost respectability. Some of them, like jovial Doctor Hutchinson, had pot bellies which put them out of court for gallantry, and others, like Rittenhouse, were as innocent as babes in arms. You could not accuse any of them of being servants either of Mars or Cupid. But they were philosophers and they had no love to lose for this government of bankers and ex-officers. They censured it in their own way by electing French scholars and the advanced thinkers of England as their colleagues, and by praising Franklin at every opportunity.

Among them Benny was quite at home. And when he felt that he was ready to publish his newspaper in the fall of 1790, it was to them, that he turned; for them that he wrote the *General Advertiser, and Political, Commercial, Agricultural and Literary Journal* as he called it first. He made it an intelligent, philosophical, and erudite paper, well fitted for the intellectuals of Pennsylvania. The Government of Pennsylvania took six subscriptions from him and the Philosophical Society encouraged him. Some of its members gave him advice, others gave him subscriptions, and all of them gave him their approval. So Benny established himself in the center of what might become a party, but as yet was only a philosophical chapter, not very rich, not very influential, and frowned upon by those in authority.

There was nothing firm to which Benny could attach himself. On the one side were all the money, all the power, all the popularity, and practical-minded men who knew what they wanted; on the other side were unpractical people who ratiocinated or drowsed while they listened to learned discourses. Between Stenton and the State Department, the State Department and the Government of Pennsylvania, the Government of Pennsylvania and the American Philosophical Society, there were friendly feelings, but no coöperation. Doctor Logan was not at all sure that Mr. Jefferson always said quite all he thought, Mr. Jefferson did not find General Mifflin quite respectable, and General Mifflin knew that in politics old doctors were a dead weight.

There was no counting on them. Poor Benny was left very much to himself. The Federalist middle class did not want him and the Democratic aristocracy took no interest in him.

His family did not help him much. His father went to the grouse grounds, his mother went visiting, his brother William was finishing his studies at the University of Pennsylvania, where he had the honor of delivering "An Oration on the Natural History, culture and qualities of potatoes"; his little sisters were at school at Mrs. Pyne's; and his dear Margaret, since the death of Mrs. Kuhn, was spending long months at Somerset in New Brunswick.

He dreamed about her, in her pretty white short gown and black petticoat; and he dreamed of ways of wedding her. It was in vain that he tried to amuse himself. At balls he was absent-minded and the girls made fun of him. He preferred solitude and went for long walks along the Schuylkill and for rides in the country around Philadelphia.

The torrid summer of 1791 oppressed him. It was ninety-nine degrees indoors, and, when you went out into the street, you felt as though you were entering a damp, reeking furnace. He had not even the consolation of talking about Margaret to her brothers and sisters; Betsy was in the country, Peter at St. Croix, and Francis at Princeton. There was nothing left for him — no hope, no comfort, only work.

He gave himself up to his gazette.

A gazette in America in 1791 was not, like the newspapers of France, a periodical cry of anger or indignation; nor was it, as in England, a serious institution, almost ritual in its formulæ. It was the daily mirror of popular life. In its four pages the American newspaper announced everything: revolutions and wars, houses to let, the types offered for sale by the proprietor, runaway slaves, complete with their description, and the erring wife, whom a zealous husband denounced by inserting a notice adorned with a little devil with a forked trident and the legend, "Stop the Satyre!" and whom a more easy-going husband would content himself with naming to the public and adding, "Notice is hereby given that I am fully determined not to pay any of her debts hereafter."

All this was presented in picturesque and disconcerting disorder. There were no editorials, but there were innumerable letters from readers, discussions of all kinds, extracts from useful works, which gave all manner of salutary counsel on the art of melting Indian rubber, or the way to treat servants, or the means of attaining virtue. The paper published poetry, crime news, ship news, the decisions of the Government and reports of the proceedings of Congress, as well as those of the Assembly of Pennsylvania.

If he wanted to succeed, an editor had to see everything, know everything, and go everywhere. He had to publish whatever would shock people enough to surprise them and set them gossiping, but not enough really to upset them. Such had been the art of Franklin. At his hearth, which Mrs. Franklin made comfortable rather than attractive, he seldom stayed; he was always roaming around the town or luring all the gossips of the neighborhood to his home, to such good purpose that he always picked up the best stories in the place. There was nowhere in the world, in the eighteenth century, any paper more amusing than his.

But he was not in love. Benny was in love. How could he laugh, smile and make himself amusing when his mind was full of a charming, fleeting form, when his heart was heavy, and his imagination stuffed with dreams? Benny got up before daylight to distribute his paper to news agents and newsboys. Then he went back to bed for a little while, to dream in the sweet, amorous drowsiness of dawn. He dashed down late for breakfast, and, always surprised to find himself the last, said to Mrs. Bache, "I'm so sorry; it's funny I should be late."

Then back he went to his paper, to receive orders, advertisements and complaints, sub-edit the news, and supervise the printing. At high tide he hurried to the quays to have a look at the ships which had just arrived and tried to glean some information. Two or three times a day he visited the City Tavern and picked up the letters which had been dropped into his box.

[155]

Back he went once more. If there were mail from Europe
or French newspapers, he had to start translating. Sometimes he sat at his table for eighteen hours at a stretch, until
he was as thin as a skeleton, dying for want of exercise.
At best, he went to bed very late, with — in his own
words — a body that "aked", a mind that had "lost its
clarity", and a soul that was sick with longing.

Still, if all this labor had produced some fruit, Benny
would have been consoled for it. But competition was too
great. Philadelphia was gorged with gazettes. The *Gazette
of the United States*, published by the weighty Fenno, was
the paper of high society and official circles. The *Freeman's
Journal* was saucy. *The Mail; or Claypoole's American
Newsletter and Advertiser* was commercial and well informed. The *Federal Gazette* prided itself on its Republicanism. The *Independent Gazetteer* also was given to plain
speaking. Pelosi's *American Naval and Commercial Register*
contained commercial and ship news. The *Pennsylvania
Gazette* was an old-fashioned institution which kept its
faithful following, and the *Pennsylvania Journal* and
the *Mercury* also had their clientèle. As for the *Dunlap's
American Daily Advertiser*, enormous and formless, it
pleased business men by the scope of its information and
the quality of even its most insipid announcements. Accordingly it was the dullest, the richest and the most influential.

Amidst all these papers Benny put up a struggle as best
he could. He had neither the piquancy of his grandfather,
nor the backing of his competitors, nor the experience of
Claypoole or Brown, nor Carey's boldness, nor Pelosi's prudence. He battled against other difficulties. Sometimes he
was without news and had to borrow some from Fenno.
Sometimes he found himself without paper and had to beg

some from his colleagues. He even confessed himself beaten from time to time.

The autumn of 1791 was disastrous. The pitiless fine weather seemed to have suspended life. People stopped doing anything, or bothering about anything, or even dying, and everything came to a standstill. "I have no idea what to put in my paper," Benny complained. "There is nothing at all — not even an accident, not a duel, not a suicide, not a fire, not a murder, not so much as a single theft worthy of notice. *O tempora, O mores!*"

So he blessed the winter, which brought back the sessions of Congress and those of the Assembly of Pennsylvania. He spent long hours in the public gallery which overlooked the House of Representatives, taking notes or dreaming; for a discourse of an honorable Congressman against the tax on molasses would suddenly end under his pensive pen in his Peggy's profile.

He took his job and these long sittings seriously. He could not stand the rustic spectators who, lest they should miss anything of the spectacle, climbed on to their benches and blocked everybody else's view of the assembly. He was indignant with the Quakers who sat in the front row and kept their hats on, and who resented it if you asked them to take them off; for their religion did not permit them to uncover themselves anywhere, and it led them to wear hats with very broad brims.

This daily and almost mechanical job suited Benny and he did it well. He had none of the genius of a poet or the imagination of a great writer. He had none of the sting of a skilled pamphleteer or the fiery style of an orator. He had none of the flair which senses startling news in advance and publishes it before anybody else. He had not the eye for display which enables a newspaper page to be made up

[157]

so that a venomous paragraph or a picturesque puff stands out. With merchants he was not wily, with customers he was not effusive, with contradictors he was not sparkling, with the enemy he was not fulminating. Mr. Fenno had more authority, Mr. Freneau more spirit, Mr. Brown more dexterity.

But Benny Bache had, purely and simply, the taste for daily life and the sense of it. He had day-to-day patience and day-to-day courage; he had day-to-day intelligence and day-to-day honesty. Every day he published his paper and published it to the best of his ability; and every day his paper had, like Benny himself, a sound, decent, reasonable air about it — a friendly air. It was a good paper, which said what it knew, and knew everything that an intelligent Philadelphian did.

Mr. Jefferson had thought himself clever in getting the poet Freneau to publish a Republican paper in Philadelphia, and, in point of fact, the collaboration of these two minds gave the *National Gazette* a luster all its own. But Mr. Freneau had one of those intellects which work in vivid flashes and which the daily round repels. Once he had expressed an idea, he got tired of it — as though any newspaper public were ever in the habit of understanding anything before hearing it a hundred times over, and as though, amid all the novelties in a public print, the only ones which please its public were not those with which it is already familiar and which it is delighted to meet once more.

Aside from some scandals, which awakened echoes; aside from some indiscretions, which charmed the curious; aside from some polemics, which made the fervent more overheated than ever, the *National Gazette* remained a failure. Mr. Jefferson and Mr. Freneau had wanted to avoid mak-

PAGE FROM A NOTE BOOK OF
BENJAMIN FRANKLIN BACHE

ing a commercial sheet of it. They had succeeded and so their paper was dying.

When he started his paper, Benny Bache had only one idea: to follow in the footsteps of his grandfather and keep on following them. He had no money, but his father provided him with a little. He had no subscribers; he collected them one by one. He had no news; he gleaned it everywhere. He had no advertisements; he besought and harried his friends to give him some. He had no doctrine; he reproduced his grandfather's. He was a Franklinian.

He had no circle of his own; but he had the street on which his workshop opened, Market Street, the main street of Philadelphia, full of merchants, *émigrés*, poor people and travelers, overflowing with the life of America — that street which Mrs. Bingham's purple curtains prevented her guests from seeing and which you could not see, either, under the great trees at Stenton.

He had that and it was all he had. True, he had Margaret; but Margaret was his by right of love and Margaret brought him nothing but her love. They got married in November, 1791, very quietly; the Baches were none too pleased to see him marry such a poor girl; Betsy Markoe treated Benny, who was thought to be richer than he was in fact, to mean looks; rich cousin Markoe disapproved of the match too, and sensible and substantial people turned their heads the other way.

He was a printer and he was married. He was no longer "Caro Bene", but "Bache the printer." When the fine Allen ladies, the Baches' tenants, met him in Franklin Court in his rusty fustian working breeches, they did not bow to him, but they made remarks to him about keeping the place clean; and, when they saw him at the Assembly, they doubted their own eyes.

[159]

He lived modestly with Margaret, in a room in his parents' house. She was rather tired and she did not sing any more. He had no time now to go riding, or to wander, crazy with love and dreams, along the Schuylkill. He had got his love. His dreams had come true. He had to pay for them. He had to work.

They were all he had, — his wife, his work, and the street. He no longer had time to see his friends. He could see nothing but the crowd and it seemed to him sometimes that he sank deeper and deeper into the ever denser and denser crowd of Philadelphia.

Over the heads of the crowd, the gods were busy. You could hear the thunder of their quarrels and the murmur of their intrigues.

Mr. Jefferson had set up a General Staff. Mr. Beckley, formerly clerk to the Assembly of Virginia, and now clerk to Congress, kept him informed about what went on and what was said, and sometimes even about what was not said. Mr. Madison and Mr. Giles of Virginia, both members of the House of Representatives, agreed with him discreetly about what ought to be said, and Mr. Freneau, his secretary at the State Department as well as editor of the *National Gazette*, agreed with him even more discreetly about what ought to be published.

This discreet, trusty force of his manœuvered well. He launched it against Mr. Hamilton.

In 1791, Mr. Jefferson had an American edition of Paine's "Rights of Man" published in Philadelphia, which made a great stir, delighted the Democrats, and scandalized the Federalists extremely. A certain "Publicola", behind which pseudonym hid young John Quincy Adams, son of John Adams, undertook the task of refuting Paine. Freneau, given a free hand by Jefferson, then started attacking the aristocratic writings of John Adams, Vice President of the United States, and those of "Publicola." The Vice President did not find it agreeable to see himself criticized under the auspices of the Secretary of State; but he was more hot-tempered than vindictive and the affair did not go far. His son, John Quincy Adams, as a matter of fact, had diplomatic ambitions. It was no more than a skirmish.

During the winter of 1791–1792, Mr. Hamilton, Secretary of the Treasury, presented to Congress, and published, a great report about manufactures, in which he paved the way for the industrial development of the United States. Mr. Jefferson was a philosopher. Mr. Freneau was a poet. They had no liking for figures, and the report was scarcely discussed, except by Bache, who recalled his grandfather's doctrine and the danger of social and moral corruption involved by manufactures.

In April, Colonel Duer, the richest speculator in America, one of the greatest friends of Hamilton and the Government, went bankrupt and flung the New York Stock Exchange into a state of prostration.

A little later, notes began to appear in Freneau's paper against speculators, aristocrats, corrupt Parliamentarians, and against the man who led the dance. The paragraphs were cutting, pointed, and discreet. It was easy to guess who was the target and who was shooting with so sure an aim. Under the spur of this insult, Hamilton reared. Disguised as "An American", he replied to it. He accused Freneau of attacking the Government, out of which he made his living; and he denounced Jefferson as Freneau's patron. How could you doubt that he was right?

But, with Jefferson and Freneau, it was not so easy to put them in the wrong. Freneau published a solemn assurance that he alone edited his paper, and that Jefferson had nothing to do with it; and, some days later, he published an article denouncing Hamilton as the writer who called himself "An American." A Minister stooping so low — and for the purpose of attacking a colleague! Mr. Freneau could not get over it.

How could you doubt that he was right?

So the fight went on over the heads of the crowd, to the great regret of Mr. Washington, who exerted himself in vain to make his Ministers break away; to the great disgust of level-headed people, who could not admire either the guile of the one or the rudeness of the other; and to the great astonishment of the vulgar, who could not understand who were all these "Aristides", these "Sydneys", these "Camilluses", these "Citizens", these "Sentinels", whom they represented, whom they defended or he whom they attacked. The crowd could only feel that there was discord in high quarters. These personal quarrels with principles for weapons had something sordid about them.

The crowd contented itself with reflecting that everywhere virtuous democrats and corrupt aristocrats were at grips. It wanted graphic pictures of it all. Greedily it read the news from France announcing the *levée en masse*, the uprising of the people, the heroic measures, the fall of the King, the victory of Valmy. All this was crystal-clear. All this recalled the American Revolution.

They drank in the taverns in honor of France and Benny filled his paper with dispatches from France. He offered his public the second part of Paine's "Rights of Man", which reflected French Republican enthusiasm. He welcomed all the refugees, exiled French immigrants who came from Europe or from San Domingo, or who flocked from New York, which was too crowded, or from the West, where they were unable to establish themselves. He published their complaints, their advertisements, their poems.

As his friend, Mr. Leib, helped him with his German, he also attracted the German immigrants to his paper. His foreman Triulny kept in touch with the Irish. In short, in the motley crowd, Benny's cosmopolitan paper served as a rallying center.

Between the crowd and the Democrats of Pennsylvania, it served as a link at election time. Nobody knew quite how to handle this restless, diverse populace, and the populace, newly installed on this new soil, did not know how to act. The Federalists were in the habit of organizing private election meetings, controlled with a heavy hand. They drew up a list of names, and at their chosen moment circulated it through the newspapers. So, they used to get their friends elected.

But now the Democrats of Pennsylvania, Dallas, Swanwick, Hutchinson, MacKean, constituted a Corresponding Committee, on the same lines as had been followed during the Revolution. They wrote to all the patriots in the State to get their advice and their backing, and, with the aid of Benny's journal, they succeeded in drawing up both a list of their partisans and a list of the leaders whom they would follow.

They succeeded. Of course Washington was reëlected President unanimously, and Adams Vice President without much difficulty, but Pennsylvania sent to Congress many a man of independent mind, hostile to the Federalists.

Virginia, worked upon by Jefferson's following, and Pennsylvania, under the influence of Dallas's young Democratic following, had proved the two hotbeds of resistance. The Virginian aristocracy and the Pennsylvanian commonalty were no longer content to see the Federalist North dominating Congress by itself.

Above the crowd there was anxiety.

To save America from anarchy, Mr. Hamilton wanted to break off relations with a France in delirium. He favored active coöperation with England and even, if it were possible, an alliance. Since Mr. Jefferson, Secretary of State, was against this policy, he proposed to get on without him.

Hamilton set himself to frame the foreign policy of America together with the aid of Hammond, the English Minister, whom he saw every day. He obtained Washington's agreement that, on all important questions, Mr. Jay, Chief Justice of the Supreme Court and former Secretary for Foreign Affairs, known for his conservative tendencies and his English sympathies, should be consulted on the sly. So he attacked Mr. Jefferson on his own ground and reduced him to impotence.

But Mr. Jefferson gave him back as good as he got. While the Secretary of the Treasury was taking steps to direct the international policy of the United States, the Secretary of State was preparing to ruin his colleague's financial reputation. At Jefferson's instigation, Giles, on January 23, 1793, moved in the House of Representatives that Hamilton be good enough to present his accounts and explain his proceedings. The motion was carried.

Mr. Hamilton, who was busy at the time with a loan and some burdensome love affairs, considered that he had something better to do than draft reports. Still, draft them he did, and very fine, very imposing, and quite unintelligible to the public and to his enemies they were. His enemies took their time. Why hurry, when all Philadelphia was talking finance and floundering about in finance?

Just a few days before the end of the session of Congress, Jefferson handed Madison a paper, which he revised and passed on to Giles. The latter, thus documented, pronounced a denunciation of Mr. Hamilton's financial administration; it was arbitrary, irregular, and dangerous. The speech sounded well, and the document, reproduced immediately in every gazette in America, was meant to finish off Hamilton. He would be taken by surprise. Doubtless he would have no reply to it ready before the next session of Congress, and meanwhile six months would pass, during which the impression made would sink into the crowd. But this calculation was balked by Hamilton, who made his reply forthwith and obtained a massive majority from the House.

Hamilton and Jefferson were exchanging blows; but Washington was beginning to receive some too. By dint of hearing so much about the true Republican spirit, the populace was brought to remark that, when Washington went to the theater, an attaché, in black full dress, hair powdered and adjusted in the formal fashion, and bearing silver candlesticks and wax candles, would meet the President at the entrance and conduct him with much gravity to the Presidential box, festooned with red drapery, and bearing the United States coat of arms. At the door of the theater, the guard, in full-dress uniform, presented arms. Inside, the military escort and the police stood at attention while Mr. Washington was taking his seat heavily beside Mrs. Washington, and his gold-laced aide-de-camp bowed and the audience, with one accord, rose to their feet.

The populace had seen him passing in the street, in his big white coach, with his six white horses at a gallop, with his postilions in front and his bodyguard on either side, armed with great white wands. Would any King keep up more state?

They had heard about those receptions on February 22d, his birthday, when, after the town was awakened in the morning by the sound of cannon firing and bells pealing in his honor, after the discharge of volleys by the infantry, after a great review of the troops and the militia, the President betook himself in the evening to the ball given for him at Oeller's by the Assembly, at which all the belles of the town and all the dandies in their finest attire, all the officers in their best uniforms, and all the high officials in their best suits, thronged under the gallery, adorned with festoons and flags, where the orchestra played "Yankee Doodle" and the "Washington March."

No doubt, he smiled as a father smiles upon his children. But the acclamations of high society, its dolling up of itself, its bowing and scraping, exasperated the lower orders.

"What a monarchical farce!" they cried.

Pell-mell the populace perambulated in the streets. They crowded around carriages and before the doors of the rich. The winter was very mild; there was no ice, no storms, and the ships kept on streaming into port, coming from Europe. They arrived laden with news, which spread through the city like wildfire. France gone Republican! — The King in prison! — The King was to be exiled to the United States! — The King was to be brought to trial! — The King was to be put to death! — The King had been beheaded!

That morning a weight of sorrow brooded over Philadelphia. It seemed to all the citizens of Pennsylvania that they had just lost a member of their own family. In the taverns they talked in low voices.

[166]

BENJAMIN FRANKLIN BACHE'S CERTIFICATE OF MEMBERSHIP
IN THE DEMOCRATIC SOCIETY OF PHILADELPHIA

Then somebody burst out laughing, somebody started explaining, the papers published long and thrilling articles, and once more people started getting excited and discussing and parading. There was still talk from time to time about the "murder of Louis", and the ladies mourned his sad fate, the ecclesiastics deplored this act of violence, and the Federalists frowned; but popular enthusiasm went its way.

In Pittsburg, at Brewer's tavern, people got together and drank fifteen toasts in succession in honor of France, universal liberty, and the downfall of the black rampart of aristocracy. In Charleston, in January, they staged a procession, a prayer meeting, and a banquet, and they fired off a cannon. In Savannah there were feasting and dancing. In cold, calm Boston a procession, adorned with flags, paraded through the town an enormous ox and a gigantic bowl of punch, which helped to celebrate the glory of France, while girls in white gowns and young men cheered, and the cannon roared, and the bells pealed. In Baltimore, in Plymouth, in Princeton, in Fredericksburg, in Norfolk, there were fêtes in the same style.

But Philadelphia led the dance. The Hibernian Society organized a special fête for France, and on February 6th, the anniversary of the Franco-American alliance, the Pennsylvania militia, under the leadership of General Mifflin, Governor of the State, assembled at the City Tavern, to praise France, Dumouriez and his victories. At the head of the table a pike topped by a Liberty cap, with the French and American flags entwined, and surmounted by a dove bearing an olive branch, announced to all and sundry that this gathering was in honor of the triumph of Liberty.

For the rest, they sang in every conceivable key, they shouted in every conceivable way. Having clinked glasses fifteen times in succession already, they had the best of patriotic and culinary reasons for letting themselves go over the finest toast of all: "The Republic of France. May the spark of liberty, kindled in America, never be extinguished till monarchies cease."

CHAPTER IV

THE TRIUMPHANT FAILURE
OF CITIZEN GENET

It was then that there appeared, young, bold, brilliant and radiant with love and liberty, Edmond Charles Genet. He came as the Ambassador of the French Republic, he came as the messenger of the French people, he came as the missionary of philosophy and enlightenment.

He was not yet thirty and for the last ten years he had been famous. He was not yet thirty, and already he had served the King and the Republic, and he had traveled from Moscow to Charleston. He was not yet thirty and he was handsome.

Edmond Charles Genet had a broad, high forehead, which registered intelligence and frankness, and big blue eyes, flush with his face, which fascinated the ladies. His fine mouth, the delicate oval of his face, and his charming manners, in which mingled the open-hearted frankness of the revolutionary, the impulse of the philanthropist, and the subtle finesse of the courtier, made him so likeable that nobody could resist the attraction of his personality.

His young life had been nothing but one long series of enchantments. He owed much to his ancestors, who had given him both brains and looks. They were, for that matter, only poor pastry cooks of Burgundy; but in the Genet family handsomeness was hereditary. His grandfather was

a very comely scullion — so comely that he found an *abbé*
to pay for his studies in Paris, take him to play his part
at Sceaux, at Madame la Duchesse du Maine's, and finally
to place him in the household of Cardinal Alberoni. Here,
piously and fruitfully, he served God, the Cardinal, and
France. In this occupation he made so much money that he
was able, on his return to France, to marry an illegitimate
daughter of the illustrious family of Béarn and buy an
administrative post at Parliament.

His son was brought up with anxious care. He traveled
in England and throughout Central Europe. He made the
acquaintance of all the philosophers, and learned all the
civilized languages. At the age of twenty he made a report
which amazed Monsieur de Choiseul, and Genet was immediately taken into the government service. Whereas his father had carried on French propaganda in Spain, he concerned himself especially with propaganda against England.

It was he who, from 1760 to 1782, with nothing more
than the title of interpreter to the Ministry of Foreign
Affairs, directed all the secret activities of French policy.
Together with Franklin, he led the great attack against
England, due to which the United States won the sym-
pathy of Continental Europe and witnessed the formation
of a league of neutrals hostile to England. He was the
mainspring of Vergennes's policy, and for him he discharged hundreds of delicate missions and brought off scores
of shrewd strokes, such as the publication of the American
propaganda journal in Europe, *Les Affaires de l'Angleterre
et de l'Amérique*, the sole great source of information about
America from 1775 to 1779.

But his masterpiece was his son. Edmond Charles Genet
was born in 1763, of Edme Genet, translator at the Ministry of Foreign Affairs, and Lucie Cardon, who had been

a milliner, and a very beautiful one, and had remained very beautiful and became a fine lady. Between her and her husband reigned a love so profound that he, the famous and respected man of learning, who knew all the great minds of Europe and could write in ten languages, was a slave at the feet of this little woman, who was incapable of writing even in her own. They loved one another tirelessly and without withholding testimonies to their love, with the result that they had six fine children, of whom Edmond alone was a son.

His sisters were remarkable women, three of whom obtained posts at Court, and one of whom, Madame Campan, after being Lady in Waiting to Marie Antoinette, became the most famous schoolmistress in France. Nothing was left undone to educate these naturally gifted girls, but on the upbringing of their brother was lavished everything that the family possessed: love, zeal, attention, philosophy, religion, the favor of the King, learning, prudence, and even audacity. Day by day M. Genet watched over his son's studies. He taught him to know his way about in Latin, Greek and Swedish. He gave him instruction about how to ride on horseback, how to plait his hair, how to purge himself, and how to conduct himself at the Opera Ball.

When he was six years old he could speak Greek. At the age of eleven he translated from the Swedish Celsius's "History of Eric XIV, King of Sweden", and Nils Idman's "Researches regarding the Ancient Finnish People." At the age of fourteen he was made a member of the famous literary society, "Untile Dulci", of Stockholm, and of the Academy of Upsala, called "Apollini Sacra." At the age of seventeen the King gave him a commission as Lieutenant of Dragoons. He assumed the name of M. Genet de Charmontot, and in his fine uniform he set out to make the grand tour of Europe.

In Copenhagen the most beautiful girl in the town made him her escort to the opera, in Florence he was elected an academician of the Academia della Crusca, and in Berlin he watched twenty thousand of Frederick the Great's soldiers manœuvering. On his return, at the age of eighteen, he succeeded his father, who had just died suddenly, and, thanks to the favor of his "adorable protectress", the Queen of France, he obtained a post as secretary to the Embassy in London, and then that of Chargé d'Affaires in St. Petersburg.

On his return to France, thanks to his good looks and to another protectress, also adorable, he obtained the post of Minister of France to the United States. Madame Roland could not resist Genet's storming of her heart and Genet's brains completed what his physical accomplishments had begun.

He was given a mission which was one of the most important that could be entrusted to him; for it was a question of conveying greetings to a friendly and allied republic, and making use of it to fight against the maritime trade of England, with whom France had just gone to war. France counted on Genet, without involving the United States in the conflict, to attach them to her by an indissoluble bond, and to secure from them the corn, the wheat and the other commodities which starving France needed to feed herself — in short, to establish collaboration of the free peoples in face of the despots.

To attain this end, Genet had a weak staff, very little money, very little time, and very few contacts in America. But France counted on his appearance, his eloquence, and his Republican zeal, which was the more passionate in proportion as many people still remembered the old attachment of the Genet family to Queen Marie Antoinette. For his success, Genet counted on his star and on himself.

It wasn't an easy job. Opposing him he had George Hammond, who was not such a handsome man, but who had plenty of dignity, plenty of coolness, plenty of patience, and a hard-boiled audacity. George Hammond also had the advantage of daily intimacy with Hamilton, who told him, day by day, what was being said and done at the Cabinet Councils. Anything that Hamilton forgot to tell him he could hear through Carmichael, American Chargé d'Affaires in Madrid, who corresponded regularly with the Court of London and was quite devoted to him.

Beside him, too, Mr. Hammond had Phineas Bond, a former American citizen whose family had remained faithful to the King of England, and who had returned to Philadelphia, his home town, as consul of Great Britain. The merchants and the upper middle class of Philadelphia were very fond of him in memory of old family ties. Accordingly, Mr. Hammond had the *entrée* into high society in Philadelphia.

His consul in New York, Sir John Temple, kept him informed about the doings and sayings of the American radicals. John Temple, also born in America, was a cousin of the illustrious Lord Temple, and to this influential relationship he had owed an important post in America, where he had acted as agent for the American radicals, on whose behalf he had betrayed the English Administration which employed him. Deprived of his post in consequence, he returned to America, and there did a little spying for the English among his American friends. Now Consul General of Great Britain in New York, he kept Mr. Jefferson informed through the medium of Beckley, with whom he was on close terms, and he kept Hammond informed about what Beckley told him.

So, without having to travel very far, or even leave his own house, Hammond knew all that was going on; and he awaited Monsieur Genet without flinching.

General Washington also awaited him without flinching He was tired of disorder and excitement. He had had only too much of it for the past two years with his Ministers, and he was minded not to tolerate any more. With Jefferson and with Hamilton he had held himself in check; for one of them was his friend and a Virginian, and the other was his friend and a Federalist, and both of them were his Ministers. He could not, without losing something of his dignity, tell them just what was on his mind; but it was beginning to weigh heavily on him.

General Washington had neither pride, nor ambition, nor avarice, nor presumption; but he insisted on being respected and he delighted in being popular. He had, besides, a weakness for reading the papers. Now he had noticed for the past few months that, as a result of all this unnecessary stir, he was beginning to be less popular. People were criticizing him and he did not like it.

He wanted to silence all these importunate voices. He wanted to work in peace. He wanted peace. Young America needed peace to establish her government and set her house in order. General Washington knew very well that you can have an orderly household and a strong people only by virtue of good habits.

He was pleased to see that his people, lured by their increasing prosperity, desired peace. As soon as he learned of the August Revolution and the establishment of a republic in France, he asked his Ministers whether the French Minister should be received and whether the treaties with France should still be regarded as valid. Jefferson said "Yes", and Hamilton said, more or less, "No", and Washington made ready to receive the French Minister, but to receive him coldly. This was something that General Washington was rather good at doing.

Moreover, as soon as war was declared between France and Great Britain, he consulted his Cabinet to obtain their views. Of course, there was that Franco-American Treaty of 1778, which contemplated the guaranteeing of the French West Indies by America. But was it still valid? For that matter, the guarantee came into effect only in case of a defensive war, whereas it was France who had declared war on England.

The whole Cabinet was in favor of neutrality, just as the whole country was. Hamilton requested Jay to draft a declaration of neutrality. He transmitted it to Washington, who looked it over carefully. Accordingly, when the Philadelphia morning papers of April 22, 1793, reached the Morris mansion, where Washington was staying, and informed him that Monsieur Genet had landed and that he had been welcomed by the town of Charleston with indescribable enthusiasm, the General's first act was to open his drawer, take out the proclamation, sign it, and send it to the papers, which published it the next day. Such was the first salutation from the General to the Citizen.

The Citizen did not mind it. He was bathing in glory. The town of Charleston had fêted him as he had never been fêted before. Salvos of cannon, volleys of musketry, peals of bells, militia, clergymen, prayer meetings, women, children, bouquets of flowers, banquets, patriotic songs, fraternal embraces, processions through the town — nothing had been left undone for Genet. Never Lafayette in all his popularity, never Washington in all his glory, had been better treated. Genet felt that the heart of the American people was with him. What did he care about a crabbed old man?

From Charleston to Philadelphia, all along his route, the farmers of Carolina, those of Virginia and those of Pennsylvania, thronged around him. His heart was warmed by all this. But these were only clodhoppers; the capital was preparing something better for him.

It was in a state of ebullition. One after another, two great fires had startled and excited the city. One after another, French and English warships had been seen coming into port. Their sailors filled the street, and gave one another dirty looks. In the taverns they exchanged insults and sometimes blows. Rumors of war came from all sides, and the great enthusiasm which spread from the South, heralding Genet, his triumphal progress and his invincible charm, set fire to everybody's imagination, everybody's fervor.

Freneau and Bache had fanned the flame. They had encouraged the citizens to bedeck the city for Genet. In the harbor, the French ships had been adorned with flags and pennants. A committee was formed to receive the French Minister; and it was murmured that, if the President chose to shut himself up and plot with the Vicomte de Noailles and Talon, the emissaries of the French princes, the populace, for its part, would not be backward in showing itself in the streets around Genet, the envoy of the French people. Everything was in readiness.

On the morning of May 16, 1793, the French warships in the harbor started firing their cannon to announce the coming of the Minister. Forthwith a hundred or so of the

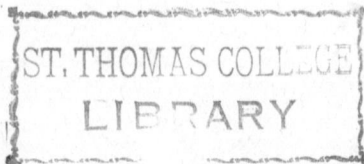

more enthusiastic Philadelphians betook themselves to Gray's Ferry to be the first to welcome him. They escorted him in procession to the City Tavern, and all day long his apartment was thronged with American patriots who had come to salute the French patriot, apostle of the liberty of the world.

In the evening, as night was falling, zealous citizens flocked to the Capitol. They were by no means anonymous or ambiguous people, but the élite of Philadelphia society: the backbone of the American Philosophical Society; Charles Biddle, who had been Secretary of the State of Pennsylvania; Doctor Rittenhouse, President of the Philosophical Society; Doctor Hutchinson, the most famous doctor in Philadelphia, and a hundred other leading citizens. They elected a committee to draft an address to Genet.

The next day, the committee, after holding a meeting at Biddle's, presented itself before the citizens of Pennsylvania, once more assembled at the Capitol. The newspapers had summoned them there in the name of liberty, fraternity, and the unity of the free peoples. In his *Advertiser* Benny had made a warm appeal to them. There were more than a thousand of them, and, with clamorous enthusiasm, they approved the address to Genet, without understanding it, or even listening to it.

Then committee and crowd, and all the passers-by whom they met on their way, and the good women who were enjoying the cool of the evening on their doorsteps, and the children in the streets who were truant from school, and playing pitchpenny — everybody, old or young, electors or apprentices or foreigners — betook themselves by way of Market Street, in the quiet of the evening which made their tumult seem still more grandiose, amplified as it was by the silence of the city in its nocturnal serenity, to Second

Street and the City Tavern, where Monsieur Genet received them. They told him of their enthusiasm, their admiration, their zeal for his country, their warm affection for his person, and their devotion to the immortal principles which he represented. Everybody talked, and sang, and embraced, and wept, and the electrified crowd was ready for a revolution, for an apotheosis, for a sublime sacrifice.

But Monsieur Genet was tired and everybody went home to bed. The children grumbled, to be sure; but that was all the trouble there was.

The next day, Saturday, May 18, 1793, the immense wave of popular affection surged towards Monsieur Genet once again. The French Patriotic Society presented him its warm homage. The German Republican Society came to tender him an address of congratulation, and in the evening at Oeller's, was held the finest banquet that anybody had ever seen in Philadelphia. It cost four dollars a cover, but nothing had been spared to combine, with that splendor which should belong to a grandiose fête, that luster which is the proper attribute of enlightened minds, and that emotion which alone can express the fraternal sentiments nourished by the hearts of citizens.

The table was adorned with an immense Tree of Liberty, pikes and Caps of Liberty. All around, entwined, the French and American flags bore witness to the union of the free peoples, while lanterns, garlands and streamers completed the setting for a fête. But the finest thing of all was Citizen Genet, with his immense tricolor scarf, at the head of the table between Charles Biddle and General Mifflin, Governor of Pennsylvania. The room was full of French officials and French officers in uniform, and citizens and citizenesses in their best clothes for this great day. All that Philadelphia could boast in the way of men of philosophical and liberal mind was assembled in this setting, and some fine ladies had even come out of curiosity; for, after all, was not Genet thirty?

Everything was in unison and the pitch was set very high. A truly fraternal spirit reigned in the hall. They drank to Liberty and Equality, they drank to the French Republic, they drank to the United States; and Citizen Duponceau, climbing on to the table, proceeded to recite an elegant ode composed for this patriotic occasion by Citizen Pichon. It was so much appreciated that the company unanimously voted that Citizen Pichon, that young Frenchman of promising abilities, be recommended to the notice of the Minister. The company on motion also ordered that Citizen Freneau, here present, should be requested to translate it into English verse, which would permit the public to understand it.

Then they drank to the State of Pennsylvania, they drank to the valiant defenders of French liberty by land and sea, they drank to the memory of the heroes fallen for the liberty of America; they drank to "the virtuous Washington — may Heaven grant to France and to the United States many citizens that resemble him!" They drank to union and perpetual fraternity between the Free Peoples, France and the United States. They toasted: "The arm of Hercules to those who combat the Hydra of despotism!"; they toasted: "May the next generation know despotism from History only!"; they toasted: "May the last freeman perish rather than bend under the yoke of despotism!"; they toasted "the years '76 and '92."

They toasted the Cap of Liberty: "May all heads be soon under one cap, that of Liberty!"; and the company, carried away by enthusiasm, shouted for the Minister to place a Cap of Liberty on his head. So he did; and then the cap traveled from head to head around the table, "each wearer enlivening the scene with a patriotic sentiment."

Now, while everybody was congratulating everybody else, the door opened suddenly, and a delegation of sailors from the French frigate *Embuscade* made their appearance. Like good patriots, confidently but modestly, they advanced and saluted the Minister, who, with all the company, had risen to his feet to greet them. He summoned them to him and gave each one of them a brotherly kiss. This was the signal for a touching and truly fraternal scene, for everybody wanted to kiss the French sailors. When they had thus satisfied the needs of the heart, they made the sailors sit down and gave them something to drink, and the company, at the tops of their voices, demanded the singing of the "Marseillaise."

Citizen Bournonville was not backward in obliging. He sang the "Marseillaise" with great taste and spirit and all the company took it up in chorus. He sang all the couplets and the whole assembly took up all the refrains. He added two couplets composed by Genet in honor of the French Navy and all the assembly sang the refrain twice more.

Feeling his heart bursting with the milk of human kindness under the stress of all this emotion, the Minister could restrain himself no longer. Standing up at the head of the table, he sang, with great energy and judgment, a song which he had composed to the air of "Vous qui d'Amoureuse Aventure." It was replete with truly patriotic and republican sentiments, and well adapted to the occasion, and it threatened tyrants with extermination.

Then, turning towards the sailors with a dramatic gesture, he handed over the Liberty Caps to them, bidding the gallant fellows defend them even unto death; and the stout fellows, electrified by the grandeur of the moment, the solemnity of the setting, and the warmth of the environment, swore to perish to the last man rather than surrender these tokens of liberty and of American and French fraternity. Then shouts, and cheers, and songs, and even the tears of tender hearts intermingled in the fevered hall. They had to get out of it.

They escorted Genet to the City Tavern, with renewed songs and hurrahs, through the evening crowd of idlers, who joined the procession and added to the enthusiasm. They cried, "God save America! God guard Genet!"

Was there any need of God's protection for him? He had the people and the genius of liberty on his side. What force could resist the strength of the people and the strength of enlightenment?

This was what he told Mr. Jefferson when he made his acquaintance. He informed him that the French Republic had charged him to fit out privateers in America to harry the English; to prepare expeditions there against the Spaniards in Florida and Louisiana and foment a rebellion in Canada; to cement the union between France and America and to sign a new treaty for trade and the revictualing of France.

When Mr. Jefferson, friendly but uneasy, shook his head, Genet smiled. People like Jefferson did not know what real revolutions were. He did not know how to handle the people. For his part, Genet was sure that he could manage the Government through Congress, Congress through the people, and the people through enthusiasm.

Mr. Jefferson, perfect patriot though he was, did not seem to know much about the people. He seemed to want to guide them without coming in contact with them, whereas Monsieur Genet was at home with crowds and liked to work with his own hands. He had just shown as much. Everything was all right with him — parades, toasts, speeches, processions, gestures, songs. He was ready for anything to fascinate the crowd and fascinate it he did.

For a man who is young, handsome, passionate, and who knows women well, it is always easy to fascinate crowds; but Monsieur Genet knew also that, to maintain his influence over the crowd, he needed working tools, and he did not overlook the fact that two of the best of them were newspapers and clubs. There were plenty of newspapers in Philadelphia already and there was no need of creating any more. It was enough for him to know how to make use of those which existed.

Monsieur Genet could choose among Freneau the poet, protected by Jefferson; Brown the business man, who was well established, and young Bache, who worked alone as best he could. Freneau was more showy, Brown was more weighty, Freneau was a poet, Brown was a business man, but Genet preferred Bache; for Bache was a journalist.

Bache became his intimate friend. What a comfort it was for Bache, after all those years of solitude and silence, once more to find a man of full-sounding mind, like those whom he had once met at his grandfather's and who had given him such a fine impression of life, such an insistent impetus of hope and eagerness! What a joy it was for Genet, after streets, and strife and subterfuge, to find himself face to face with a man who was straightforward and strong, silent and sincere, to whom everything that he, Genet, said had a real meaning, and who played with his cards on the table!

He adopted him and Bache's gazette became Genet's mouthpiece. Bache became one of his closest counsellors. New life penetrated into him and new life penetrated into his gazette. It took a sudden spurt and in two months it gained three hundred subscribers. Bache needed more, however, and with Genet he began the organization of the American masses.

It was an odd thing, a fine thing, the American crowd. All the revolutions in the world, all the disasters, all the persecutions, cast upon that soil, still virgin and vast, human débris, broken and shrinking, beaten but rebellious, who came to seek revenge or a grave, and who disembarked shivering with fear, longing, regret and want. One of the most extreme climates in the world welcomed them and added to their distress; the disorder of a region hastily colonized increased their perplexity, and the brutal simplicity of a social life rapidly organized made them at once submissive and sullen.

Those who found their way to the West could let themselves be soothed by the silence of the countryside or give vent to their wrath in the solitude of the frontier. Those who stayed in the towns could only shout, drink, sing and play politics. In face of the dominant class and race, the Anglo-Saxon, instinctively they grouped themselves racially. There was the Society of the Sons of Saint George for the English immigrants, the Society of Saint Andrew for the Scots, the Society of Saint Patrick or the Hibernian Society for the Irish, the Germanic Society for the Germans, and in 1792, when the great influx of French began, the French Benevolent Society was organized.

So the poor people grouped themselves and helped one another a little; but this scarcely gave them power, though it was the beginning of electoral combinations. These societies did not commence to play an important political rôle until the time when the Tammany societies were formed. Tammany was an old Redskin, whom Pennsylvania

legend designated as one of the Indian chiefs who had sold
land to Penn, and who was suspected of duplicity, drunkenness, incurable laziness and some other picturesque vices.
But all this was guesswork, and history can only suspect
Tammany of never having existed.

This did not prevent his name from becoming popular,
serving as sign for the fishing clubs along the Schuylkill and
for patriotic societies, and finally being taken up by a
group of patriots, tainted with philosophism, who, after
the Revolution, founded a popular society in New York.
No saint gave them patronage except the old drunkard
Tammany; they belonged to no particular race, they had
no doctrine except liberty and philanthropy, but gradually
they became the rallying center of the immigrants.

While the upper classes, merchants, bankers, lawyers and
landowners, looked askance at them, Tammany opened its
arms to the newcomers. It enrolled them at once, and let
them take part in its meetings, where there was informal
discussion of political problems, or where from time to time
some member raised a general question: "Ought not death
as the punishment for crimes in society to be abolished
except where it is the punishment for murder?" —
"Whether the adoption and use of a National dress
would be a National Benefit in the United States?" —
"Whether the existence of a Convention of the people,
either in concurrence with or in opposition to the will
of the existing Government, would necessarily destroy that
Government?"

So the immigrants familiarized themselves immediately
with the boldest ideas. They were instructed in the art of
politics. They were given enlightenment; even a museum of
history, natural philosophy and ethnography had been established for their benefit, in which they found snake skins,

the portrait of Saint Tammany, and the works of Thomas Paine.

But, above all, by a master stroke in reply to the provocation of the superior, arrogant Anglo-Saxons, the members of Tammany declared themselves autochtonous, the true heirs of the soil, the only real Americans, since their patron was Tammany. For the great fête days, accordingly, they dressed themselves as Indians. They painted themselves red, rigged themselves out in blankets and feathers, and then, armed with bows and arrows and tomahawks, they leaped and shouted through the streets, to the great amazement of respectable citizens.

More astonished still were some real Indians when, having come to New York on a delegation to Congress, they encountered these unknown, heterodox and unexpected brethren of theirs. They treated them to dirty looks and the ice would never have been broken if Indian Redskins and Redskin Irish had not got together around an immense bowl of punch.

These war dances, these drinking bouts, and these parades were by no means so puerile as they might have seemed. They enabled the leaders of Tammany to stimulate their followers, to give them a sense of their own number and their strength, to draw them out of the drifting crowd and form them into a group, to make them react against the hostile environment in which they found themselves, and finally, when the time came, to get them to vote.

Like all the associations in which the Irish element was dominant, the members of Tammany hated England and venerated France. Their center was in New York, but they had branches throughout the country and a strong organization in Philadelphia, which greeted Genet on his arrival. Genet appreciated it, but he realized that Tammany, which

[185]

was very well suited to a commercial city like New York, was by no means so well suited to intellectual and Quaker Philadelphia.

In the environment of the American Philosophical Society and with the help of a group of cultivated Quakers, there was born in January 1793, another association, which fitted better into the Pennsylvania setting and atmosphere. The "Democratic Society" was still an embryo, but it had the seed of growth. It was, in short, the heir to the societies formerly founded in Philadelphia to discuss political questions, and in particular to the "Society for Political Research," which met at Franklin's house from 1788 to 1790. But the Democratic Society was more open and more active.

Genet galvanized it. He constituted a solid and substantial General Staff for it, whose elements he assembled from the American Philosophical Society and the Government of Pennsylvania. He found a rank-and-file for it among the *émigrés* and immigrants of all kinds. Rittenhouse, president of the American Philosophical Society, and the most famous man of learning in America, was its president. Dallas, secretary to the Governor of Pennsylvania, was the principal member of its Corresponding Committee. On its board of directors figured Teutons like Rittenhouse and Doctor Leib; French, like M. Duponceau; Scots, like Dallas; Irish, like S. Bryan and J. Smith; Americans of old stock, like B. F. Bache, and Jews, like Israel Israel, the lawyer who had the honor to be its treasurer. So everybody had his place.

But its essential organism was its Corresponding Committee, whose duty it was to get in touch with the public and with the other Democratic societies and to influence public opinion. Its basis was the "Rights of Man"; its program, "to teach the peoples to dispose of themselves"; its method, "to watch the Governments, whatever they were, whatever they did"; its ultimate goal, "the federation of the free peoples in a universal fraternity and the annihilation of the despotic Hydra"; and its immediate object to eliminate Hamilton, break Federalism, and intimidate Washington.

It met every week to discuss political problems, vote resolutions and addresses of blame or praise, send them to those in authority, celebrate the victories of the peoples, scrutinize the actions of the Government, and draw up addresses to the other Democratic societies. In fact, a regular chain of them had been formed. There were more than twenty-seven of them, scattered throughout all the territory of the Union and in all the States. But the most influential, apart from the Mother Society of Philadelphia, were the German Republican Society, also of Philadelphia; the Democratic Society of Lexington (Kentucky), which had as its particular object the opening of the Mississippi and the West to Americans; and the four Democratic societies of Virginia, which were the most implacable against the English.

Jefferson had nothing to do with this movement and his lieutenants had nothing to do with it either. Madison did not figure in it, Freneau held himself aloof, Beckley hovered around without risking himself too close. While all the Pennsylvanians, from George Logan to Bache, and from Charles Biddle to Doctor Hutchinson, rallied to it with enthusiasm and delighted to mingle with the crowd of patriots, the Virginian leaders abstained. They had no taste for a crowd of people, they were no townsmen, and Jefferson could feel that a storm was brewing.

Mr. Washington had had quite enough of all this pother. He held that the people should reign, but have no right to rule, and it was very disagreeable for him to feel spied upon in everything he did, in everything he undertook, in everything he meant to do. He had a very clear consciousness of public opinion and read the papers carefully. The least popular hostility annoyed him. The idea of an organized hostility exasperated him.

For that matter, Citizen Genet's ways in themselves exasperated him. In his attitude towards him, Citizen Genet was at once deferential and patronizing, admiring and cavalier. Citizen Genet treated General Washington as a young angel might treat a Divinity who had become a little feebleminded. But Mr. Washington, who was far from feebleminded, was making ready to treat Citizen Genet as an experienced schoolmaster treats an impertinent pupil.

It was clear that Genet had the people on his side. From every corner of the Union they sent him addresses. The working men of the towns kept on fêting him. The peasants of the countryside were devoted to him too, out of Republican enthusiasm and also because the French Republic was making large purchases of wheat. Juries acquitted the French privateers whom the magistrates sent before them. Accordingly General Washington acted firmly, but prudently. In the first place, he made sure of his Cabinet.

One day when there was to be a Cabinet Council, Mr. Jefferson was very much surprised to see General Washington arrive early and slam the door behind him. The General came over to Jefferson's table, thumped it with his fist, and, usually reserved though he was, launched into a long, violent and haughty diatribe. Finally he flung a newspaper on the table and desired Jefferson to tell him "who wrote this" and who was this "swine of a Freneau."

Naturally, Jefferson could not tell him. He never wrote

for the papers, and it was contrary to all his principles to pay any attention to the papers, even if one of them happened to be published by a clerk of his own Ministry, paid by him and chosen by him. So he had nothing to say. He was very sorry that he could not reply to the General. But the General was in such a state that he persisted in requesting, requiring and even demanding an answer.

It was a painful scene, and Mr. Jefferson made a sorry story of it to Doctor Logan, under the great trees at Stenton. Doctor Logan often thought about it afterwards. Mr. Jefferson never forgot it.

Mr. Jefferson, all in favor of France though he was, could not approve Citizen Genet's audacities, and after this scene he disapproved them more and more every day. He went so far as to drop a hint to him; but Genet had always known that Jefferson was virtuous and weak and he paid no attention to him. He went straight ahead; with him he had the people, and right, and the genius of Liberty. He made ready his expeditions, bought his wheat, and fitted out his privateers. An article of the treaty of 1778 appeared to give him title to do all this; and he drew attention to all the American privateers which had been armed, repaired and manned in France before France intervened in the War of Independence. Between free men there was mutual understanding and mutual help.

But the Minister of Great Britain was far from admitting this interpretation of the treaty of 1778 and he had no difficulty about convincing Mr. Hamilton and Mr. Knox. General Washington, who for that matter was himself no longer very sure about the validity of the treaty of 1778, now that there had been a change in the régime in France, would not admit Citizen Genet's interpretation, which compromised the maintenance of peace and the trade of American ports. He consulted his Cabinet. Without exception it sided with him.

He desired Monsieur Genet to stop issuing letters of marque. Monsieur Genet was too polite and too deferential to say "No" to an old man. He made his bow; but he was too good a patriot not to go on fighting against despotism. So he went on fitting out ships. Mr. Washington, however, was a man who stuck to his point; and, just when the *Petit Démocrate*, which had been equipped at Philadelphia, was about to quit the port, he forbade Genet to let her go. The Government of Pennsylvania associated itself with Washington's action.

Genet had the weakness to say that the ship should not sail. He had the still greater weakness to let her sail.

One may sympathize with Genet. The weather was very hot in Philadelphia and he was in a round of one fête after another. On the Fourth of July, on the occasion of the American national festival, the French Patriotic Society and the whole town celebrated Liberty, and Citizen Genet. On July 14th it started over again. In the *Journal*, "Juba" insulted Hamilton and Noailles and lauded Genet to the skies. Throughout the country they were planting Trees of Liberty, sporting the tricolor cockade, donning the Cap of Liberty, and singing the "Marseillaise" and the "Ça Ira". They were subscribing to send wheat to France; they were thronging to enroll and harry the English. In the streets of Philadelphia, citizens and French sailors mauled English sailors, and sometimes there were heads broken. It was hot, and they were singing, and toasting, and embracing.

So Monsieur Genet let the *Petit Démocrate* sail. It was a mistake. He let her sail, and he told his friend Dallas that, if "Old Washington" annoyed him, he would appeal from the President to the people. It was a fine phrase, and

"A PEEP INTO THE ANTI-FEDERAL CLUB"

Dallas was a friend of his, and Jefferson had certainly told Genet that Congress was on his side; but still, it was a mistake.

"Old Washington" assembled his council of Ministers and asked them for their views. They were all beginning to feel their ears tingling with all this racket. Besides, it was stifling hot. They all agreed that the American Government should demand the recall of Monsieur Genet from the French Government, which could now scarcely refuse it. Monsieur Genet had lied to the Government to which he was accredited.

So long as the people were with him, Citizen Genet was not afraid of the President. While he awaited the meeting of Congress, he went on influencing public opinion and pursuing his great schemes. As a matter of precaution, he sent his Government a report in which he denounced Washington, whom he treated with disdain as a Lafayettist, and Jefferson, whom he accused of being a timeserver. Then, without asking Washington's assent, and in defiance of Jefferson, who had advised him to the contrary, he made public the impassioned, insulting letter which he had sent to Washington, and Washington's cold reply.

It was another fine gesture and it started a frightful fuss all over the country. The Federalists waxed indignant about it, Jefferson was dismayed, and the fieriest of the Democrats triumphed over seeing Washington arraigned before the tribunal of world opinion.

But this was not enough for Citizen Genet. Without turning a hair, having thus fired the powder train behind him, he set off for New York, where a French fleet had just arrived. He had decided to launch it against Newfoundland. There it was to capture the six hundred English fishing boats. Thence it was to sail and round up the

English commercial convoy as it came out of Hudson's Bay. Then it was to bombard Halifax and destroy the English frigate anchored there as a guard ship. Next it was to sail south, enter the Gulf of Mexico, and occupy New Orleans, where the population was ready to welcome it. Finally it was to return to New York, there to receive from the hands of Citizen Genet the laurels which belonged to Republican conquerors.

So Edmond Genet said; so he dreamed. But, instead of his great fleet laden with the spoils of Newfoundland and Halifax and Montreal and New Orleans, what he saw putting in its appearance first was a wretched, pitiable fleet, hundreds of vessels of every sort and kind, bringing from Cap Français the unfortunate white colonists who had succeeded in escaping from the burning, sacking and massacre to which the Negroes had given up the town. They landed on the American coast a deplorable, desolate, disconcerting horde, a querulous and exasperated herd, bearing with them a few remnants of their wealth or their comfort: a little gold, a goat, an old Negro slave, some books, a clock, and an inexorable hatred of revolutionary ideas.

The American people received them with pity, kindliness and generosity. Shelter was found for them, subscriptions were taken up for them, the State of Pennsylvania provided relief for them, and the Federalists were very loud in their compassion for these French victims of the French delirium.

It showed their kindness. It showed how horrible the French Revolution was.

The heavy, stifling summer, in which heat waves succeeded one another without respite, dampened enthusiasm, blunted the edge of quarrels and benumbed energy. Philadelphia was torrid and stinking. In the lower wards, around

Water Street which ran along the river, where the Negroes and the poor whites lived, where unsanitary wooden huts and filthy hovels huddled together, the air became pest-laden.

First, there were a few cases of sickness; there often were, in this dirty corner of the city. Then people died, plague-stricken within a few days, or a few hours, and their bodies turned black, repulsive in their stench. It was yellow fever.

It gained ground more and more. It seemed to make its way from house to house and to increase with the heat of the days. In August a dozen people a day were dying; at the beginning of September they were carrying a score a day to the cemetery, and by September 15th it was more than seventy. On October 11th there were one hundred and nineteen deaths.

Panic seized upon the city. The rich fled to their country houses. The poor trembled in their homes. They did not dare to go out, they did not dare to visit their neighbors, they purged themselves, they sniffed smelling salts, they tried not to swallow their saliva, if they happened to encounter a suspected case, for, so the physicians said, if you came in contact with a contagious person, you should always spit afterwards. Empty houses began to be seen, doors stood gaping, the streets were deserted and silent, and gloom brooded over the crossroads. There were no longer carriages. If any vehicle rumbled over the stones, it was the death cart.

Doctors multiplied. Doctor Rush purged his patients and gave them ipecac, and so did Doctor Hodge. Doctor Kuhn advised bitter tincture and laudanum, Doctor Wistar preferred a camomile treatment, whereas Doctor Carson recommended feeding up with highly spiced dishes. Others held

[193]

by cathartics, others again by emetics, and many recommended mercury potions, which had considerable effect, for, if you did not die, they left you ill for several months; while still more encouraged their patients to drink hard to keep their spirits up. In short, they were full of zeal and remedies; but they could not prevent Doctor Wistar and Doctor Carson from falling sick or Doctor Hutchinson from dying, together with four thousand five hundred of his fellow citizens.

Twenty thousand persons had fled the city. On Bush Hill a hospital was established for the contagious poor, and two citizens, the Frenchman Stephen Girard and the American Peter Helm, took charge of it. About the streets wandered abandoned children, starving orphans. There was soon so great a number of them that shelter had to be provided for them also. The poor immigrants, German, Irish, and French, died by hundreds. Alexander Hamilton was caught by the contagion and thought he was going to die. Four members of the committee for the relief of indigent patients caught it and did die. The city was mute, mournful and moribund.

General Washington had taken refuge at Mount Vernon, General Knox was gone, Mr. Jefferson was living in the country near by, Citizen Genet was in New York. The shops were shut, the doors of the Ministries were closed, and only the lawyers felt it their duty to stay at their desks to help their clients to make their wills. The few people who still lived in Philadelphia lived only on death and for death.

It was only as a dying echo of the fêtes and the agitations of the summer that the French celebrated the first anniversary of the establishment of the Republic on September 22d. It was in but a small company that they went

[194]

aboard a ship in the harbor, the *Ville de l'Orient*; and, even after they had drunk a little, and speechified a little, and toasted a little, they still did not dare to let themselves go or make much noise. They fired only a triple salvo, and its noise seemed to spend itself idly, incongruously, in the silence of the city.

Bache reported this in his paper. Then he set off for the country. He had souls in his keeping. He did not want to risk either the life of his dear Margaret, or that of his fine youngster Franklin, his eldest son, born in 1792, or those of his four apprentices and his seven workmen, for the sake of publishing a paper which would circulate only amid corpses and which only the moribund would peruse.

So the silence of the city became complete.

And, as the yellow fever ravaged the other great centers, or threatened them, it may be said that the whole of the United States fell into silence.

And the great enthusiasm which had swept the whole American people toward Citizen Genet fell into silence too.

CHAPTER V

THE DAWN OF THE *AURORA*

IT was during this silence, during this dejection, that Genet's enemies fell upon him. Dallas had told Mifflin what Genet had said about appealing from the President to the people, and Mifflin had related it to Knox, Knox had passed it on to Hamilton, and Hamilton had conveyed it to Jay and King. In the course of August, Jay and King, at Hamilton's instigation, published a solemn declaration in which they quoted and denounced what Genet had said. Then all the Federalist papers took it up and circulated it throughout the United States. The Federalist papers were dominant in Boston and in Connecticut. The stronghold of the Democratic papers was Philadelphia; but the Democratic Press, overwhelmed by the heat and the yellow fever, found itself in no position to reply with the eloquence, the power of persuasion, which the occasion demanded. Bache tried to fight back, but with no great success; and Genet felt around him a wave of disapproval.

It was all very well for Dallas to declare that all that Genet had said was that he should appeal from the President to Congress. It was all very well for Genet to spread himself in protestations of his innocence and the perfidy of his enemies. He felt that he was being persecuted and he was eloquent about it. His gestures remained grandiose but they interested the public less.

Genet himself had less time to devote to his gestures.

He had other things to worry him. He had, indeed, met at New York that great fleet of his which was to ravage Newfoundland, bombard Halifax, seize the English convoy and take New Orleans; but he found it in a state of mutiny. Its sailors had just come from San Domingo, where the Republican authorities had tried to compel them to act as arbiters between the whites and the blacks, and to protect the latter. They could not see things that way, for, sailors though they might be, after all, they were whites. So they refused to obey, and, in desperation, they were withdrawn from San Domingo and transferred to New York, where Genet met them.

Genet talked to them, Genet embraced them, Genet gave them banquets and Caps of Liberty, promises and hopes. The sailors adapted themselves to all this, they embraced the Minister, they applauded him, and they gave him back promise for promise — so much so that Genet was able to write to France that the sailors' "bounds of philosophy" had been overshot, but not their "bounds of patriotism." He proceeded to try and invoke their patriotism.

He held up before the sailors the vision of an expedition to Newfoundland, a bombardment of Halifax, a taking of New Orleans; but the sailors, whose souls were not romantic, remained unmoved and even frigid. Then Citizen Genet flashed before their eyes the prospect of their return to France, to the bosom of their families, amid the plaudits of all patriots, with their great fleet and the immense convoy of San Domingo, laden with wealth. The sailors, used to being at sea and accustomed to being away from home, were not in the least elated by the thought of seeing their families again. They said that they were quite ready to sail and to accompany the convoy — so long as they were sure that they would not meet the English fleet.

[197]

Genet negotiated, reasoned, argued, but there was nothing doing; and, when he proceeded to give orders, the sailors mutinied. He had discovered the bounds of their patriotism. He suffered for it in his patriot's soul.

He was to suffer more. At the end of autumn, the yellow fever stopped raging, Washington returned to Philadelphia, Jefferson went back there, the whole Government re-established itself there, and Congress resumed its labors. Immediately Washington sent a message to Congress relating what had happened during the summer, and politely, prettily and promptly, the two Houses of Congress approved the President's action. There was no need for Citizen Genet to appeal from the President to Congress. Before he did so he got his answer.

He was to suffer still more. When his letter denouncing Washington, and the letter from the American Government denouncing him, arrived in Paris, his friends had fallen, the *Girondins* were outlawed and being hunted down, and Robespierre, who now held power, had no use for them. Robespierre did not hesitate. He accepted forthwith the kind gift which Washington made him, and he invited Citizen Genet to return with all speed to Paris, there to present his accounts and no doubt, a little later, his head.

Citizen Genet was a hero, ready to give his life for his country, for liberty and for justice; but his accounts were complicated and he felt no desire to present them forthwith. He was not in the least inclined to suffer an undeserved death. That, however, was what awaited him in France — not the least doubt about it. If this were the case, he preferred marriage, and he had somebody in view in America.

General Washington might have stood in his way and dispatched him to France, as Robespierre desired. But General Washington was a profound politician, who knew that a vanquished enemy who retreats is more dangerous than a vanquished enemy who stays on the field. General Washington was also a man of taste, who knew that pity for a man who has insulted you is a rarer pleasure and a more complete revenge than wrath.

Genet stayed in America, and he married Miss Clinton, and he made a very good farmer.

In the presence of this catastrophe, the Democrats were dismayed. The man who had succeeded in forming the crowds of the cities into a solid block and flinging it at the Federalists had fallen. He left a great gap behind him, and apparently there was nobody to replace him. They consoled themselves by saying that the Democratic Party still had its great philosopher, its great artist in intellectual and parliamentary manœuvers, Thomas Jefferson. They were wrong. Thomas Jefferson, too, was lost to the Democratic Party.

For the past two years Thomas Jefferson had been saying that he wanted to retire. He had talked about it to General Washington; and the General, while he tried to dissuade him, let him see that he found this desire of his quite natural. The incidents of the summer, the agitations of the autumn, the digs and the blows of that year 1793 had left the Secretary of State bruised all over. He had by no means forgotten certain scenes. He insisted on retiring and the President bowed to his decision. Mr. Hamilton drew the conclusion that this was a victory for the right party and a success for the President.

He had a right to think so, since Mr. Freneau followed his chief into retirement, and the *National Gazette*, which had given the General so much trouble, ceased to appear.

[199]

Jefferson vowed that henceforth he would concern himself with nothing but his tobacco, his cows, and his pigs; and Mr. Freneau proposed to navigate over seas less stormy than politics.

By that coolness of his, so firm, so artfully armed with anger, the General had rid himself of his most dangerous enemies.

His kindly coolness was also to rid him of the most dangerous of his friends. Mr. Hamilton declared that he would shortly retire — that he would have retired already if the state of affairs had let him. The President, while deploring his departure, let him go.

Mr. Hamilton needed to make a living. He could not do so in politics. Mr. Hamilton, it would also seem, found the struggle less exciting now that Mr. Jefferson was gone. Above all, Mr. Hamilton knew that General Washington would never give him what he wanted, what he dare not ask, or mention, or even hope, but what he must still desire.

So the General had made a clean sweep.

Only a few journalists still importuned him. Only the Democratic societies still kept their eye on him. Those of the East cried out against the English, because they were pillaging American ships and disorganizing the trade of the United States by their privateering. Those of the West stormed against the English, because they maintained their garrisons in the forts of the West, and against the Spaniards, because they refused to open the Mississippi to the Americans. Those of the West and those of the East alike denounced the incapacity, the idleness, the negligence and the lack of patriotism of the Federal Government.

Certain newspapers acted as an echo to them; and of all

the Democratic papers, the one which the Genet affair, and the creation of the Democratic societies, and the campaign against Washington had thrust into the front rank was Benny Bache's paper. They did him the honor to consider him a danger. When Jefferson retired after four years of struggle, when Genet disappeared after ten months of battle, they left scarcely anything solid behind them but the Democratic societies and Bache's *General Advertiser*.

Benny found himself no longer on the right side of the line where he had once wanted to be; but, where he was, there he was henceforth the leader.

And who should say that he had chosen wrong? He had the street with him, the living soul of the city. In his paper echoed all the rumors of the town, and the town was a whispering gallery of the passions that his paper spread through it. His public was all that world of small folk that disgusted the Federalists and that Jefferson loved, but only at a distance: Tammany, the workers, the mechanics, the Democratic societies, the militiamen, the vulgar, the rabble; and the rabble, awakened by Genet, excited by the Democratic societies and Benny's paper, the rabble, all enthusiasm inside and all rags outside, paraded the streets.

On January 1st, the Second Regiment of the Philadelphia Militia assembled and acclaimed Genet. On February 6th, the officers of the regiment celebrated the anniversary of the French alliance by a dinner at Richardet's, and the sailors of the *Ville de l'Orient* were escorted right through the town by a band; while at Oeller's the French Patriotic Society gave a fête, and the captain of the *Ville de l'Orient* received American and French patriots on board.

On March 11th, the city merchants, meeting at Mac-Sheane's Tavern, sent an address to Congress protesting against the proceedings of England. On May 1st the Democratic Society and the German Republican Society celebrated the spring, humanity and France in Israel Israel's garden. The Fourth of July and the Fourteenth of July were full of the roar of salvos, the pealing of bells, the clamor of the crowd in the street, the tramp of processions which succeeded one another around the places of worship and across the squares and crossroads.

At the theater, on the demand of the audience, the performance of the "Widow of Malabar" was interrupted for the singing of the "Ça Ira", and the audience rose to their feet to listen to the "Marseillaise." In the House of Representatives, when a patriotic speech resounded through the crowded chamber, thunder-claps of applause burst from the public galleries. In the street, on their doorsteps, the little children played with Caps of Liberty.

Citizen Genet had fallen and was gone. Monsieur Fauchet had arrived. His manners were genteel and gentle. He was unassuming and discreet. He went to see General Washington and they had an amicable talk. At the end of the interview the General was so touched that he was moved to an outburst of tears. Monsieur Fauchet recommended his partisans to treat the General with consideration. He begged them in a public address not to embarrass the Federal Government in any way. Let them keep quiet, and let England have her head; she would work better for France than Monsieur Genet had ever been able to do.

England, by an Order in Council issued in November, had just ordered the seizure of all the American ships which traded with the French West Indies, and more than a hundred American vessels had been captured by the English cruisers. New York, Boston, Philadelphia, Baltimore and Charleston seethed with wrath and indignation. In Congress, Mr. Madison made an eloquent protest and demanded reprisals. The Federalists themselves were nervous. There was much discussion, and finally, on March 26th, Congress voted one month's general embargo in American ports.

The crowd applauded and acclaimed; but the seamen protested. They paraded the streets with flags and bands. They went and shouted outside the Governor's residence. Detachments of soldiers had to be posted at the street corners. At the junction of Market Street and Second Street, opposite Benny's house, there were cannon and guards, and when a pretty girl passed by, the soldiers made rude remarks. O Philadelphia, City of Quakers, city of brethren and fraternal love, whither was gone thy Spartan purity, whither thy peace?

With the burgeoning of spring, everybody's mind took fire. Pitt was burned in effigy at the street corners, and downtown, at the sign of the Black Bear, the proprietor of the Exhibition of Figures in Composition at Full Length, "to render the Exhibition pleasing and satisfactory to his patrons", added the attraction of the execution of the late King of France, together with his Queen, the whole performed true to life. Young and old, everybody seemed to have caught the fever again. The great carnival of 1793 seemed ready to start once more. Everybody was talking about a war with England.

But General Washington remained serene. He thought things over and weighed them, and he took the advice of his counsellors, the Federalists. Then he decided to send Mr. Jay to England, to make one more effort to keep the peace. Mr. Jay was a good diplomat, honest and cold, who had known how to get a good deal out of England in 1783 and also how to make himself respected by the English. He had guided American foreign policy well from 1784 to

1790, and, though he was now in the Supreme Court, he had never lost sight of national problems.

The Democrats hated Mr. Jay, because Mr. Jay clad himself with genteel elegance, and because his manners were as finical as they were frigid. They reproached him with having thought, and said, that America had not observed the terms of the treaty of 1783 with exactitude — which happened to be true — and they resented the fact that he did not seem to care about the West. But, above all, they could not forgive him for his visible coolness towards France and democracy.

They demanded of the Federal Government whether there was nobody in America but Mr. Jay who could dispense justice, control the country's foreign policy, and do any other urgent job. They were sarcastic and bitter; but Mr. Jay had already gone. Mr. Jay had arrived in England, where the King received him very graciously, and Mr. Jay had sat down to table with Mr. Grenville, deeply affected by all the attentions of which he was the object. Around that table peace reigned.

In America war still reigned. Philadelphia remained indignant, the gazettes kept up their shouting, and Benny led the dance. In the West there was insurrection. People objected to paying the excise. After protesting, they raised their voices; after raising their voices, they mauled a few officials; after mauling some of them, they tarred and feathered one of them. Then they exchanged shots with revenue officers and finally they proceeded to organize meetings under arms. There was talk of secession, of an armed uprising, of resort to force.

The boldest spirits wrote to Philadelphia to obtain the support of the Democratic leaders and try to convince them that the moment for boldness had come; and in Governor

Mifflin's office there were long and anxious conventicles. Could this unfortunate event be turned to advantage? Could they profit by these critical circumstances to make Washington realize that the people wanted a government more democratic, closer to themselves? They talked, they hesitated, they consulted Randolph, Jefferson's successor, they sounded Fauchet. Could they act? Had they the means to act? Ought they to act?

While the Governor of Pennsylvania hesitated, while among the leaders of the West some pressed for conciliation, others for audacity, and their followers fumbled, General Washington made up his mind. He armed. He made ready an army of fifteen thousand men, and he and Hamilton proposed to show these insurgents of the West what a Government meant. His decision, his prompt action, impressed the country. The people of the West, after all, were only people who had lost their heads; and nobody wanted to compromise himself for their sakes, nobody wanted for their sakes to gamble with the fate of the Union.

The Federalists overwhelmed these rebels with upbraidings, the Democrats pleaded extenuating circumstances for them, and the Democratic societies, while approving their motives, condemned their proceedings. In the upshot, it was much ado about nothing. The people of the West did not even defend themselves. They dispersed, hands were laid on their ringleaders, and they were brought to Philadelphia much as a couple of policemen hustle a thief along; and so Hamilton made a kind of triumphal entrance. Washington participated in it only by a salute.

Washington was reserving himself for another occasion. When Congress reassembled, he addressed a message to it in which he denounced the Democratic societies. He saw in them the cause of all the trouble and the origin of the up-

[205]

rising. He incited national sentiment, which was aroused against the insurgents, to turn upon these societies and overwhelm them. He wanted to strike down the last of his enemies, the last center of resistance, of hostility to himself; and the crowd of Federalist partisans, Federalist pressmen, and Federalist leaders followed his lead with enthusiasm. In Congress a motion against the Democratic societies was proposed. Never had Genet himself been attacked in such terms. Congregationalist preachers, Presbyterian ministers, and Episcopalian priests denounced them from the pulpit.

The Boston newspapers amused themselves by pointing out that once again Washington and the French Government were of one mind, since the Convention, after the fall of Robespierre, had just suppressed the Jacobin Society. Monsieur Fauchet, who felt the hour of his disgrace approaching, said nothing.

The societies replied. Each one of them issued a manifesto. But the most persuasive was that of the German Republican Society. It protested and it affirmed that "all governments are more or less combinations against the people, they are states of violence against individual liberty, originating from man's imperfection and vice; and, as rulers have no more virtue than the ruled, the equilibrium between them can only be preserved by proper attention and association; for the power of government can only be kept within its constituted limits by the display of a power equal to itself, the collected sentiment of the people."

So the Society proclaimed its legitimacy. But its voice spent itself in silence. Again autumn had passed over Philadelphia. Again yellow fever had brought death and doubt back to the city; again the crowd felt itself crushed and chastened; again, in Congress, the advocates of England had gained the upper hand; and again Washington had rallied the mass of opinion around him.

Mr. Jefferson, on his estate, waxed indignant; but he was out of politics. He never wrote for the papers. He merely wrote letters and urged his friends to write to the papers. But his friends had written so much during the past two years, they had talked so much, that they were tired of talking and writing. They replied to Mr. Jefferson with politeness, but without hope.

In his workshop Benny went on working. He had become used to clamors, to defeats, to victories, to yellow fever. He had become used to long nights of work and to the affronts of high society. He had become used to being hard up. He had become used to fighting; for now he was fighting for his country, and for the memory of his grandfather, and for his wife, and for his two children, Franklin who was two years old, and Richard who had been born that autumn, during the yellow fever.

He had got used to everything; and now, now that, on the anvil of men and things, he seemed to have forged and found something that he had long been seeking; now, at the end of 1794, when Jefferson was gone, when Freneau was beaten, when Genet was laid aside, when Fauchet awaited his disgrace, when Gallatin was proscribed, when the Democratic societies were in process of dissolution — now he rechristened his paper, rejuvenated and renewed, *Aurora;* and on the front page of it, instead of the nondescript device of old, he placed, fairly and squarely in the middle, the fine sign of a rising sun.

[207]

Book Four

RISE AND DEATH

CHAPTER I

LIBERTY CAPS, LIBERTY POLES

THE crowds shouted in the streets. They danced the "Carmagnole"; they sang the "Ça Ira". They sported French cockades, they flaunted French passions, they went crazy over French victories.

France was a positive obsession. She was found everywhere. At the end of Cherry Alley, between Third Street and Fourth Street, in the Long Room beneath Mr. Poor's Young Ladies Academy, at the sign of the White Lamb, Monsieur l'Egalité presented Citizen Sans Culotte and Monsieur l'Aristocrate in their act. Before a wonderstruck audience, "these two *automates*, the only ones which ever appeared on this Continent", came slowly out of their heavy sleep. With stiff, precise motions, the life-sized figures bowed all around, they stretched their legs, they tumbled over a horizontal bar, they turned somersaults forward and backwards, they did the splits, they cut capers. Then they started dancing a minuet, a gig, a country dance, a quadrille.

Suddenly, the music began playing the "Carmagnole". Monsieur l'Aristocrate stopped dead, while Citizen Sans Culotte gamboled his finest and the impressario gesticulated, and the crowd shouted. Amid this tumult, despite the chidings of his master, the threats of the public, and the cries of the women, Monsieur l'Aristocrate stood stubborn

[211]

and could not be prevailed upon to dance the "Carmagnole".
Little by little he fell back into the immobility of nothing-
ness. They sang the "Marseillaise".

Not far away, on the corner of Second Street and Callowhill Street, at the sign of the Black Bear, you might go and
see the death of Louis XVI. There you saw "the late King
of France, together with his Queen, taking her last Farewell of him in the Temple, the day preceding his execution."
The King was represented standing; his Queen on her knees,
overwhelmed with sorrow and ready to faint, "the King
looking tenderly at her." Then you saw the scaffold on
which he was to be executed, with the King standing in full
view of the guillotine. Before him was a priest on his
knees, with a crucifix in one hand and a prayer book in the
other, and beside the guillotine stood the executioner,
awaiting his hour.

At a signal, the priest rose to his feet; the King laid
himself on the block, where he was secured; the executioner
turned and prepared to do his duty. At a second signal, the
executioner dropped the knife and in a second severed the
King's head from his body. The head fell into the basket,
and you could see the King's lips, first red, then turning
blue.

It was a well-staged spectacle, perfect in its performance.
The inventor, an Italian by the name of Columba, boasted
that "the whole is performed to the life," and that "the
workmanship has been admired by the most professed
judges." The proprietors added that they desired only to
please and satisfy their patrons, and humbly hoped for
the encouragement of the public. For children it was half-
price.

For more than six months, three times a day, they beheaded Louis XVI for the delectation of the Philadelphians,

who for fifteen years had found it their joy to admire and venerate his portrait in the Great Hall of Congress.

Now they went to the theater to applaud the taking of the Bastille. There you could see La Fayette, Bailly, the National Guard and the Sovereign People. There you could see Monsieur Moreau de Saint Méry calming the crowd. There you could see the victors in procession and the vanquished in their shame, the prisoners in the drunkenness of their deliverance and the despots enduring their expiation.

The audience cheered and clapped in delight. The whole theater stood up and sang the "Ça Ira". On the stage the actors took up the refrain, and from galleries to stalls the audience roared the "Marseillaise". Everybody was stirred and thrilled, and one day even the President of the United States was seen there, in company with the Minister of France, sharing in the popular fervor.

Sometimes the intoxicated crowd in the top gallery shouted at some aristocrat in the stalls: "Get up and bow!" One man started the cry, then the whole gallery roared it, and, if the haughty fellow did not obey, they began throwing beer bottles at him and spitting at him with shrewd and certain aim. And they kept on singing the "Marseillaise".

France was everywhere: at banquets as at balls. There was fine gossip about that great repast at which the Democrats served a roasted pig. They presented it on the table, pink and trim, in its own juice. They called it Capet and stuck a Liberty cap on its head. It was carried around to each of the guests, who, after placing the Liberty cap upon his own head, pronounced the word "tyrant" and gave the poor little grunter's head a chop with his knife. Then, to the cheers of the guests, the host cut off its head. After that,

[213]

they embraced one another and toasted one another; and they sang the "Ça Ira".

France pursued you out into the country. When the stage-coach stopped, they showed you the Liberty tree that the farmers had just planted. In the town square they took you to see the Liberty pole around which the country children came on Saturdays to dance the "Carmagnole".

If you stayed at the City Tavern, you found France again around the smoking hearth. While you waited for your coffee or your whisky, everybody discussed the news and talked about France. If a traveler chanced to be French and if he was recognized, the whole company threw themselves upon him.

"So you're French?" they cried. "Well, then, you're a friend of ours, a dear friend of ours! All of us would die for the French; we're all good Republicans here, and we'd like to kill the English. It would be a good job, wouldn't it? Ah, our dear, dear friend!" They repeated to one another: "He's a Frenchman, the dear, good fellow! Well, if he's a Frenchman, he must drink grog with us!"

And they brought a bowl of grog, and the enthusiasm was so great that the bowl of grog was never big enough to quench all that affection, and after one first bowl of grog for France they ordered a second, a third, and a fourth, until America slid under the table and France held her stomach, as happened to Monsieur le Duc de La Rochefoucauld Liancourt, whose stomach was about as deficient as his head.

France was everywhere, red and dazzling. On the Lancaster road an Englishman kept an inn which he had called "The Beheaded Queen of France." On its sign you could see Marie Antoinette standing up, with her head on the ground beside her, and out of it spurting a fine flow of red blood.

There was no forgetting France. Every week, every day, the gazettes published reports of her victories and her conquests, biographies of her generals, and extracts from her philosophers. The whole year was nothing but a round of French festivals: in January, the anniversary of the death of the King; in February, the anniversary of the Alliance; in May, the festival of Tammany and of French fraternity; in July, the American and the French national festivals; in August, the anniversary of the Revolutionary triumph; in September, the anniversary of the foundation of the Republic. The better to share in all this glory and exaltation, people bought the Revolutionary Calendar at Benjamin Franklin Bache's, the printer in Market Street, and learned those new names of the months, ringing and rustic.

In Congress, whether it was a question of commerce, industry or agriculture, whether it was a question of diplomacy, of relations with the Dey of Algiers or with the Indians of Kentucky, of the whisky duty or the prerogatives of the Executive, of the bank statute or eternal principles, they always ended by talking about France, discussing her and disputing about her.

In drawing-rooms, in between two quadrilles, or when you drank tea with the ladies, it was still France that kept on cropping up. You might hate France; but there was no chance of getting away from her. She broke everywhere upon the shores of America.

Her exiled priests brought her Catholic religion to Baltimore, just as her booksellers in flight circulated her books in Philadelphia. Monsieur Ambroise Varinot from Cap Français made the Philadelphians familiar with the Franco-Italian refinements of Greek fire and other fireworks. Monsieur Brillat-Savarin revealed the delights of French cooking to them, Monsieur Héraut introduced them for

[215]

the first time to ices and ice-cream, Monsieur Bastide sold French umbrellas, Monsieur Bartault French lacework, Monsieur Ducomb French perfumes, Monsieur Claudius Chat French jewellery, Monsieur Crespin French drugs, Monsieur Balbaud in Vine Street French buttons, Monsieur Duparc in Chestnut Street French hats, Brugeille brothers French jugs, Monsieur Boissière in Front Street French shoes. Monsieur Quesnet, Monsieur Gaspard Cénas, Monsieur Sicard taught dancing *à la française*, Monsieur Lemaire fencing *à la française*, and Madame Garreau and Monsieur Guynemer from Cap Français undertook to teach American youth of either sex *à la française* in a French atmosphere.

In their houses everybody put on French wall paper and drank French coffee. General Washington himself had a French cook. And he displayed on his sideboard a key of the Bastille, which he showed to his visitors. It was very big and rusty.

You might hate France, but there was no forgetting her.

She had got into the American people's blood: she became a passion, an obsession, against which it was vain to try to fight. The Federalist Party could not help it. The Ministers of New England might denounce France, but they could not stop people talking about her. The merchants might curse her, but they could not resist her fascination. The government journalists might accuse her, but they had to write about her all the time.

France was a tyrannical fashion, a mania, a kind of epidemic without a cure. Nobody could even direct the course of it — the French in America less than anybody else.

They watched their country becoming a legend with a mixture of alarm and embarrassment. The Royalists preferred to bury themselves in the country and hide themselves there, to try and forget, to console themselves for the hardness of the times by the sweetness of the passing moment, and for the cruelty of an old people by the charm of a young people. They found their pleasure in plunging into the great silent forests, or else in cultivating a solitary farm, where the Indians came in the evening to ask for gifts. They liked this hospitable country, this eager, negligent, nonchalant, generous nation which had welcomed them. But they wanted to rest, not to act.

The Girondin and Jacobin refugees, for their part, might have worked upon the masses and given a more concrete form to this worship of France. But some secret force prevented them.

They had their headquarters in Callowhill Street at the house of the good Monsieur Moreau de Saint Méry, onetime president of the electors of the Paris district, one-time Constituent, one-time great man, who to save his head had quit his country and lost his glory. He could not get over it. Still, he had a loving wife, a chaste daughter Heloïse, a sensible niece Uranie; he had many friends and a philosophical soul, which raised him above superstition and disaster.

Even so, during the months that followed his arrival in America, where he first had to make his living by branding boxes on the quays, he could not help shedding a tear on every box he branded. Later he had the joy of being able to start a bookshop in Philadelphia, and of succeeding in grouping around him all the fugitive Frenchmen who had enlightened minds.

There you might find Monsieur de Talleyrand, with his limp and his raillery; Monsieur le Duc de la Rochefoucauld in his threadbare clothes; Monsieur Demeusnier, who talked so well about everything and especially about himself, so much so that he said "I" in two syllables — "*Ey-e*"; Monsieur de Beaumets who took unto himself a wife; Monsieur Volney who looked like a skinned skunk; good Monsieur de la Colombe with his military dignity; and wily Monsieur d'Hauterive, who had once been a count.

They met around Monsieur Moreau de Saint Méry's Madeira. They sipped it slowly, and they lavished eloquence, wisdom, sentiment and virtue upon one another. They talked a great deal about France, which they could never forget. They talked about this revolution of hers, the origin of their greatness, the cause of their exile. They also talked about America.

She did not please them. Doubtless she was a land of refuge, but they found themselves lost here. The small fry were too coarse and unresponsive to eloquence. The fashionable world was too stiff and too English. To these Frenchmen, who had a taste above all for ideas, or at least for the high sound of ideas, this nation eager for action, creation and land remained a mystery. They drew the conclusion that America was materialistic.

They could not forgive her for being indifferent to their own greatness. Monsieur Moreau de Saint Méry recalled with bitterness that he had brought to this barbarous New World one of the finest adornments of modern civilization, the clyster; and yet they treated him as a shopkeeper and would not let him attend the fashionable gatherings of the "Assembly." Monsieur de Talleyrand, who never forgot that he had been a Bishop, a Constituent, and a man of influence, and who was very well aware that he was one of the deepest of men here below, felt himself slighted that General Washington should refuse to receive him. He thought it impertinent that the baker above whom he lodged should consider the exotic mistress whom the former prelate

[218]

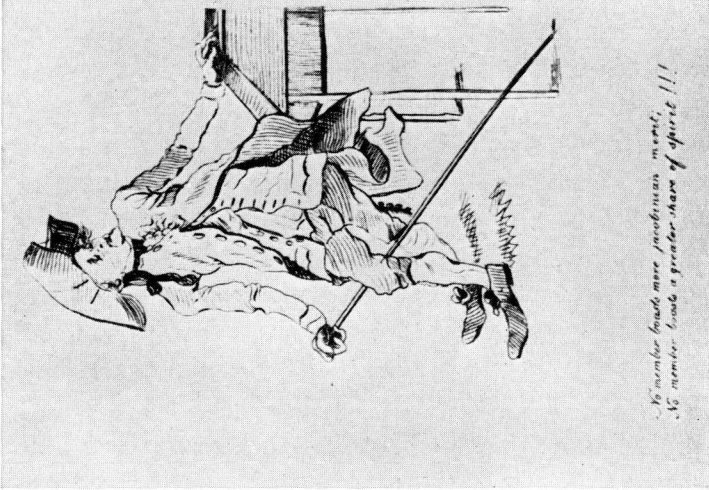

TWO CARICATURES TAKEN FROM THE "REMARKS ON THE
JACOBINIAD" (BY J. S. J. GARDINER), BOSTON, 1795

had chosen for himself as too exotic, and raise his visage, white with flour from his kneading trough, to make faces at the bishopric Negress.

The raucous, indeterminate, motley rabble of America displeased these Frenchmen. Her passion for action shocked them. All their lives they had been dominated by words, words brilliant, impressive, profound, which had ended by becoming their very soul, their system of morality. Since Americans did not understand these words, Americans must be without principles or morals.

Only Mr. Hamilton interested them, because he was witty and cynical, and, as he was very hospitable, they were glad to visit him. They could go and see Mr. Jefferson too, though he was reserved and not very frank. But the rest of America was a desert to them, for they could find no audience in it. They preferred to speculate like Monsieur de Noailles, deal in real estate like Monsieur de Talleyrand, fit out ships for the Indies like Monsieur de Beaumets, or sell books, ink, and emetics like Monsieur Moreau de Saint Méry. They ignored the crowd that shouted in the streets.

Monsieur Fauchet, the Minister of France, ignored the crowd no less. Monsieur Fauchet was virtuous, modest and young. He was born to be the perfect official and, though he was only thirty, he fulfilled his destiny. He minced about Philadelphia, and paid respectful, unctuous little calls upon Mr. Washington, who understood nothing about the crowd either and was moved almost to tears when he compared the touching genteelness of Robespierre's envoy with the emphatic arrogance of Genet and Girondin.

Monsieur Fauchet had long, quiet, intimate interviews with Mr. Randolph, the Secretary of State. The two of them, friendly, cordial, but no fools, unbosomed themselves to each other, without altogether ignoring the fact that they

THE TWO FRANKLINS

had more than one bottom to their hearts. Thus Monsieur
Fauchet gleaned feelings, confidences, confessions, which he
described with great care to his Government in interminable,
elegant dispatches. They left him no time to concern himself
about the crowd that shouted under his windows. In any
case, he distrusted the crowd. Had not Genet burned his
fingers over the crowd? Had not Mr. Jefferson compromised himself over the crowd?

Mr. Jefferson, indeed, had retired, and the vain noise of
the world now reached him only like a distant echo. He
went in for agriculture, philosophy and architecture; he
wrote letters and occupied himself with his family. He
was dead to the ambitions of politics. Let nobody come and
talk to him about them; let nobody importune him any
more. "The crowd", they told him, "venerate you, celebrate
you, demand you." But Mr. Jefferson turned away. He had
never been present at a popular meeting, he had never participated in the activity of the Democratic societies, he had
never liked the bustle and the hustle of the hustings.

He asked nothing. He was quite satisfied to watch Mr.
Hamilton and Mr. Washington and the rest of them wearing themselves out in the vain game of politics, in wrestling
with circumstances from which there was no escape, in the
tornado of popular demands and plebeian tempers. He was
quite content to write for the benefit of posterity precise
notes in which he put down what he knew, and to watch
the clouds gliding over the vast horizon of Virginia. He
was very far away from the crowd.

You could not count on Mr. Randolph to guide public
opinion. Mr. Randolph was not a man of decided mind and
he was by no means a man of moral courage. He had made
war on the Constitution and then he had rallied to it. He
passed for a Democrat, but he had been highly favored by

Washington, who had got him accepted as Secretary of State, even though Mr. Jefferson, when Washington consulted him, had told him flatly that Mr. Randolph's affairs were supposed to be involved, and had then relapsed into a silence which was eloquent.

No, Mr. Randolph was not one of those men who carry the people with them; he was rather one of those who, if the case arises, denounce the people. When Washington had condemned the Democratic societies, Mr. Randolph, Secretary of State though he was, had not thought it at all beneath his dignity to publish, under the pseudonym of "Germanicus", a series of articles in which he raised the hue and cry. Everybody knew it and the Democrats shared the opinion of the Federalists about Mr. Randolph. He was not born to lead the crowd.

The Democratic societies had tried to lead the crowd. They had done it with plenty of boldness and but little experience. Still, they might have succeeded, after a certain length of time, in shaping the formless passions of the masses and giving a direction to their restlessness of mind. Unfortunately their career had been suddenly cut short by Washington's anathema.

The blow was too much for them. The Democratic societies vegetated. The oldest and the strongest of them, that of Philadelphia and that of New York, preferred to merge gently into the Tammany Society. The members of Tammany were Democrats, too, but they were Irish Democrats, and this conferred a special strength upon them.

In the struggle of races which was in progress in the United States, the Anglo-Saxons were the race that queened it. Everybody knew it, and it would have been useless to try to do anything about it. The Government — Washington, Jefferson, Hamilton, Knox, Randolph, Pickering, Wolcott, etc. — were Anglo-Saxon. High society was Anglo-Saxon. The merchants and the bankers, the leading clergy and the high officials were Anglo-Saxon. An instinctive sense of discipline united them, maintained them as a solid group, over against that motley rabble in which all races and all colors merged.

Neither the Germans nor the French could fight against them. There were too few French and the French were too individualistic to form a body. Any group of French was never anything more than a tornado of factions. The Germans were numerous but they were passive and humble. So long as you let them live their family lives in peace, so long as they had their fine fat farms with their fine fat cows and their fat coaches to take their fine fat wives to market, they let themselves be led by the nose.

The Irish were far from letting themselves be led by the nose. They were many, they were restless, they were poor, and they liked political activity just as much as work. You could not bluff them, like the French, with fine speeches, and then make fools of them. You could not utilize against them the instinctive sense of discipline which was in every German. The Irish were a compact group, which nothing could break up — not even threats, not even defeat, not even contempt, not even their own internal quarrels. Nothing could break up Tammany.

The members of Tammany absorbed the Democratic societies and went their way without troubling to give any explanation. They cried, "Long live Washington!" who had just condemned them, together with the other political associations, and they treated him with much respect, while awaiting their opportunity to throw him overboard.

They knew how to handle crowds. But they were too Irish to handle all the crowds there were, and the Democratic

Party, if it were to survive, if it were to win, needed all the crowds there were. French, German, Welsh, Irish — it was all these crowds that danced the "Carmagnole", that sang the "Ça Ira", and that wanted to vote for a new America.

Who was to guide them?

"Here am I," said Benny; "and all I want is to serve." *Surgo ut prosim* — so said his paper; such was its motto.

Benny was a full-grown artisan. Benny was no longer a child. He had let his beard grow to give himself an air of responsibility. But those eyes of his, "fair and softy", always gave him away, and Margaret had made him cut off his beard, which did him no good and only frightened the children. Benny was a toiler. In his fustian breeches, in his leather apron, Benny labored in company with his workmen, and he was one of them.

Out of all the Franklin family he alone was left in Philadelphia. His father and mother, on their return from England, had settled in the country, and at Settle Farm they led that kind of life, placid and sleek and a little dulled by happiness, which is the property of lovers, of the wise and the lazy. Around them their children, supple and strong, formed a crowning joy for them. Louis and Sarah, Richard and Deborah were confident and care-free. Everybody knew them in the neighborhood because they were friendly, because they were good-looking, and because they had been seen swimming up the river, the whole lot of them, boys and girls together, against the current for five miles.

William, for his part, was gone. Strong like the rest of them, he had wanted to see Europe and make the pilgrimage to France. At Le Havre he had been arrested and put into prison because his papers were not in order. Then, as they had neglected to guillotine him and he had no money, he shipped aboard a privateer. She took prizes and he became rich. Now, in Paris, he was leading amid the *incroyables* and the *merveilleuses*, the life of a successful privateer. He drank, he toasted liberty, and he sang the "Ça Ira".

Benny had been supple enough too. He had swum in the sea, and the rivers, and the great lakes. Now he toiled amid the crowd. Now, bending over his forms, leaning over his desk, Benny was getting stiff.

He had to fight against hatred and against contempt, against poverty and against intrigue. He had to fight also against himself, against that yearning, veering heart of his, which any joy flooded and mastered, which any sorrow overwhelmed; against that need of his for love and dreaming, which kept him for hours with eyes half closed and lips half parted. He had to fight against his taste for believing in people and his instinct for trusting them. He had to learn to distrust himself. He had to educate himself in indignation, instruct himself in anger, and get used to all the fine, virile hatreds.

Benny drove himself and stiffened himself. In the reeking atmosphere of his printing house, with its stale smell of ink, damp paper and dirty clothes, he could never have stood it if he had not had Margaret, always at hand, always clean and pure, in whose presence he could breathe all the perfumes of a better life. Benny could never have managed to fight and win if he had not loved his setting, and this young woman who had accepted the daily task, and this great, clamorous crowd, which surged around his workshop, which brought him its curiosity, its passions, its desires, and which took from him his time, his strength and his zeal.

To him the crowd was far from being something squalling and sniffling, as it seemed to the Federalists and to the genteel Democratic minds of Virginia. Benny knew the crowd from having rubbed elbows with it in Geneva, in Paris, in Passy. With the crowd, in the Place Louis XV, he had hailed the first balloons in this world; with the crowd, in the plain of Plainpalais, he had hailed the triumphs of democracy. Like the crowd, he was made up of desires and hopes which had come from all the corners of the earth. Like the crowd, he saw in France the mirage which intoxicated him, his mind and his heart.

What mattered theories, the balancing of power, the dreams of philosophers, the arguments of jurists and subtleties of statesmen? France was a force, a dance or a song, which filled men's minds with hope, which swelled hearts with courage, which unleashed desires and pressed against all barriers. In Benny Bache, as in this eager and awkward people, France was all his youth, invincible, insatiable, intoxicated with expectation and promise.

For Benny and for the crowd, France was a stimulus. The crowd was a mass of emigrants, a confused whole, which was conscious of its exile and realized its disappointment. There would never have been any Democratic Party if the Federalists had not despised so much the Irish, the Germans and all the rest of them. No doubt one would have seen parties developing in Congress, and there would have been drawing-room debates; but the mass of the people would not have felt its dull anger rising against the rich, the merchants and the well-born. There would never have been that gulf of hatred between the two parties, or that desire to hurt one another, to drag one another in the mud, to destroy one another.

The American mass at this time was just like a domestic animal whom his master has hurt and offended. In America the Anglo-Saxons had both power and prestige; their lan-

[225]

guage was that of the nation, their religion reigned over the country. They wanted their prejudices to dominate it as well.

"Right-thinking" newspapers waged war on the Irish patriots, on French ideas, on the German language, and on old Franklin. They were never tired of jeering at that old trimmer, that old philosopher, who could neither pray like anybody else, nor rally to sensible, constitutional ideas like anybody else, nor bow down to the morality of anybody else.

"Franklin," they said. "Oh, yes; Old Lightning Rod!" And they added, with a laugh, "Benny Bache, Young Lightning Rod!"

Like the crowd, Benny was affronted. Like the crowd, he was poor. He had no slaves and estates, like Mr. Jefferson or Mr. Madison; no fine house, like Mr. Burr; no imposing office and pompous title, like General Mifflin or Alexander Dallas, Secretary to the Governor of Pennsylvania.

Benny was simply "Bache the printer." His father lent him a little house to live in, a corner for his printing shop. From time to time Richard Bache advanced him a little money to buy new fonts or to repair the printing press. Sometimes, from St. Croix, his brothers-in-law the Markoes sent him a few barrels of rum or molasses to help out with his housekeeping.

But as a rule Richard Bache had something better to do than waste his money for the benefit of that printer, his son; and the Markoe brothers-in-law, what with their debts, their lawsuits, the tornadoes, the blockade, the privateers, the war, the fall in prices, the rise in freights, the revolts of slaves, the embargoes, the shipwrecks, the yellow fever, judged it wiser not to send him anything. They let their money rest — and their debts grow. They sent Benny a few hopes and plenty of advice. They had only too much affection for him. It would have been madness to spoil it by talking about money.

So he had to do without it. Without money, without support, without family, without confidants, Benny went on working alone on his *Aurora*.

He had the crowd. The crowd felt that he was close to them, and they knew him. He had been seen at the Democratic Society, where he was a member of the Corresponding Committee. He had been seen at the ceremonies in honor of Genet, and at the patriotic festivals. At the time of the yellow fever, he had been one of the last to leave and one of the first to return. He was always to be seen in the streets, mingling with the people, humble as themselves, young as themselves. In summer, when the heat fell upon the city, when the dust blinded passers-by and choked the street, Benny went from door to door to ask all his neighbors to throw water into the street, to sprinkle it and keep it a street alive, fresh and cheerful.

Benny knew the street, Benny knew the crowd; and, all alone, he talked to the crowd.

CHAPTER II

"MR. JAY'S INFAMOUS TREATY"

GENERAL WASHINGTON did not move about the streets much. He had too much work to do and he stayed shut up at home.

Sometimes, for the sake of his health, he went riding on horseback, followed by his grooms. Sometimes he was to be seen passing in his fine coach-and-six, globular in shape. Before the amazed eyes of the gossips, he sped past like a meteor, dazzling the good people, who had never seen such a fine carriage, all cream-colored and ornamented with Cupids supporting festoons and wreaths of flowers. The figures and flowers were beautifully covered with fine glass which protected them from the dust and sparkled in the sun.

From his capacious coach the General saluted in kindly fashion; but his grave gaze, charged with secrets of State, scarcely saw that moving crowd. He looked straight in front of him.

His mien grew more and more serious every day. Far from accustoming himself to power, he seemed to find it more and more of a burden as the months of his Presidency rolled by. He complained about it to his confidants. One might suppose that supreme power was too heavy a weight for his republican soul, or that the tumult of parliamentary life, and the outcry of public opinion, were becoming unendurable to his aristocratic soul. Only his sheer love for his country, his inflexible discipline, still kept him going;

but weariness made his steps heavy, and so it did the movements of his mind.

He was less supple of mind than he had once been. He showed himself at once less ready to listen to those who gave him advice, less disposed to suffer those who might raise a point of criticism, and more apt to lend ear to adulators who gave him the support of their sometimes cunning eulogies of him and their insinuating obedience to him.

General Washington, without desiring it, or even realizing it, had become Hamilton's ægis and the Federalist Party's hero. What he wanted was greatness and stability for America, and the merchants, the middle classes, the financiers and the clergy seemed to him the only real props of order and the only repositories of the national spirit in the New World. But the merchants, the middle classes, the financiers and the clergy belonged to the Federalist Party, which had in Hamilton its champion, in John Jay its oracle, in Morris its treasurer, in Rufus King and Fisher Ames its parliamentary tribunes, and which adopted Washington as its tutelary Deity.

In America, whither flowed both emigrants frightened away by the wars of Europe, and English capital in flight from the long European conflict; in the United States, which Europe's years of turbulence and bloodshed enriched with all the spoils of the Old World and in which commerce was advancing by leaps and bounds, the Federalists, whose wealth kept on growing and who held by peace more firmly every day, ran the country's business along with their own. Washington was grateful to them for it and he collaborated with them. He knew that these business men would support the Constitution, that they would develop the resources of the country, that they would maintain order,

[229]

and that they would be progressive. He was grateful to them for what they were doing for America, and for the deference which they showed towards himself.

He knew that, if they were to prosper, they needed peace and a trade treaty with England. English money at this time was flowing into America and fecundating it. English industry equipped towns, farms and factories. English credits kept the functioning of American finances stable and regular. The English fleet, mistress of the seas, alone could make navigation safe for American ships; and the English army, master of all the strategic points of the West, was in a position either to let loose the Indians upon all the frontier villages or, on the contrary, to let peace and prosperity reign there.

Short of taking England by the throat and creating a new governing class in the United States, it was essential to make life possible for the existing American upper class by an agreement with England.

General Washington could not avoid it. He owed it to his partisans to follow them, to his faithful friends not to let them down, to his political General Staff to carry out their plans.

This was why he sent to England Mr. John Jay, Judge of the Supreme Court of the United States.

Mr. John Jay was a tall man, upright and rather thin, who thought himself an upright great man. His black eyes, penetrating and serious, and his fine aquiline nose had a majesty which was made still more impressive by his hair, tied behind and slightly powdered, and by the black dress which he always wore. The expression of his face was exceedingly amiable, and his manner very gentle and unassuming.

There was an intense modesty about him which you noticed at once, but which impressed you as soon as you observed how pointed his chin was, and which ended by intimidating you. Everything about Mr. John Jay was perfect, and there was no excess about him except his excess of modesty which you could not help thinking was a lesson to the world and also the expression of a secret weakness.

However great Mr. John Jay may have been, the idea which he had about himself was still greater. However upright and simple his soul may have been, the image of it which he made for himself was still more upright and simple than the reality. Other Americans were Anglo-Saxons, freed from England. Mr. John Jay was an Anglo-Saxon who, before freeing himself from England, had been a French Huguenot anxious to free himself from France. These two revolts of his, that of the Protestant and that of the insurgent, far from coinciding, clashed to some extent and created a conflict in him.

He himself did not realize that, as a Frenchman who was an enemy of France, he could not altogether hate England, who had served him to free himself from France. He did not appreciate that, for his own part, he knew France too well to love her with that fine, vague, flexible enthusiasm which had invaded other Americans since 1778; and that, for all he might call himself John Jay, he was too little of an Englishman to hate England knowingly and deeply, as did other Americans, the Anglo-Saxons of America.

Mr. John Jay knew himself to be the soul of justice. He drew the conclusion from this that he was a righteous man. So he was imperturbable, invulnerable, and, when he was wrong, free from any remorse or any reticence.

[231]

During his negotiations for the peace of 1783 with Franklin and Adams, he had exercised a singular mastery over the American delegation, for he was the simplest and the coolest member of it. John Adams, always hot-headed and usually indignant, and Franklin, always enthusiastic and usually sentimental, submitted to the ascendancy of the Huguenot; and when the English delegates had convinced him, without much difficulty, and without much veracity either, that the French wanted to fool the American delegation, John Jay had no trouble about carrying his colleagues with him. The English were so delighted over this that they paid a very high price for this moral success, and Jay returned to America wearing the laurels of the ideal negotiator.

Ever since that day he had towered over the foreign policy of the American Government. For six years he had been Secretary for Foreign Affairs, and afterwards, as Judge of the Supreme Court, he had been consulted by Hamilton and Washington whenever a particularly delicate problem in foreign policy presented itself. Now, Chief Justice of the Supreme Court though he was, he was sent to England to obtain the evacuation of the English military posts in the West, already promised by England in the treaty of 1783, respect for American ships, the indemnity due for the spoliations of the War of Independence, a trade treaty and a general agreement. He was given wide powers and they counted on his prudence.

Such, at least, was the opinion of his peers. It was not at all the same thing with the people. The people hated Mr. Jay, for Mr. Jay had the gift of unpopularity. This might have derived from that pointed chin of his, or from his black dress, or again from that smile of affability which he wore on his face and which expressed only too clearly a virtue satisfied to feel itself virtuous, a humility only too conscious of itself.

However that may be, the people of the West were persuaded that Mr. Jay would betray them and that he had not the least desire to obtain the English posts in the West for the United States. The people of the East were persuaded that Mr. Jay, Justice of the Supreme Court of the United States, by accepting the post of Envoy Extraordinary and Minister Plenipotentiary to the Court of London, had agreed to couple functions which belonged respectively to the Judiciary and the Executive, and by so doing had infringed upon the very spirit of the Constitution.

The Democratic papers heaped coals of fire upon him. The crowd shouted in the streets. In his own good city of New York a number of distinguished and respectable citizens ordered a stuffed likeness of this evil genius of Western America to be made, dressed in a courtly manner, all in black, and installed it in a pillory. In its hand was held a notice which proclaimed, in Latin and in English: "No man e'er reached the heights of vice at first." After they had danced the "Carmagnole" around him a little, they ordered him to be guillotined, "which was dexterously executed," and then set fire to him, "which finding its way to a quantity of powder, which was lodged in his body, produced such an explosion, that after it there was scarcely to be found a particle of the *disjecta membra plenipo*." Then they sang the "Ça Ira".

Mr. Jay cared little for all this. He was at the Court of St. James's, where Lord Grenville had received him with extreme affability. The King was no less amiable and all the officials paid him little attentions. Did they not know him for a friend of England? He alone, perhaps, was still

[233]

unaware of the fact; but, for that matter, there was no need for him to be aware of it.

They put Mr. Jay at his ease. They talked to him about France, and about the American Democrats, just as Englishmen talked among themselves. They gave him to understand that they had full confidence that his sense of justice would enable him to see their point of view. He replied that they were quite right. They let him see that they counted upon him, and he showed them that they might, since, before sending his Government the most delicate dispatches, he submitted them to Lord Grenville, so as to be sure of not making any mistake. He never made any mistakes, it seemed.

For the rest, Mr. Jay was beaten point by point during these negotiations. They were difficult to carry on, for America wanted to avoid a war, while England was not much afraid of one. They were rendered still more difficult by the proceedings of Hamilton, whose intimacy with George Hammond, the Minister of England, led him to reveal to Hammond the secret principles and intentions of the American Government. To Lord Grenville, John Jay's mind was as transparent as his instructions, his intentions, and those of his Government.

So, while storms raged all winter, cutting America off from England for weeks, while Philadelphia was scourged by a biting cold, in a nice warm room, in which a fire crackled softly and serviceably, Mr. Jay and Lord Grenville, in the friendliest fashion, fixed up the most detestable treaty that America had ever signed.

American ships remained subject to all the vagaries of the English Admiralty. The trade of the United States remained under the tutelage of the English Admiralty, while the United States opened their ports to English ships.

The English Admiralty did not agree to make any reparation for the American ships which had been seized and put under sequestration, nor for the American sailors who had been pressed into service in the English fleet.

It was true that England promised once more, as in 1783, to hand over her military posts in the West. She set the door of her West Indies ajar to small American ships and she opened her East Indies to American traders. But in return she obtained an indemnity for her Loyalists, "most favored nation" treatment for her commerce with the United States, the entrance of her ships of whatever tonnage into the ports of the United States, the exclusion of French privateers from American ports, and the right to exercise close surveillance over the whole sea-borne trade of the United States.

English diplomacy had negotiated a treaty which would in no way embarrass the English Admiralty in the war which it was carrying on with France.

Mr. Jay was not, indeed, enthusiastic. He was simply satisfied. That went with his natural modesty.

General Washington, who had less natural modesty, when he received the treaty, late in the spring, was neither enthusiastic nor satisfied. His first act was to hide the treaty in a drawer to prevent anybody from seeing it or taking a copy of it.

To Mr. Hamilton the treaty came as a shock. By dint of railing against France, he had reached the point of forgetting all about England. By dint of talking to Hammond, he had ended by believing that Hammond thought the same as he did, whereas in fact he had come to the point of generally thinking the same as Hammond, but the Jay treaty was too much for him. He was surprised and rather shocked. It was a bad treaty.

[235]

Mr. Randolph, the Secretary of State, was still more shocked, and with his unfavorable impression there was mingled some hope. The President had paved the way for this treaty with his Federalist counsellors, who were not fond of Randolph and of whom Randolph was not fond, either. The treaty was extremely bad. That might be a lesson to the President.

It was clear also that the treaty put the country, and Mr. Randolph himself, in a delicate position towards France; for it was clear that it violated the spirit of the Franco-American treaties of 1778, and it was probable that it violated their letter too. But Mr. Randolph need not concern himself too much about this. France was very far away, and the French were very busy guillotining one another, making war, and changing their Ministers.

After Monsieur Genet, it was Monsieur Fauchet's turn to prepare himself for disgrace. Robespierre was dead and the suave Monsieur Fauchet had to go. Randolph did not regret him, for he found him underhanded, mock modest and boring. But, little as he might like the French Minister, Mr. Randolph did not like Jay's treaty any the better.

Only Mr. Hammond and Mr. Jay had a real affection for the treaty. Mr. Hammond waited impatiently for its ratification, which was to be the culminating point of his diplomatic career in the United States. He was under recall, to make place for a man less brilliant, but also less arrogant, who was to make a fresh start.

Mr. Hammond waited impatiently.

Monsieur Fauchet was burning to know what was in the treaty.

General Washington was much perplexed to make up his mind what he ought to do with this treaty. He kept it in his drawer and waited.

The people moved in all directions. They shouted for a sight of the treaty. It was known that it had arrived. It was said that it was execrable. They gossiped about it, they discoursed about it, they declaimed against it. But nobody knew anything about it. So they kept on shouting.

Finally Mr. Washington made up his mind not to make up his mind but to see what the Senate had to say. He submitted the treaty to it under pledge of secrecy and every Senator promised not to divulge anything about it.

The month of June was hot and so was the treaty. But Mr. Hammond's house was cool and hospitable. He entertained a great deal that month. He was very friendly, sometimes even fawning, often ingratiating; his silver shone, his glasses scintillated, his cooking tasted good, his arguments were excellent while Monsieur Fauchet, struck dumb by fear of the future, was unable or unwilling to act.

The crowd, of course, kept on shouting in the streets. They celebrated the victories of France. At Oeller's they dined in honor of the French Republic, the Batavian Republic, and the Republic of the United States. They toasted universal liberty and drank three healths fifteen times over to stimulate it. Then they went to bed, and neither Jefferson on his plantation, nor Mifflin at his desk, nor Bache in his workshop, nor shrewd Beckley in his office, nor poor Fauchet in his Legation, knew anything about the text of the treaty. President Washington spared the emotions of the Sovereign People.

Finally, on June 24, 1795, the United States Senate ratified Jay's treaty by the requisite majority, rejecting only one article of it whose terms were too manifestly in violation of the treaties of 1778. Despite Mr. Hammond's dinners, the Senate itself could not work up any en-

[237]

thusiasm. It had done its job against its will. But it had done it.

Again Washington had to make up his mind. He began by deciding to wait a few more weeks. He shut the treaty up again in the drawer whence he had taken it out to show it to the Senate and he took counsel with Randolph. Look at the treaty how he might, he could not find it good, or honorable, or satisfactory, or encouraging. It was a wretched treaty.

As a treaty it had only one quality: it was a treaty. But was this quality sufficient to justify the President of the United States in signing it and so making it operative? What should he do?

Mr. Washington, whenever he was embarrassed, read the newspapers. On this occasion he found an interesting piece of news in them. As soon as the treaty with America had been drafted and signed by the negotiators, His Britannic Majesty had issued an Order in Council, in accordance with which all ships carrying food to France were to be regarded as contraband of war. Thus the treaty was complemented and all trade between the United States and France was abolished.

This was the more toothsome a titbit in that the great victory of France in 1778–1783 had consisted in bringing the maritime nations of Europe to accept the principle that a neutral flag covered merchandise. The United States had applauded this acceptance. The Franco-American treaties contained such a clause, and the French were bound to respect the American ships carrying merchandise to England, in accordance with their treaties of 1778; whereas, according to their treaty of 1795, the English had the right to confiscate all American ships carrying merchandise to France. Grenville's manœuvers had proved a brilliant success.

[238]

It was such a success that General Washington was startled by it. He gave a further turn to the key of the drawer where the treaty lay hidden, and he deliberated with Randolph, who really struck him as quite level-headed, now that Hamilton and Jay seemed to him less prudent than he would have thought.

While they deliberated, Fate took care of the treaty.

Or, rather, it was Monsieur Adet.

Monsieur Adet was the new Minister of France in Philadelphia. He was thirty-two years of age and a clever chemist. He was well-mannered, intelligent, vivacious, clear-headed, and a bit too romantic.

His predecessor told him about this treaty, whose text had not been shown to him, but which quite clearly meant the ruin of the Franco-American alliance. His informants declared that Mr. Hammond had secured a favorable vote on it by financial procedure on which morality frowned. By the same procedure, Monsieur Adet persuaded a Senator to divulge the treaty. He had to make haste, in order to startle public opinion and forestall Mr. Randolph, who was preparing to communicate the text to a journalist of his own choosing. Monsieur Adet wanted to take the Government by surprise, to make an impression on public opinion, and to communicate Jay's treaty in a frankly Democratic paper, which would know how to feature what called for featuring in it.

Monsieur Adet took steps to keep in his own hands the text of the treaty which, by a happy chance, Randolph had entrusted to him, and which was the only copy that the American Secretary of State had at his disposal. There was no danger, therefore, of Randolph's communicating it to the Press. Meanwhile Mr. Mason, Senator from Virginia, and a friend of Monsieur Adet's, showed the copy of the treaty which he had to Benjamin Franklin Bache.

Benny had always imagined that the treaty was deplorable. He had said as much; but he had not expected to be proved right to this extent. When he got this document, which he had so much wanted to see and which now came into his hands at last, he was beside himself. First of all, he made a summary of it for his paper, for Mason at the outset would not authorize its publication *in extenso*.

On the morning of June 29th, the *Aurora* circulated throughout Philadelphia a brief, but exact and complete, summary of this curious document. The American people read it with amazement. They were so surprised that they could not believe their eyes. People said, "Bache is faking." Then Bache obtained Mason's authorization to publish the text as a whole. Hastily he printed it as a pamphlet, and his paper offered it to the public on July 2, 1795, by way of honoring the anniversary of the Declaration of Independence!

At last the country knew what it was that President Washington had been hiding from it for the past two months, and why he had been hiding it.

The country was so profoundly astonished by it that at first it was silent.

The crowd stopped shouting. Through the silent streets they hurried to get the news. From seven o'clock in the morning Benny's printing house was besieged. You might have thought it was a fair day. Market Street and the market booths in front of his shop were jammed by the waiting crowd. Silently, seriously, men thronged outside the door. They could not wait any longer. They knocked for it to be opened.

When the treaty was put on sale, it was one long procession of buyers, come from every part of the town, come from the country, come from the near-by towns. Benny's workmen did not know which way to turn; Doctor Leib, who had insisted on lending him a helping hand at this critical moment, worked his hardest, but still could not satisfy all the customers; and Mrs. Bache beamed, proud and dazzled, not sure whether she was standing on head or heels.

As for Benny, after working all day and all night long to print his edition of the treaty, he had made big bundles of them, and he had set off with them at four o'clock in the morning in the stage-coach for New York. Missionary of the national indignation, he was on his way to spread it throughout all the North of the United States, that stronghold of Federalism. He was on his way to pass in review the forces which were fighting against England and to fan the fire of their enthusiasm.

The road was dusty, the ground was hard, and in that odd vehicle, a sort of wagon on springs, in which you perched high, with its dozen travelers crowded on the four parallel seats, badly protected from the sun and the dust by the board top and the canvas curtains, it was in vain that you tried to doze. The awkward, angular packages placed under the seats left no room for the travelers' legs and bumped against their shins over every stone.

The monotonous, flat landscape, with its little hills, its poor little farmhouses scattered here and there on a rise, its little sickly thickets, and the uniform line of its wooden fences, presented nothing to charm the eye or distract the mind. The jolting of the wheels over the stones, the rasping of the leather straps against the wooden shafts, the noise of the canvas curtains flapping in the wind,

[241]

made it impossible to talk. It was a sour summer's dawn in that lurching vehicle where Benny found himself isolated with his own deed of daring.

For the first time in six years he found himself back on the roads. For the first time in his life he was traveling over the highroads of this country of his which he did not know; and for the first time he, who had hitherto passed humble, silent and bowed through the tumult of revolution, war, and disaster, was now on his way through the peaceful summer countryside, bearing in him and with him the wrath and the storm which he was to spread throughout the whole nation.

The countryside was peaceful and the fields were yellowing in the sun. The nearer he approached New York, the richer the country seemed. Despite the jolting of the stage-coach, Benny enjoyed his sense of liberty, the sense of strength that he carried within him, and the simple majesty of this great country, this young country, his own country.

In it he was at last the leader and the guide he had always dreamed of being. In it he could at last see shining that love of liberty in which his grandfather had given him his first lessons, and of which he, Benjamin Franklin Bache, was now the High Priest.

It was eleven o'clock at night, and the moon at its full stared at itself in the immense extent of the Hudson, prolonging the shadows of the ships' masts to infinity, filling the port and the silent streets with perfect peace, when the stage-coach reached New York. But at the inn a messenger awaited Benny.

The courier whom he had sent on ahead of him, bearing the pamphlets which contained Jay's treaty, had sold every one of them. There was not a single spare copy in the city. Already two of the New York papers had reprinted the text, and the city was thunderstruck. The Federalists did not dare to say a word. The Democrats did not know how to give vent to the wrath that filled them. There was not a moment to lose. It was essential to circulate the treaty, and indignation, far and wide.

Benny spent only one night in New York. While in Philadelphia, on that Friday the 3d of July, the populace emerged from their surliness to manifest their disgust; while, in a great black mass, they surged towards the port, threatening to pillage and burn an English ship; while the carpenters and workers from the suburbs poured into town to demonstrate in front of Washington's house; while, recoiling before a barrier of troops, they swept back into their suburbs and there, amid shouting and din, to the tune of the "Ça Ira" and the "Carmagnole", burned Jay's effigy — at this time Benjamin Franklin Bache, over the stony roads, through the summer heat, was hastening towards Boston.

He passed through the quiet, dainty little towns of New York State, and the pretty white villages of Connecticut, with their neatly painted wooden houses and their simple, genteel churches, whose sharp steeples dominated the townships and seemed to rest, clear-cut and severe, upon a sky of well-washed blue. Everything was heat and peace. They stopped to eat cherries at the crossroads. They called a halt at the village greens to have a drink with the carpenters, patriotic and diligent, who were setting up Liberty poles and adorning them with tricolor festoons for the Fourth of July.

In the evening they arrived at Stamford. They ate, they drank, they talked; and, before going to bed all together, without taking off their boots, in the big common bed at the inn, opposite the stars that you could see through

[243]

the open window, they talked about the treaty. Benny told them all about his mission.

They listened to him. They followed his telling; and soon there was nothing to be seen around him but faces aflame, eyes flashing with anger, fists clenched. "Oh, those English!"

On a corner of the table the good Mr. Seaman, Mayor of Hartford, signed a paper and thrust it into Benny's hand. "The day after to-morrow," he told him, "is Sunday, and you will find all the stage-coaches stopped, and all the villages closed against travelers. But make haste, take a post chaise, and, with this permit, nobody will hold you up. Make good speed. Be in Boston as soon as may be."

Around them, in the torrid summer night, grasshoppers and crickets made a shrilling noise so loud that it was like the sea in storm; and this sound mingled in their fevered dreams with Jay's treaty.

At three o'clock in the morning, Benny was on his way again. The stage-coach rolled slowly through the snug little towns of Connecticut, which were peacefully celebrating American liberty and the favors of the Eternal.

In Philadelphia the militiamen, the patriots, the Democrats, the old Whigs cursed Jay in their toasts, denounced the English, and glorified France. Through the streets the mob paraded a transparent painting, with the figure of John Jay upon it. "The figure was in full stature, holding in his right hand a pair of scales, containing in one scale American Liberty and Independence, kicking the beam; in the other, British Gold, in extreme preponderance." In his left hand Jay held "a treaty of Amity, Commerce, and Navigation, which he extended to a group of Senators, who were grinning with pleasure and grasping at the treaty. From the mouth of the figure issued these words: 'Come up to my price, and I will sell you my country.' " At night they burned it.

In New York an immense procession hoisted the French flag, marched about the city with drums beating, and, after collecting a vast multitude of townsfolk, urchins, gossips, shopkeepers, burghers, swept like a gigantic wave to the Battery, where they burned Jay's treaty in solemn form.

Late at night Benny arrived at Hartford. In the inn the patriots, sitting at table, proposed to celebrate Independence Day by a long Bacchic session, and they invited him to join them. But the exhausted traveler fell into his bed, from which he had to get out again before dawn to set off once more in his post chaise, along with his eight hundred pamphlets, and gallop all through the Sunday calm, through villages with shuttered houses, with church belfries pealing, with streets empty and sedate — from Hartford to Springfield, from Springfield to Brookfield, from Brookfield to Spencer, from Spencer to Worcester — without stopping except to change horses, without resting, without thinking about anything but Jay's treaty and American Independence. At Worcester he slept heavily but briefly.

In the morning he was still all yawns when, before he took the stage-coach, while he was still at breakfast, a stout, imposing man and a somewhat dried-up lady came and sat down beside him. It was a vast figure of a man, even heavier than he was majestic, and even more bouncing than he was heavy; for there was something petulant about the way he moved. Benny recognized John Adams, Vice President of the United States, in company with Mrs. Adams.

Mr. Adams was friendly with Benny, whom he had known as a boy at Passy; and Mrs. Adams was affable with Benny, who had once played with her son in the gardens of France. They talked about the weather and the state

[245]

of the roads. They also touched on politics, and Mr. Adams, in friendly fashion, asked the young journalist whether they knew anything about the treaty in Philadelphia.

"Oh, just a little," replied Benny.

"Well," said the Vice President, "once the people know about it and they have tried it out for a few months, everybody will like it very well."

Then he gave the young man a farewell salute which resembled a benediction. He set off for Braintree. Benny set off for Boston.

He arrived there about two o'clock in the afternoon of that Monday, July 6, 1795. The town was all in an uproar. The papers had just received and reprinted the analysis of the treaty which Benny had published on June 29th. The patriots had at once summoned a meeting of townsfolk in Boston to discuss the treaty and solemnly condemn it, if need be. The Federalists had instantly retorted that there was no occasion for discussing a document which was but ill known through the medium of a publication certainly fraudulent and doubtless truncated.

There was strife. Quarrels and threats had free course. The fury of the patriots was great; but the monocrats were well organized, numerous and impressive. Nobody could tell who was going to carry the day.

Benny arrived about two o'clock. He was bringing the text of the treaty. There was no denying it. He put it on sale, he had it reprinted and reproduced by the newspapers, he sent it to the neighboring towns, he dispatched extracts from it to newspapers at a distance. He brought copies of it in person to influential Democrats in Boston: that illustrious old man, Samuel Adams, Governor of the State; Doctor Jarvis, the tribune of the Boston Democrats; and Benjamin

[246]

Austin, the Radical pamphleteer, to whom no Federalist dared to stand up. All of them received Benny with enthusiasm. From house to house they took him to see the Democratic leaders. From tavern to tavern they escorted him, so that he might tell his story there and fan the courage and the patriotic zeal of the Bostonians.

They never got tired of toasting him, listening to him and questioning him. Was it true that the English had corrupted a number of Senators; that Reed of Carolina had received fifteen hundred pounds' worth of plate; that Gunn of Georgia, in order to obtain a favorable treaty with the Indians, had had to submit to Hammond's conditions? Was it true that English gold ruled in the American Senate? Was it true that men bearing the highest names had let themselves be seduced and that the country had been betrayed by its most illustrious servants?

Was it not true that Jay had signed the treaty, that Washington had submitted it to the Senate, and that the Senate had ratified it, without daring to show it to the people?

Now the people had seen the treaty and the people condemned it. When the town meeting assembled in Faneuil Hall on July 10, 1795, the Democrats hoped to arrive at a solemn condemnation of Jay after a careful examination of his treaty, and the Federalists hoped to ward off the blow by having a commission appointed. But the crowd did not see things this way. They had read the treaty; they wanted to vote on it at once.

Doctor Jarvis spoke. He recalled the clauses of the treaty; his sonorous voice scanned his attacks upon it; often he interrupted himself, as though overwhelmed by the shame of the words that he had to pronounce; and the audience was carried away by his eloquence and dominated by these silences of his. There was no delay. When Jarvis cried, "All those who approve the treaty, hold up their hands!" in the silent hall not a hand was raised. When he said, "All those who disapprove the treaty, hold up their hands!" everybody in the hall stood up.

In vain Federalists and monocrats tried to explain, to excuse, to soften, to obscure, to turn the blow aside. It was useless: in Federalist Boston the treaty was unanimously condemned. Nay, more, they appointed a committee which drew up a long remonstrance to the President of the United States. Launched from the citadel of Federalism, a reasoned denunciation of Jay's treaty, embodied in seventeen articles, was addressed to President Washington and dispatched to him by special couriers.

The whole country echoed Boston. Throughout New England the town assemblies met and condemned the treaty. In all the newspapers of the continent it was cursed and banned. "Atticus", "Civis", "Sidney", "Caius" and a hundred other patriots under classic and sonorous pseudonyms published article after article, riddling it and detailing all its infamies. New York, following Boston's example, had a great gathering of its citizens, who flayed the treaty, hooted Hamilton and cursed Jay.

Benny was present at this gathering. Then he returned in haste to Philadelphia, where he organized a similar one. Its success was striking. Six thousand persons attended it, manifested against Jay, and passed a unanimous vote in favor of an address to the President. In the evening, in the city squares, they burned the treaty. At Charleston, in South Carolina, the whole town assembled to denounce it. At Lexington, in Kentucky, it was the same thing.

From one end of the Union to the other the citizens assembled and voted addresses to the President, begging him

[248]

not to sign a treaty which would cover the country with shame and sacrifice the liberty of the nation to the greed of its merchants. The shops closed in token of mourning. Workshops were shut, and consternation reigned everywhere.

CHAPTER III

THE STRANGE STORY OF MR. RANDOLPH

GENERAL WASHINGTON was aghast.

True, he had never liked this treaty, and it would give him no pleasure to sign it. But up to this day he had seen no way of withholding his signature, without disorganizing the party of law and order in the United States forever, and without running the risk of war with England. Now he could not see any way of signing it either, without raising the country against him and without giving the French the impression that he was taking sides against them.

It was vain to plead that first in New York, then in Boston, and here and there elsewhere, Chambers of Commerce, and merchants' associations started petitioning in favor of the treaty. They were only a tiny minority. Their manifestations, indeed, stressed the most disagreeable side of the treaty, which was denounced as a low-down deal whereby John Jay had sacrificed many legitimate interests and long-standing claims of the United States to obtain commercial security. The newspapers were able to prove that, out of sixty merchants who had voted in New York in favor of the treaty, only eighteen had been in the American ranks during the War of Independence. The others had been lukewarm or neutral, or were recent immigrants or old Loyalists.

George Washington could clearly feel around him in

Philadelphia, and in Virginia among his neighbors, the reprobation of everybody — even sound people, even loyal Federalists. The whole country regarded the treaty as a cowardly abandonment of its old ally and as meaning the ruin of its trade in wheat with France, which had been so lucrative during the past two years.

Sailors saw in it a repudiation of all their demands and a betrayal of the most sacred rights of the American marine, which was to be constrained to bow down to England's supremacy and accept her theory of blockade, instead of maintaining the principle of the freedom of the seas for neutrals. The townspeople were indignant that English industry should obtain all the advantages, while America received nothing in exchange. The people of the West themselves distrusted the fine promises of the English to evacuate their military posts, and they denounced the ambiguous rôle of the English commanders, who kept up underhand incitement of the Indians everywhere.

As though to justify all these complaints, the King of England, without even informing Washington in advance — Washington learned it from the papers — added to the list of articles forbidden as contraband of war all American foodstuffs intended for France. Nobody could make any mistake about it any longer: Jay's treaty clearly meant the rupture of the Franco-American alliance. It was an instrument of war against France.

Despite the opposition of Wolcott and Pickering, the President decided to follow Randolph's advice. The Secretary of State finally triumphed over his colleagues. On July 13th Washington instructed Randolph to tell the Minister of England that the treaty would never receive his signature so long as the Order in Council of the King of England was not abrogated.

[251]

Always polite, always ingenious, Hammond suggested a solution on the spot. The King of England would suspend his Order in Council, Washington would sign the treaty, and then the King of England would reëstablish his Order in Council. In this way everybody would be satisfied. But Randolph, after referring the matter back to Washington, was instructed to inform Hammond that the President of the United States would never sign on these conditions.

The heat of summer fell upon the city and fever grew among the crowd. On July 24th a great concourse of people assembled in the gardens of the Congress Building. Under the stimulus of Benny, returned in haste from Boston and arrived two days before, all the Democratic leaders had come together. They harangued the crowd. No Federalist dared to reply to them. No Federalist dared even to mingle with the crowd. They voted an address of indignation to the President, and marched in procession to the Consulate of France and then to the Legation of France, where they gave three cheers for Adet.

Next the crowd proceeded to the Legation of England, where they burned Jay's treaty and hooted Hammond, who from his windows watched this curious and picturesque spectacle. Finally they went off to break Mrs. Bingham's windows, and when Monsieur de Noailles, impetuous and chivalrous friend of hers, charged the crowd on horseback single-handed to disperse them, they tore up cobblestones and started stoning him.

The anger of the crowd and the heat of summer, reached so high a point that General Washington could not stand them any longer. He decided to instruct Randolph to draw up a memorandum for the Court of London, while he went off himself for a rest at Mount Vernon.

For the first time in his career Washington retreated be-

Courtesy of the American Antiquarian Society

"His lean left hand he stretched, as if to smile,
"And, manful, groped his breeches' with his right."

Say, who for Larning, ever equalled I?

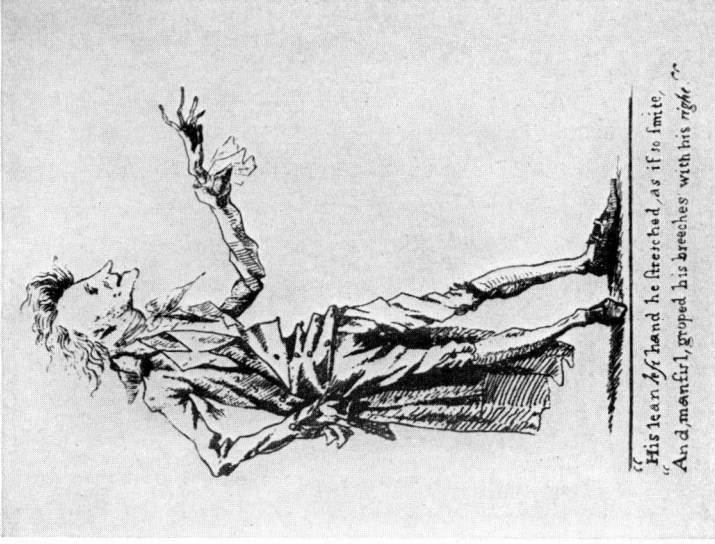

TWO CARICATURES TAKEN FROM THE "REMARKS ON THE JACOBINIAD"
(BY J. S. J. GARDINER), BOSTON, 1795

fore the crowd. For the first time he wrote: "To sum up the whole in a few words, I have never, since I have been in the administration of Government, seen a crisis which in my judgment has been so pregnant of interesting events; nor one from which more is to be apprehended, whether viewed on one side or the other. . . . It would seem that the opposition is in a manner universal, or that those of different sentiments are supine or intimidated; which would make ratification a serious business indeed."

For the first time General Washington found against him a hostile public opinion which even his popularity could not shake. In face of the avalanche which Benny Bache had let loose, the President of the United States prepared to give way.

But George Hammond by no means regarded the game as lost.

George Hammond had his faults. He was supercilious, he was stiff, and his fine manners bordered on impertinence. But he was plucky and obstinate. He had a cool head, a hard heart, and he was lucky.

In three weeks he had to embark on his return to England and he wanted to take the treaty back with him. He wanted to have the business settled before he left. But Mr. Randolph, whom he had never liked, seemed to be master of the situation and barred the way to him. Hamilton, who had once served him so well, did not seem to enjoy Washington's confidence in the same degree as before. Wolcott and Pickering were impotent. Hammond must act himself, promptly and directly.

Luckily for him, his Government had just sent him an excellent weapon. On March 28, 1795, in sight of the coast of France, off Penmarch, the French ship *Jean Bart* was chased and seized by the English frigate *Cerberus*. The captain of the *Jean Bart* hastened to throw into the sea the papers that he had on board, but he did it so hurriedly and carelessly that the papers came to the surface for a moment and an English sailor dived in and fished them out. They were Monsieur Fauchet's last dispatches to his Government.

Unluckily for France, Monsieur Fauchet was conscientious. He kept his Government informed about his smallest actions, his smallest feelings; and, as he had a taste for literature, he did so in a rich, eloquent and moving style. In the dispatches thus seized, he told Robespierre that Mr. Randolph had called upon him for the purpose of telling him how the American Government had mismanaged affairs in the West and made a mess of the situation in that region. Monsieur Fauchet also described, for the benefit of the "Incorruptible" [1], the suggestion which Mr. Randolph had then made to him that he should buy some influential politicians in order to give these events in the West a turn favorable to France — a turn which, for that matter, would do no harm to the real interests of the United States.

Monsieur Fauchet had not been able to profit by this good advice, for he was short of money. He drew from this, for the benefit of his chiefs, a twofold conclusion — first, that they ought to send him more money, and, next, that the Americans were not a moral people. In a happy couplet, which sounded well and gave a good idea of the literary taste and the moral worth of the Jacobin Minister, he wrote:

"Thus with some thousands of dollars the Republicans could have decided on civil war or on peace! Thus the con-

[1] It was the nickname given by his admirers to Robespierre.

science of the pretended patriots of America have already
their tariff!"

The English officers who read this dispatch of Fauchet's
found it amusing. It might come in useful and they transmitted it at once to the Foreign Office. There Lord Grenville read it carefully and found it very interesting. It
should be useful. He dispatched it without delay to George
Hammond, who received it and read it eagerly. It was a
godsend. It would come in useful on the spot.

Still, it was rather delicate for an English Minister to
transmit to the American Government the denunciation of
a Minister of France, who accused an American Minister of
dishonesty and boasted about having refused to buy him.
Badly handled, the business might have unexpected results.
If you acted too timidly you might look like a spy; if you
proceeded too boldly you ran the risk of looking like a
blackmailer.

Mr. Hammond acted without delay, without hesitation,
without omission, and without haste.

He knew that Mr. Wolcott did not like Mr. Randolph.
One fine evening, after dinner, Mr. Hammond took the
letter about Randolph out of his pocket and showed it to
him. Mr. Wolcott read it over with a mixture of satisfied
surprise and delighted consternation. He lost no time in
showing it to his colleague, Mr. Pickering. The two men
decided that Mr. Washington should know of it.

So, henceforth, Mr. Hammond was out of it and the
affair was in good hands. There could be no question any
longer of international complications or diplomatic repri-
mand.

These two men of the North could not contain themselves
for joy at the idea of giving a lesson in morality to their

colleague of the South. These two counsellors of Washington's, who felt themselves neglected by their master, could not fail to find some pleasure in proving to him that the counsellor whom, to all appearance, he preferred was a rogue. By acting in this way, they would be conforming to the demands of their patriotism, of their moral sense, and of their jealousy. What man would have resisted?

General Washington could not resist either.

He had left Mount Vernon, where the importunate clamor of protest against Jay's treaty had pursued him. He had returned to Philadelphia for the purpose of getting in touch with his advisers, seeking their counsel and doing something quickly. You could not let public opinion run riot in this way without trying to calm it or control it.

Washington did not meet Mr. Randolph immediately on his return, but he met Mr. Wolcott, smiling and mysterious; and Mr. Wolcott lost no time in showing him Fauchet's dispatch, together with the translation which Mr. Pickering had made of it, with more zeal than elegance. The General read this document attentively.

Mr. Randolph was a friend of his, a neighbor of his, and his personal *protégé*. Mr. Randolph owed to General Washington his advancement in his political career, which was approved neither by the Federalists, because of Randolph's hostile attitude to the Constitution, nor by the Democrats, because of his blind personal devotion to Washington. Mr. Hamilton had been reserved about Randolph. Mr. Jefferson had had his reticences about Randolph, which General Washington no doubt recalled at this critical moment. General Washington knew that Mr. Randolph's personal affairs were supposed to be embarrassed and that he had often been accused of lacking in honesty.

General Washington read Fauchet's dispatch with the

greatest attention. The next day, August 12, 1795, he once more asked his Ministers, assembled in Council, for their advice about Jay's treaty and its ratification. He ignored Mr. Randolph's objections to ratification and rallied to the thesis of Mr. Wolcott and Mr. Pickering, which was the British thesis.

On August 14, 1795, Washington signed the treaty. Then, with a majesty which bordered on solemnity, he desired Mr. Randolph to be good enough to hand this document to Mr. Hammond. He withdrew without saying more.

So it was that Jay's treaty was ratified, which broke the Franco-American understanding, and which the American people reviled.

Mr. Randolph could not believe his eyes or his ears. He was naïve enough to let this be seen by Mr. Hammond, who was too much of a gentleman to smile, though he was human enough to find some fun in it. Monsieur Adet, who was immediately informed, could make nothing of it all, either; but he was as furious as he was disgruntled. He had thought the game was won.

Everything was cleared up on August 19th.

That morning Mr. Randolph was working at home, and he was making ready to call upon the President about nine o'clock as usual, when Mr. Kidd, the President's major-domo, arrived to desire him not to do so, but to come at half-past ten instead. Mr. Randolph assumed, with a smile, that the President was going for a ride. At half-past ten, when he presented himself very punctually at the President's, he was surprised and annoyed to find that Wolcott and Pickering were ahead of him and already with the President.

[257]

"Some silly mistake of Kidd's, curse the fellow!" Mr. Randolph said to himself; and he prepared to make his excuses to the President. But for these excuses of his there was no call.

When he went in, Washington's solemn appearance, the grave but gloating faces of his colleagues, and their overdone courtesy towards himself, warned Randolph on the instant that something was going to happen, that the scene was set and the scenario ready, and that he was assigned the leading rôle.

After a few awkward, confused remarks, General Washington made up his mind. He took a paper out of his pocket and handed it to Mr. Randolph. "Mr. Randolph," he said to him, "here is a letter which I beg you to read, and about which you will give such explanations as you see fit." Randolph ran his eyes over the paper. "An intercepted letter!" he cried. Washington nodded his head.

Mr. Randolph read it carefully; but he had, in short, nothing very definite to say, no very clear explanation to offer. It was all so long ago. He had forgotten all about it. This solemn setting, the hostility of his colleagues and of the President, the suddenness of the attack upon him — all this froze his memory, his imagination, his reasoning faculty.

He neither stammered nor flushed; he neither confessed nor wept. He remained very upright, very calm, and very vague. There was nothing to show that he was either guilty or innocent, but everything to show that he was a gentleman.

He merely affirmed that he had never had any dishonest communication with Fauchet and that he had never asked him for money or received any from him. He added that he would put his defense in writing.

Washington requested Wolcott and Pickering to ask him questions. Pickering had nothing to ask; he sat rigid and asked nothing. Wolcott, too, was rigid; but as a matter of politeness to the President, he asked some question of no particular importance. Then Washington desired Randolph to withdraw into the next room.

After waiting for nearly an hour, he was summoned back into the study, where Washington had been taking counsel with Wolcott and Pickering. The President informed him that he should put his explanation into writing. Randolph retorted that such was already his intention. He added that he tendered his resignation. None of them seemed to be either surprised or grieved. So they parted.

Mr. Randolph's career was finished and Mr. Randolph himself was finished. He knew it; but still he fought stoutly to save what he could save of his honor. He went in search of Monsieur Fauchet. Monsieur Fauchet had just left Philadelphia. Mr. Randolph went after Monsieur Fauchet. He overtook Monsieur Fauchet at Newport, ready to embark at any moment aboard the frigate *La Méduse*, which, before weighing anchor, awaited only a favorable wind and a convenient mist to hide her from the English cruiser standing outside the bay.

Mr. Randolph went to see Monsieur Fauchet at his hotel at nine o'clock in the morning and Monsieur Fauchet promised to furnish him forthwith with certificates of his honesty. Mr. Randolph should have them the very next day. The very next day, not having received these certificates, Mr. Randolph went back to the hotel.

Fauchet was gone, and they told him that *La Méduse* had weighed anchor. She had vanished into the mist, together with Monsieur Fauchet and his certificates of Mr.

[259]

Randolph's honesty. Faced with this last blow of Fate, Mr. Randolph felt himself floored.

Nevertheless, before he set out on board *La Méduse* Monsieur Fauchet had indeed drafted these certificates. He sent them to Philadelphia for the approval of Monsieur Adet, who finally handed them over to Mr. Randolph. At Mr. Randolph's disposal were also put any documents he might desire in the archives of the Legation of France, and in the archives of the American Secretary of State.

But Monsieur Fauchet's certificates were not of very much use to him. In them Monsieur Fauchet, with an eloquence which was incontestable, but more touching than it was convincing, affirmed Mr. Randolph's absolute honesty. Monsieur Fauchet explained that the agents whom Mr. Randolph had advised him to bribe were flour merchants, who might be in a position to reveal to him the secret intrigues of the English in the West. But the flour merchants struck public opinion as being somewhat befloured; and so did Mr. Randolph's honesty.

Mr. Randolph published his defense. In it he affirmed that he had never taken any money, which was obvious. In it he maintained that he had never requested any for himself, which was probable. In it he protested his honesty, in which nobody was interested any more.

For that matter, Mr. Randolph knew this himself quite well. All his pamphlet aimed at was not excusing himself, but proving that all this business had no other object but to ruin him, to intimidate Washington, and to obtain his (Randolph's) dismissal and the signature of Jay's treaty by Washington: a twofold object which had been attained. Randolph's pamphlet was rather long-winded, but it was clear and convincing.

Randolph had begged Madison and his other Democratic

friends not to take up his defense. They did him this favor, and without making any bones about it either, it would seem. Only a few Democratic journalists took up the cudgels for him, and later a crook by the name of Callender put up a clever *apologia* for him. But, in short, nobody took much trouble about him, for nobody had liked him much and nobody had had much confidence in him — nobody except one man, who, for his part, could not forget him so quickly or resign himself so easily.

George Washington had made Randolph's career. Randolph was his personal choice, his own friend. After Jefferson's retirement, Washington had imposed Randolph on the Democrats, who suspected him, and on the Federalists, who distrusted him. He had collaborated with Randolph in an intimate kind of way, less as a chief with his subordinate than as a father with his son. Washington had trusted Randolph and he had an affection for him.

Randolph's downfall went to Washington's heart. It diminished Washington as a political leader and as President of the United States. His choice of Randolph was the first serious mistake with which his party could reproach him. It was also the first time that, by an imprudent appointment, he had risked the reputation of the United States in the eyes of foreign Powers.

Washington felt all this so deeply that in this crisis, a leader so full of strength and coolness as he usually was, he let circumstances get the better of him, and became the plaything of a hard, haughty diplomat like Hammond, and of a pair of Puritans, inconsiderable enough, like Wolcott and Pickering. He could not contrive to save either his friend, or the prestige of his country, or his own personal prestige.

Randolph sent him his pamphlet. Washington read it

with great care. He read it over again and annotated it; but he had no reply to make to it; and the two men never met again in this world.

Jay's treaty was signed.

Mr. Hammond voyaged across the Atlantic to receive, at the hands of Lord Grenville, the reward which he had so richly earned. He obtained it, and it conferred upon him a kind of title to the quality of a great man which he otherwise could never have held, and which his later life proved to be a misfit.

Monsieur Fauchet voyaged across the Atlantic, aboard *La Méduse*, making ready for the punishment which doubtless awaited him. But there was no punishment for him. They did not realize in France that Monsieur Fauchet's eloquence and his ill-timed stickling for morality had stamped the soul of General Washington with the seal of implacable alienation from France, and that Monsieur Fauchet, with his willy prudence, had done his country more disservice than the imprudent Genet. But Monsieur Fauchet drafted documents well, he never bribed anybody without written orders from his chiefs, and he kept his accounts in order. He was made a prefect and he had a fine career.

Triumphant England had her treaty. She had beaten France. Thanks to her fleet, she had made her diplomacy respected, and through her diplomacy she had secured recognition of the supremacy of her fleet. Henceforth she was cock of the walk in the United States. It was no longer only in Mrs. Bingham's drawing-room that people dared to sing the praises of England, but in all the merchants' shops and on the sidewalks of the main streets.

England had won. But she had humiliated Mr. Randolph,

she had dishonored the American Secretary of State; and many an American resented it.

Thanks to the Fauchet-Randolph scandal, General Washington, Mr. Hammond and the Federalists had been able to impose Jay's treaty on the American people. But they could not calm their anger. Instead they deepened it and envenomed it.

It was true that the Democratic leaders were silenced or eliminated. Jefferson sulked on his fine estate at Monticello. Gallatin, compromised by the revolt in the West, still held himself aloof. Nobody mentioned Randolph any longer, Monroe and Paine were in Europe, and Madison preferred to wait. But public opinion, aroused by the newspapers, had gained consciousness of its strength. It had been overridden, but not vanquished.

The Democratic leaders were eclipsed; but, mingling with the crowd, Benny Bache stirred up the crowd. The crowd still shouted in the streets. Henceforth they shouted the words that they read in the *Aurora*. They took up the refrains that Benny Bache taught them.

CHAPTER IV

BENNY BACHE AND GEORGE WASHINGTON

It was then that Benny attained glory. It was then that he became famous. It was then that he compromised himself in the eyes of "right-thinking" people, that he burned his boats in the eyes of fools, and that the crowd nearly burst themselves cheering him.

Benny Bache damned himself then, because he said what he thought while other people lied, and because, on their behalf, he said what they thought. He then lost his good name and many friends. But at least Benny Bache did not lose what some other people lost.

In 1795 General Washington was the most famous man in the world, and the greatest, pending the rise of a little general, who still called himself Bonaparte, and was still doing little jobs for a government that he despised.

Washington was very great; but he was very lonely in 1795. Never was a leader so much alone as Washington was in 1795. He had had friends once, good neighbors with whom he hunted, drank, played cards and pool, and with whom he went to the races. He had lost almost all his friends — almost all the Virginians, the comrades of his sports and his political struggles, of his military campaigns and of his labors for the nation.

Virginia rejected the Federalists, cursed Jay's treaty, and denounced its defenders. Washington's old friend Thomas Jefferson was so indignant, when he thought of all the

[264]

harm done by Washington and by that infamous treaty which he had imposed on the country, that he cried: "Curse on his virtues, they have undone the country!"

Jefferson cried it aloud — when he was alone — and whispered it when he was in company. But Washington had good ears and he knew what Jefferson was thinking. He even guessed what he was doing.

Washington perceived all that the people around him were thinking and feeling; and that gave him a cruel time of it in 1795. When he broke and repudiated his friend Randolph, he knew what harm he was doing him, and he saw very well that he was alienating from himself the only man, good or bad, venal or pure, who, amid all these selfish politicians, had an affection for him into which entered a kind of tenderness and yearning.

But, if Randolph could never tear that affection out of himself, neither could he prevent himself from saying of the General, in that pamphlet in which he laid bare their former intimacy: "His is a temper which, under the exterior of cool and slow deliberation, rapidly catches a prejudice and with difficulty abandons it."

Only the General's death permitted Randolph once more to enjoy that old affection of theirs. As long as they were both alive, it remained dead. It was not the only thing the Jay treaty killed.

All the brilliance of Washington's younger life was dead. Once he had been the idol of the French. Lafayette venerated him as a loving son venerates his father. The Marquis de la Rouairie, the bravest man in France, saw in him an incomparable hero; and the Chevalier de Chastellux, noblest, most philosophical and most enlightened of writers, said of him: "He is a god; everything about him is godlike."

[265]

Now Lafayette was in prison, the Marquis de la Rouairie had been torn to pieces by the revolutionaries, Monsieur de Chastellux was dead, and Monsieur Genet, Minister of France, had called Washington "the old Washington." Monsieur Fauchet considered him crafty, Monsieur Adet regarded him as a traitor, in the *Sentinelle de Paris* Monsieur Louvet denounced him as "an enemy of his old friends, and a friend of his old enemies." Everything that came from France was bitter and insulting.

What came from England was not much brighter. Hammond had treated Washington with a polite irreverence which bordered on contempt. Hammond's Secretary at the English Legation had said of him: "He possesses the two great requisites of a statesman, the faculty of concealing his own sentiments and of discovering those of other men. A certain degree of indecision, however, a want of vigor and energy, may be observed in some of his actions, and are indeed the obvious result of too refined caution. He is a man of great, but secret ambition, and has sometimes, I think, condescended to use little arts, and those, too, very shallow ones, to secure the object of that ambition. . . . I have never heard of any truly noble, generous or disinterested action of his; and, what is worse, his own State, Virginia, has less affection for him than any other part of the United States."

The General, besides, was by no means unaware that the Federalists, men of the North, who served him, sought above all to serve themselves through him, whether it was Hamilton, Rufus King, Fisher Ames or Cabot. With them he could never find himself on that footing of frank friendship which springs only from intimate and spontaneous understanding, or from long community in the habits of childhood. To Hamilton, Washington was always the chief,

[266]

indispensable, respected, but whom you always distrusted a little, because his rank placed him above you, when you thought that you ought really to be above him.

This was what Hamilton meant to convey to the Duc de Liancourt when he told him that the President had, in short, not much brains, not much learning, not much education, but good judgment and great common sense, and a prudence which appeared to be the principal trait of his character and the guide of his actions, political and personal. This was also what the Vice President of the United States thought; but all these qualities Mr. John Adams could not prize very much, for he did not possess them himself, and he knew it very well.

In 1795 Mr. Adams and the Federalists, Mr. Hamilton, Mr. Wolcott, Mr. King, Mr. Morris, all considered that Mr. Washington was growing old and that he lacked strength of will; for they had been afraid of seeing him refuse to sign Jay's treaty, and to bring him to do it they had had to resort to extreme measures, which indeed were not very agreeable. The Federalists could not do without Washington; but, if they did not fail to make use of him, to defend him, sometimes even to exalt him, among them he was, so to speak, a prisoner rather than a leader.

For the Democrats Washington had become an enemy, or rather *the* enemy. The Democrats knew very well that the Federalist Party was bound to fall to pieces and weaken if Washington disappeared. They knew also that the Federalists, led by Washington and profiting by Washington's still very great authority, would always succeed in rallying a majority in the country. If the Democrats wanted to win, or even to survive, they had to attract Washington to themselves, or else force him to quit political life.

Jefferson had tried to regain the influence which he had

[267]

once had over Washington and bring him over to the
Democrats. His failure had been so pitiful that never could
the two men forgive each other. Randolph had tried to lead
Washington gently over to the side of the Democrats. He
had come near his goal, only to fail shamefully.

Henceforth nobody could dream of wresting Washington
away from the influence of Hamilton and the monocrats.

There was nothing left to do but compel him to quit.

Such, indeed, was the obsessing idea of all the Democratic
leaders from this month of August, 1795 until Washington's death. One can discern it in Jefferson's and Madison's
letters, in Randolph's pamphlet, in Monroe's messages and
in the manifestoes of the Democratic societies, in anonymous letters to the papers and in Freneau's poems. It was
the Democratic Party's fixed idea. But, the more its leaders
talked about it among themselves, the more they were
afraid of talking about it in public. The more they judged
Washington's retirement indispensable, the more careful
they were to do nothing which would reveal their hostility
to him. They encouraged one another to action, and they
waited on events.

Benny Bache was only one among these leaders. But he
was twenty-six. He had been brought up in Geneva, where
they had taught him that you must always say what you
think. He had associated with his grandfather, who had
set frankness high among the virtues. He was a democrat,
who believed sincerely in unburdening your soul and crying
from your heart. He had a naïve faith in the wisdom of the
people, among whom he lived himself, and he set them
over against Washington.

The other Democratic leaders were Parliamentarians.
For his part, Benny was a "Jacobin." He wanted the people

to govern themselves directly and express themselves explicitly. He wanted to see the disappearance from political life of all individual wills which were too strong, which could not yield to the desires of the masses. He wanted to see the disappearance of all personalities which were so great that they isolated themselves out of contact with the crowd.

So Benny Bache attacked Washington.

From all directions, in that summer, in that autumn, of 1795, people sent him articles aimed at Washington. He published them. "Hancock" accused the President of treating the will of the people with contempt. "Belisarius" told Washington: "Believe me, Sir, your fellow citizens are not mere moulds of wax. . . . Stripped of the mantle of infallibility and possessing nought of the *jus divinum*, you appear before them a frail mortal, whose passions and weaknesses are like those of other men."

"Pittachus" rallied the President for a spoilt child. "Miles" reproached him for that royal tone which he affected. "Atticus" and "Gracchus" could see nothing in him but a despot, a pale, poor imitation of the Georges of England. As for "Valerius", he was more brutal and more definite:

"Is there an American who, after reflecting on these facts and attending to a crowd of additional ones, which must press on his mind, has the baseness to offer incense to those who tell us that honor consists in an uncomplaining submission to insults, and public virtue in forming a close union with those who insult us? Yes, Sir, there are such men: men who had never merited the indignation of 'Valerius', had not your dark schemes drawn them from a state of safety and obscurity. They may hereafter regret, in the anguish of despair, and on a relapse of virtue, that they

have sacrificed their peace of mind to the fruitless attempt
of enslaving their country. For, Sir, we are free, and are,
with one mind, determined to remain free. Your voice
may have been heard when it called to virtue and glory,
but it will be lost in the tempest of popular fury, whenever it shall speak the language of lawless ambition. The
American People, Sir, will look to death the man who as-
sumes the character of an usurper."

All autumn long, all winter long, in Benny's *Aurora*,
which was reproduced by the Democratic papers throughout the Union — the *New York Argus*, the *Boston Chronicle*, the *Kentucky Herald*, the *Carolina Gazette* — and all
the smaller weeklies, tireless, pitiless, the "Pittachuses",
the "Atticuses", the "Valeriuses", the "Hancocks", the
"Millions", the "Belisariuses", and anonymous letter writers
succeeded one another. All of them repeated to Washington:
"Shame, shame upon you!" All of them, openly or covertly, bluntly or tactfully, gave him the same counsel:

"If you could for a short time put off your suit of buckram, and condescend to that state of humility, in which you
might hear the real sentiments of your fellow citizens, your
next levée would be the last. . . . You would save the
wreck of character now crumbling to pieces under the
tempest of a universal irritation, not to be resisted."

In Virginia, in Massachusetts, in Pennsylvania, in Connecticut, in Maryland, even in far-off Maine — everywhere
resounded attacks upon Washington, and always they came
from Philadelphia, from the *Aurora* which was the center of
the Democratic Party, the focus of the campaign against
Washington. Through Beckley, Jefferson was in communication with Bache. Through Beckley and through Logan,
sometimes even directly, Monroe, the Jacobin American
Minister in France, sent Bache notes and articles to

publish anonymously. Paine wrote for him and entrusted Bache with the sale and circulation of his books.

Bache was accused of receiving from the Minister of France the price of one hundred subscriptions to send his paper to France, and eight hundred subscriptions to distribute it gratis in the United States. For his part, he despised calumnies, threats and insults. When the Secretary of State informed him that henceforth the Government would cease to take the six subscriptions which served to refresh American diplomats in Europe with *Auroras*, Bache replied that little he cared; he would send them his paper at his own expense, and so he did.

He also made a present of it to Washington, who could not stand the sight of this sheet in the morning, and could not help opening it. John Adams was a subscriber, and he read it with delighted wrath, for he at least derived pleasure from Bache's indignation.

In all the market towns of the United States, Democrats and small fry devoured the *Aurora*. One woman wrote to Benny: "I thank you for your *Aurora*. I welcome it every evening as I would a pleasant, intelligent friend. You can't think how delightful it is, in this Region of Aristocracy, to meet a little — I had almost said: treason!"

There was, indeed, treason widespread everywhere in America in 1795; but there was none of it in the case of Benny Bache. He alone fought without any mask.

Mr. Randolph had been betrayed and he could not help taking his revenge. He published his defense, which was a denunciation of Washington, and he signed it. But about the same time there appeared a letter signed "Calm Observer", in which it was insidiously asked whether Washington, disinterested as he appeared to be and though he had refused any salary, had not in fact received a salary and even exceeded the sums which were constitutionally allotted to him. The "Calm Observer" was perfidious; but he was well informed. Beckley and Randolph knew who he was.

Wolcott and Hamilton were spurred to action. They hastened to send explanations and refutations to the *Aurora*, in which "Calm Observer" had published his letter. They had to admit that General Washington, embarrassed in his personal finances and overwhelmed by the cost of keeping up his state, had, indeed, received advances from the Treasury which exceeded the amount of his annual salary. There was, for that matter, nothing scandalous in this; but it was enough to satisfy the keen hostility of the Democrats and to make Washington turn pale.

At the same period there was republished in Philadelphia, from Bache's printing house, a little book, "Letters of General Washington", which was full of relish. Intermingled with letters serious or blameless were to be found some of an amorous nature, crude enough, and they were signed "Washington." They had first been published during the War of Independence by the English, who claimed to have seized them. They had, indeed, seized them, but they had also falsified them. They had revised them and added to them.

Bache republished these letters now in order to unmask Washington, the betrayer of America, to the English. Such is the circular course of human hatred, perfidy and cruelty. None of them is ever wasted. They hang fire but they burn out slowly and at length.

From Europe came back another piece of perfidy to add its sting to all those that tormented Washington. In France, Gouverneur Morris, Federalist Minister of the United States, was not on good terms with Thomas Paine, once an American patriot, still an American citizen, and now a strong Girondin deputy in the Convention. When his Girondin friends were proscribed, Paine was himself imprisoned, at the instigation of Robespierre, who did not like him. At once Paine wrote to Morris to demand the diplomatic intervention of the United States in his favor.

Undoubtedly he had a right to it, though it was droll to see this ardent Republican have recourse to a Monarchist to get himself out of the clutches of the Revolution. Morris enjoyed the comedy of the situation but he added tragedy to it. He informed Deforgues, Robespierre's Minister of Foreign Affairs, that, at Paine's request, he was writing to inform himself and learn for what reasons Paine was in prison and why he should remain there. The letter was courteous, and there was something comic about seeing a Monarchist whom Robespierre's blood-thirsty brutality disgusted, thus so politely putting one head more at his disposal.

But in the end it was Robespierre who was sent to the guillotine. Paine was saved. He returned to the midst of his friends. He had influential friends, he saw Morris's letter, and he wrote a pamphlet against Washington, whom he accused of having plotted his death with Robespierre and having betrayed the most sacred rights of friendship. He sent his pamphlet to Benny and Benny published it.

It seemed as though all Washington's present and all his past too were rising up against him. There was republished also in Boston the story about his first campaign, about that tragic incident when in a clearing at dawn he and his soldiers opened fire on a French detachment, at a time when there was peace and the French were under a flag of truce. The incident had been explained and it had been forgotten; but in 1795 it cropped up again. Bache published

[273]

it, the other papers wrote about it, and the crowd discussed it.

The campaign against General Washington ended by bearing fruit. The whole country was buzzing with it. Washington had ceased to be the supreme arbiter and the supreme model. He was dragged into the strife of parties. Unable to stop his ears, or to close his eyes to these sheets that some ill wind kept on always thrusting upon him, he was unable either to dismiss the disgust, the weariness and the discouragement which filled his soul.

He complained to his friends. He wrote to Jefferson a letter of reproach. He let himself go in the presence of his confidants. He, who had withstood all the attacks of a relentless enemy, weakened before public opinion. Now he could no longer help listening to the crowd. He listened and he heard the crowd shouting in the streets.

The crowd was singing the "Ça Ira". The crowd was brandishing Benny's *Aurora*. At the street corners they were making bonfires of Jay's treaty. With the French cockade in their hats, they were dancing the "Carmagnole".

CHAPTER V

"PORCUPINE" AND "LIGHTNING ROD"

THEY had broken Mrs. Bingham's drawing-room windows. They were in course of breaking Mr. Washington's glory. They were in course of breaking everything, and, the way things were going, there would soon be nothing left.

The Republicans had broken Mr. Hamilton, who had gone into retirement in high dudgeon. The Federalists had broken Mr. Jefferson, who was gone never to return. The Federalists and the English between them had destroyed Mr. Randolph, who had disappeared for ever.

Now the Republicans were applying themselves to eliminating Mr. Washington. It was all very well to shut your doors; you could still hear them. It was all very well to shut your windows; they broke them for you.

The time had come to do something about them. The Federalists could not get on without Washington. Washington represented, in the eyes of all Americans, and of the whole world, order, peace, and greatness. Washington was the symbol of American nationality, the flag around which everybody rallied instinctively. The Federalists would never have been able to constitute their party and keep it in being without him. Now, if Washington lost his prestige, if Washington retired from political life, the Federalist Party would be left impotent, headless, moribund.

Washington and his glory had to be saved. But how was it to be done?

Once it was easy. When Jefferson was available, you could always attack him. But Jefferson had retired to his estates and there was no excuse for attacking him. There was a lack of Democratic leaders whom you could attack. There was a lack of Federalist leaders who could attack. There was no Mr. Hamilton to strike the public eye any more, no Mr. Jefferson. There was no official and well-known leader who led the dance any more.

The Federalists had not to deal with Jefferson, or Madison, or Gallatin. They had to deal with public opinion, such as Bache had made it: the opinion of the American people.

They had to condescend to the crowd and talk to the crowd, now that the crowd had started breaking ladies' windows and would not respect General Washington any longer. But Mr. Hamilton had never talked to the crowd. He was a colonel, a lawyer, a great statesman; but he was not a tribune of the people. Mr. Jay was no tribune either. He was dry; he had no voice. Handsome man that he was, eminent as he was as a bookbinder, General Knox was no leader of crowds. Mr. Robert Morris had succeeded in moving Congress from New York to Philadelphia, but he was dumb in the presence of the crowd, and, besides, there were nasty rumors circulating about his land speculations. Mr. John Adams's belly was bigger than his prestige, and he had no contact with the masses. Mr. King, Mr. Ames and Mr. Cabot were distinguished men but they had nothing to do with the masses either. Mr. Bingham knew how to give a dinner but not how to make a speech or write an article.

Mr. Washington, no doubt, knew how to silence everybody; but he had nothing to say.

Nevertheless, the time for saying something had come.

[276]

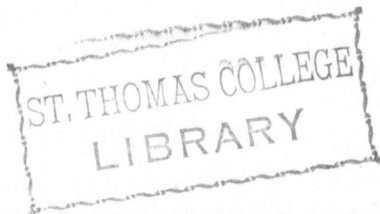

If you did not want some day — and soon — to be submerged by the crowd, you had to go down into the streets. You had to talk to the crowd. You had to go into every house and talk to everybody.

Only a newspaper could do it. Only a newspaper man could make a success of it.

Once, no doubt, Mr. Hamilton and the Federalist leaders would have chosen the upright Mr. Fenno to defend sound ideas and maintain good doctrine. But Mr. Fenno was heavy-handed. His paper was ponderous. He bored everybody, including even himself, it seemed. He was all right for publishing official communications. He suited well enough for printing and circulating those admirable letters of "Camillus" which Hamilton drafted to defend Jay's treaty.

But it was better for Mr. Fenno not to try and be witty or bombard his adversary. The only projectiles he could use were cobblestones, and he handled them with the grace of a bear. He took up Washington's defense with plenty of courage, and thundered against the papers that attacked the Father of his Country. He merely overlooked the fact that he had himself republished in his own paper the article which he blamed other papers for printing. When he tried to be funny, he was grotesque. When he was not in the least trying to be funny, he succeeded in being so only too well. His news had gone rancid, his articles stank of the midnight oil, and his jokes had a taste of dust about them.

Fenno could not save the party. But nobody else presented himself as its savior either. Noah Webster in New York was better. He had plenty of erudition, but he did not always digest it himself, and his public never digested it at all. In Boston Russell was a good journalist; but he

[277]

was also a good Bostonian, and that did not suit the rest of the country.

The Federalists knew nobody who was enough like themselves to defend their ideas sincerely, and different enough from themselves to make himself heard by the crowd. Throughout the whole of America they could not find anything that suited them. They could not find anybody.

But William Cobbett found himself; and he found them.

He was a sergeant major in the King of England's army. He was a fat man. He was sandy, with little, steel-blue eyes such as whitebait have. He had coarse hands and a ruddy, clear complexion such as you sometimes see in peasants. His small, oval head, on top of his fat, massive body, gave you no hint of anything but a brute. But, when he looked at you, you got quite a shock from the lightning that flashed in his eyes.

If there had not been a glint of genius about him, William Cobbett would have been just a brute. He said what he thought. He ate what he chose. He drank what he wanted. He liked what pleased him and anything that he did not like he loathed.

With all this, he was as straightforward as any bull. Noisiness, disorder, vice, jealousy, evil — all this set him mad. He could not stand it. However far off he might see it, he charged it. He gored it, he trampled it, he bit it; and, if he thought this was not enough, he flung all the weight of his heavy body upon it. He had a genius for brutality and an animal instinct for nobility.

William Cobbett was one of the miracles of England. Only very old and very rich lands — England, France, Germany, Italy — possess in the folds of their soil such reserves of intellect, of refinement and of pride that sometimes, without seeking it, without knowing it, some simple, earthy soul may unearth a treasure. He remains a peasant. He will never be anything but a peasant; but he has become a peasant of genius, in whom the genius of his country lives and shines with a dull, pure radiance, with a refinement incorruptible in its brutishness.

The animal vigor of the race picks up the intelligence of the élite, without passing through that long apprenticeship which society usually demands, and without submitting itself to the discipline that the mind usually accepts in order to become creative. Such human beings never have the coherence, the unity, of the great authors of their country. The forces which they carry within them remain incoherent forces. They rival one another rather than collaborate. But they exalt one another and they give the man concerned an incomparable luster. They make him a solitary, a fighter, an adventurer.

William Cobbett was this kind of an adventurer.

He was a peasant, a son of peasants. He had herded cows, fed pigs. He had danced on his village green in Surrey, and he had made love to farm girls, who had not found him exceptional. He had been to fairs and he had seen the diligences going by on the highroad. One day he had even set out for London. He had worked in Kew Gardens. But, garden for garden, he preferred those of his own village. He went back there. Once more he tilled the ground, and rubbed beasts up, and groomed them down. Once more he dreamed dreams. Once more he set off.

He discovered the sea. He wanted to be a sailor; but the recruiting officers of His Majesty had no use for him. They were afraid that he had simply seduced some girl and was trying to avoid marrying her. So William Cobbett the farm laborer, who could not become a sailor, became a lawyer's

[279]

clerk. He could neither read nor write, but he could sweep out an office as well as the next man; and he picked up some shreds of learning.

But, if it came to sweeping, he still preferred his village; and he preferred the sea to the art of sweeping. He tried to enlist again and this time he had better luck. Unfortunately, he made a mistake in a matter of detail. Instead of His Majesty's fleet, he enlisted in a careless moment in His Majesty's army, and so found himself a private at his regiment's depot in Chatham.

He still had to sweep, and rub up, and groom down. William Cobbett would have been bored if he had not learned to read and write in order to amuse himself. They made him a corporal and they sent him with his regiment to Frederickstown in New Brunswick.

His writing was good, his conduct excellent, his zeal exemplary; and he became a sergeant major. It was then that he completed his education. He learned the niceties of the English language, he learned arithmetic, he learned the wretchedness of men by studying his soldiers, and the vileness of men by observing his superiors, who cared about nothing but swindling over rations, getting a graft on purchases, and making a profit on supplies. Cobbett learned the art of writing in order to instruct his subordinates, for whom he drew up an English grammar, and in order to chastise his officers, against whom he prepared a formal complaint.

On his return to England he left the army, published his grammar, and launched his accusation. He was discharged with glowing certificates, and his grammar was a success, but his denunciation was no such thing. To avoid unpleasant consequences of it he had to quit England. His first crusade had failed.

Cobbett established himself in France. He would have liked her very well, apart from her Revolution. But he could not stand its disorder and he set off for America. There he settled and liked her well enough, despite the disorder which the American Revolution also had left behind it. Then he became a teacher, and he taught French *émigrés* the English tongue, with so much success that he was able to support himself, his wife, and his family.

But that cursed American Revolution importuned him. It rang in his ears. It kept on cropping up to worry him, annoy him, infuriate him. He could have put up with America very well. Her people were good fellows, her climate was a good climate, and her population came of sound Anglo-Saxon stock, hard-boiled, hard-working, hard-fisted. Cobbett could have got along with America quite well, but for this reek of revolution.

But America was infected with Jacobinism. Everywhere Cobbett heard people lauding France and the Revolution. He saw the crowd dancing the "Carmagnole", heard them singing the "Ça Ira", and watched them revelling in the streets with their French cockades.

Soon Cobbett could not hold himself in any longer and he started on his second crusade. He attacked the Revolution in America. He did not attack America, he did not even attack France, he did not attack the American Revolution, since it was over. He did not attack it — because it *was* over. But he attacked Revolution — any still existing Revolution that he encountered in his path in America.

When he met Mr. Priestley, Unitarian clergyman and English politician in flight; when he saw him exchanging compliments, toasts, and revolutionary homilies with the Democratic societies of New York, the members of Tammany, Congressmen and Senators, artisans and professors,

[281]

Cobbett could not stand it. He burst out. He told the Americans that they were fools and Priestley that he was a scoundrel.

This tickled the Americans. Cobbett published his pamphlet in Philadelphia and it had a great success. Its publisher found it going so well that he begged Mr. Cobbett to continue. Now Mr. Cobbett, once settled in Philadelphia, had every ground for continuing. Philadelphia was the Fourteenth of July every week, the "Marseillaise" every day, the "Ça Ira" all day, and the "Carmagnole" day and night. They kept on warming his ears for him.

Mr. Cobbett let himself go. For his own pleasure, for his own satisfaction, for the joy of saying what he thought and saying it brutally, he published first some pamphlets, and then a review. Finally he opened a shop on Second Street, opposite Christ Church and not far from Benny Bache's.

It was a fine shop. It was big, it was bright, it was comfortable, it was imposing, and it made you look at it. Cobbett left nothing undone to make it known. He had the best books of Europe and the finest engravings. He had, above all, a shop window without precedent.

One of its casements was adorned with portraits of all the Kings and Queens on whom Cobbett could lay his hands, not excluding Louis XVI or Marie Antoinette, who were in a prominent position; but the center was reserved for His Majesty King George of England. In the opposite casement you could see all the most notorious criminals, bloody Marat, brutal Lepelletier, Ankarström, who killed the King of Sweden, and among them, in the two places of honor, Priestley and Benjamin Franklin. In a little corner Cobbett had made a place for Fauchet, who could not fail to adorn such a fine collection.

A third window presented to the astonished eyes of the

Philadelphians all the English Generals, Admirals, Bishops and Ministers you could imagine, with Grenville and Pitt lording it in the middle. Finally, the last window was devoted to instructive and educative scenes, such as the Taking of the Bastille, the Feast of the Supreme Being, and the Sacking of the Tuileries in August, with the corpses of the Swiss Guards whom harpies were despoiling and mutilating. The Philadelphians had something to gape at.

They gaped, and some of them shrugged their shoulders, others grumbled, a few applauded, but plenty of them were furiously angry. Cobbett received insulting letters, threatening letters, letters intended to intimidate him.

He was not easy to intimidate. When he saw that he had succeeded in making a scandal; when he was quite sure that the Philadelphians had not failed to remark the happy coupling of Franklin with Marat and Ankarström; when he could not doubt that they had appreciated the honor he did them in presenting to them publicly, for the first time since 1776, the venerable image of His Britannic Majesty, William Cobbett went ahead. The crowd could not ignore him now. The Democrats must know of him, and the Federalists, myopic as they were, could not help noticing him.

Cobbett founded a paper, *Porcupine's Gazette*, and he attacked.

He attacked Benny Bache. He took him by the throat. He hated him hard; he hated him intimately. Cobbett knew how to insult Bache and how to hurt him. He rallied Bache on his big, "sleepy", girl's eyes, his emphatic Republicanism, and his manners of an aristocrat turned market gardener. He called him "good Master *Surgo ut prosim*", for this was the motto of Bache's paper, or "Young Lightning-Rod", for Franklin was "Old Lightning-Rod".

[283]

Cobbett told Bache that he was a scoundrel, a hireling of France, an atheist educated in immorality by a grandfather who was a master of the art, a wretch who had incited the rabble of Philadelphia to burn Cobbett's shop and cut his throat, a traitor who could neither respect Washington nor serve his country.

Then Cobbett added jocosely: "I wish to avoid all personality whatever. Our readers, and especially those of this city, know already everything that is worth knowing about you and me. Nothing that we can say will alter their opinions of us; and, for altering our opinions of one another, that is a thing not to be thought of. I am getting up in the world, and you are going down; for this reason it is that you hate me, and that I despise you; and that you will preserve your hatred and I my contempt, till fortune gives her wheel another turn, or till death snatches one or the other of us from the scene.

"It is therefore useless, my dear Bache, to say any more about the matter. Why should we keep buffeting and spurring at each other? Why should we rend and tear our poor reputations to pieces, merely for the diversion of the spectators? A great number of persons, rather lovers of fun than of decency, have already pitted us, and are prepared to enjoy the combat. Let us disappoint them; let us walk about arm in arm: many a couple, even of different sex, do this, and at the same time like one another no better than we do.

"Your pride may, indeed, reject the society of a British corporal, as you very justly style me; but, my dear Sir, whatever we have been, we are both now of the same honest calling. Nobody looks upon you as the grandson of an ambassador and a philosopher. People call you (they do indeed) Ben Bache the newsman; nothing more, I assure

[284]

you. And, as they have no regard to your illustrious descent, so you may be sure they will not long remember the meanness of mine. . . ."

But, despite this cordial leave-taking, Cobbett could not tire himself of talking to Bache, and some weeks later, he made a burlesque will and left Bache a legacy. "Item," said Cobbett, "to Franklin Bache, editor of the *Aurora* of Philadelphia, I will and bequeath a small bundle of French assignants, which I brought with me from the land of equality. If these should be too light in value for his pressing exigencies, I desire my executors, or any of them, to bestow upon him a second part of what he has lately received in Southwark (a beating); and, as a further proof of my good will and affection, I request him to accept of a gag and a brand new pair of fetters; which if he should refuse, I will and bequeath him in lieu thereof — my malediction."

Cobbett had clearly seen that the Democratic Party drew its breath from Benny Bache, and that it lived on the memory of Franklin and could not do without the glory and the stimulus of France. He waged war daily on Franklin and on France. With his sergeant-major's soul and his pamphleteer's genius, Cobbett did what the Federalist Party had never been able to do. In his sonorous, hard English, he lashed the crowd and made them listen to him. He talked their own language so well that the very insults which he hurled at them were a kind of pleasure and rasped the throat like a gulp of very dry gin.

To the Irish he recalled that they were poorer than the pigs in their native land. The French he advised to go home and see whether they still had their heads on. The Americans themselves he told that they were the sons of convicts, graciously sent to these new shores at the expense

[285]

of His Majesty, thanks to their good fellow countrymen sitting on juries.

To everybody at large he declared: "I am out of all patience with the *Swinish Multitude* of this place. Those fine-sounding words *Liberty* and *Equality* have hurt this place more than the British army and the yellow fever.

"I cannot get along the streets for crowds of ragamuffins, tatterdemalions, and shabby *freemen*, strolling about idle, who, if they had masters, might be employed in something useful both to society and themselves. Go to the Statehouse or Congress Hall; the galleries are filled with a respectable group of idle oyster-men and lounging apprentices, superintending the proceedings of Government. Go to the Courthouse; it is crowded with vagrants who have nothing to do but study law. You cannot squeeze into an auction room for idle vagabonds, who are glad of something to stare at. Every rascal in the city who can steal half a dollar you will see in the chief seat at the theater. A funeral, a house on fire, a ship-launch, a speech, a birthday, or a quarrel in the streets, collects them in thousands.

"Perhaps the poor devils are starving with hunger and cold. Would it not be a kindness to themselves to take their liberty from them? And a material advantage to the public to whip them to their work? . . . O for monarchy, despotism, slavery, or any species of government, that will conduce to the happiness of mankind! . . . If I can rid the streets of these dirty swine, I shall be the best scavenger in the city. John Farmer tells his hogs that the Devil took possession of the swine long ago, and has not left them yet. The devil of lounging possesses the swine of Philadelphia. I wish the Gadarean devil would enter them, and conduct them into the Delaware."

The crowd of Philadelphia took a lot of killing, and

[286]

even Cobbett's insults did not decide them to give up living, to lie down and die. It took more than that to intimidate them or tame them. But, surprised and amused by his violent diatribes, they gave ear to this language of his, which was not what they were accustomed to hear among the Federalists; and Cobbett took advantage of the fact. He circulated among the crowd insults, calumnies and defamations against Franklin.

Cobbett understood the spirit of crowds; and he realized that the Jeffersons, the Madisons, and the Monroes might be parliamentary leaders, but that only the legend of Franklin was a popular legend and the soul of the Democratic Party, just as the legend of Washington was the soul of the Federalist Party. He set himself to dirty, to ruin, to efface, to annihilate the memory of Benjamin Franklin.

Can you not see, he said, that Franklin was an atheist, a scoundrel, and a libertine? He was an atheist — everybody knows that; there is no need to prove it. He was a scoundrel. Did he not, with the connivance of Deane and the French, speculate on the traffic in arms and munitions during the War of Independence? Still, if he had been a generous scoundrel, if he had put this money stolen from the State to good use, one could forgive him more easily. But he was an avaricious scoundrel, who at the moment of his death was pleased to leave to the hospital of Philadelphia old debts, at usurer's rates, which it was impossible to recover. He was a libertine. One knows very well how he spent his money. " 'Increase and multiply' is an injunction that this great man had continually in his mind; and such was his zeal in the fulfilment of it, that he paid very little attention to time or place or person."

Any occasion was good enough for Cobbett to bring a denunciation against Franklin, to crack a joke against

Franklin. But Cobbett preferred those occasions when he could prove to the crowd that, after all, Franklin was not one of themselves. Once he succeeded in this to perfection. Cobbett described the home of his own grandfather, Cobbett the Surrey farmer. Then suddenly he interrupted himself, and wrote, with great humility:

"Every one will, I hope, have the goodness to believe that my grandfather was no philosopher. Indeed he was not. He never made a lightning-rod nor bottled up a single quart of sun-shine in the whole course of his life. He was no almanach-maker, nor quack, nor chimney-doctor, nor soap-boiler, nor ambassador; nor printer's devil; neither was he a deist, and all his children were born in wedlock. The legacies he left were his scythe, his reaphook, and his flail; he bequeathed no old and irrecoverable debts to an hospital; he never *cheated the poor during his life* nor *mocked them in his death.* He has, it is true, been suffered to sleep quietly beneath the green sward; but, if his descendants cannot point to his statue over the door of a library, they have not the mortification to hear him accused daily of having been a whoremaster, an hypocrite and an infidel."

Tirades like these made Benny mad. Jefferson could not read them without a sense of shame. Public opinion frowned on them and the Federalists were careful not to praise them. They contented themselves with subsidizing them, spreading them and giving them the assent of their silence. They were delighted to see Bache's campaign to present Washington as a false Republican answered by Cobbett's campaign to present Franklin as a false and foul Democrat.

It was easier for the Federalists to encourage Cobbett's campaign against France openly. Despite her popularity, France still had old enemies in America, Puritans and Anglo-Saxons conscious of their stock; and she had ac-

quired new ones just because of her popularity. They were
tired of hearing her praises sung and disturbed by hearing
her doctrines preached up hill and down dale.

So they were glad to find first in Cobbett's review, and
then in his newspaper, a regular feature, "French Bar-
barity", with very precise descriptions of the Lyons massacres, the Paris massacres, the Vendée massacres, the Nantes
drownings, and the other divers horrors with which the
French Revolution adorned its philanthropic career. They
found pleasure in reading in Cobbett's pages the story of
France's overt invasions in Italy and across the Rhine, and
her covert invasions in Geneva and Holland, under the
heading "French Fraternity."

How could you help laughing when, in his paper, you
came upon a piece of news like this: "The scarcity of eggs
in Paris is so great that the Directory have actually passed
a decree, ordering that all the *hens* and *pullets* in France,
who do not each lay two eggs per day, shall be transported
to *Cayenne* as *incivic poultry* in the pay of Pitt and Co;"
and you found this comment upon it: "This seems incredible
at first sight, but it is not so bad as *offering premiums* to the
women who should bring forth *Twins*"? So against France
Cobbett contrived to invoke both ridicule and the prejudices
of Anglo-Saxon modesty.

He had no lack of sticks with which to beat her. Genet
had given him one by making public his instructions, which
denounced Vergennes as a corrupt diplomat and Louis XVI
as a blind despot guided only by hatred of England. Cobbett had only to carry on the anti-French propaganda begun
by the French revolutionary diplomats; and, since they
were hateful in the eyes of a good part of the American
population, it sufficed to prove that the rest of the French
were like them, or worse than them, and the game was won.

Cobbett knew the crowd-mind and its temperament very well. He knew that it is never responsible, but always emotional or frolicsome, peevish or ready to be humbugged. Never did he present the crowd with a serious picture of France. He turned her into a scene of tragedy or a burlesque. He published reports of the Terror and cracked jokes about the civic festivals.

One summer, when the flood of civic festivals had burst over Philadelphia with even more exuberance than usual, and Bache had filled his paper with them, Cobbett presented a parody of them. That summer, at the same time as the civic festivals, Philadelphia had been regaled with the presence of a pig of great erudition, which had the greatest success, and about which Bache's *Aurora* wrote in these flattering terms:

THE LEARNED PIG

The docility, tractability, and sagacity of many animals, such as the Dog, Horse and Elephant, has been as much the theme of conversation as the stupidity and stubbornness of the Pig has been proverbial.

This little animal forms an exception to the general rule; for he not only equals any, but excels all the above in their most eminent qualities.

He will read, write, spell, tell the Hour of the Day, distinguish colors, the number of persons present, etc., etc. And what is more astonishing, any Lady or Gentleman may draw a card and Keep it concealed, and the Pig without any hesitation will discover the card drawn from another pack.

You could see him for a quarter at Mr. Cook's, corner of Market Street and Third Street, between Cobbett's shop and Bache printing house.

When the pig departed, Cobbett perpetrated this parody:

[290]

LEARNED PIG'S DEPARTURE

Yesterday, being Sunday, the *Learned Pig* took his departure for Trenton. He was conduced as far as Harrowgate by a select party of Sans-culottes, where, we are informed, they were regaled with a trough, filled with the choicest washings of the kitchen.

The greatest hilarity prevailed during the entertainment, and a number of patriotic toasts were drunk, among which the following are worthy of particular notice: 1. The French Republic, one and indivisible. 2. Thomas Jefferson, the historian of the Bull, and the *man of the Swine*. . . . 6. Ben Bache and bribery. 7. Thomas Mifflin, J. A. Dallas, and Randolph, and success to all others *who deal in meal*. . . . 9. Blair McClenachan, the first of hogs. . . . 11. May the enemies of the swine never save their bacon!

(The Pig having retired.)

12. The Learned Pig — may each of us, his fellow-citizens, soon equal him in knowledge, as we already do in beastliness!

The company broke up about six in the evening, and we have the pleasure to add, that they retired to their homes in the utmost good order, not a chop or the mark of a tusk being this morning visible on any of their jow̓ls.

So the battle went on, from door to door, from day to day, from gazette to gazette. The Democrats were far from leaving Cobbett without reply. In the year 1796 alone a dozen pamphlets and a print against him appeared in Philadelphia: "The Blue Shop, or impartial and humorous observations on the life of Peter Porcupine", by James Quicksilver; "A Pill for Porcupine; The Impostor Detected", by J. Tickletoby; "A Roaster for P. Porcupine", by Sim Sanculotte; "The History of Peter Porcupine"; "A Picture of Peter Porcupine"; "A Plumb Pudding for the humane, chaste, valiant, enlightened Peter Porcupine", by M. Carey. In the print Cobbett appeared accompanied by the Devil, John Jay, and the English lion, while Liberty

wept on a bust of Franklin, and the American eagle folded
his wings.

In the *Aurora* Bache accused Cobbett, or let him be accused. Cobbett was a deserter, he had been flogged before
the troops, he did not pay his taxes, he was an English spy,
he was a hireling of Hammond, Bond, Jay, Hamilton. He
had sold himself to the Devil.

The better to get the better of him, an obscene and
blasphemous pamphlet was published in Cobbett's name.
There were threats of burning his shop, breaking his windows, giving him a hiding. But nothing happened; and, in
the storm of insults that were thus exchanged, Cobbett's
voice made itself heard the loudest, because he was the
commoner clay and knew all the rudest English words.
Soon his review, his bookshop and his paper became the
biggest in Philadelphia.

Only the *Aurora* still stood up to him, for Bache alone,
like Cobbett, had the soul of a crusader. Throughout all the
year 1796 they found themselves face to face, and face
to face they fought.

They fought about Monsieur Adet. To begin the year in
a way that would embarrass Washington and impress the
public, Monsieur Adet offered Congress a French flag.
Monroe, the American Minister in France, had offered an
American flag to the Convention, and it had been solemnly
hung in the hall of the Convention. Washington could
not refuse to receive a French flag and allow it to be offered
to Congress; but neither could he find this pleasant, nor
could he enjoy the pompous, fraternal speeches which had
to be exchanged on such an occasion. He was chilly, and
the Senate was chilly; but the House of Representatives
was warm. Adet took advantage of this. He presented a
magnificent flag and sent a triumphal message.

Bache was tireless in describing this flag: "It is tricolor, made of the richest silk and highly ornamented with allegorical paintings. In the middle, a cock is represented, the emblem of France, standing on a thunderbolt. At two corners diagonally opposite are represented two bomb-shells bursting, at the other two corners, other military emblems. Round the whole is a rich border of oak leaves, alternately yellow and green, the first shaded with brown and heightened with gold; the latter shaded with black and relieved with silver; in this border are en-twined war-like musical instruments. The edge is ornamented with a rich gold fringe. The staff is covered with black velvet crowned with a golden pike and enriched with the tricolor *cravatte* and a pair of tassels worked in gold and the three national colours." At the sight of it the Democrats massed in the galleries trembled with joy and enthusiasm. What a triumph for the Republic!

But Master Porcupine wrote: "I saw a Democrat, who was so fully persuaded that the flag was the harbinger of fate, that he began to anticipate the torments of the world to come. Never did I before behold such dreadful symptoms of a guilty conscience. He was as white as paper, his knees knocked together, his teeth chattered. He wrung his hands and rolled his eyes. . . . His voice was like the yell of the inhabitants of the infernal regions: 'Oh, Franklin Bache, Franklin Bache!' "

Thus Porcupine tried to turn the purest enthusiasm into derision. He was but half-successful. Washington succeeded better. He decided that, the better to honor and preserve the flag, instead of leaving it in the Congress Hall it should be put in the Archives of the United States. There were as yet no Archives of the United States; but it was easy to hire an out-of-the-way loft, where the flag could rest in

peace and solitude, sheltered from all eyes but the spiders'.
Monsieur Adet judged that General Washington was
making a fool of him. He was right. He complained. He
was wrong. The laugh was not on his side.

He tried to get the House of Representatives on his
side. In February, 1796, Washington had promulgated
Jay's treaty and ordered the country to observe it as the
law of the nation. It remained for him to apply it; but for
this he needed a vote of the House of Representatives
authorizing the necessary expenditure. Now the Democrats
were in a majority in the House, and Monsieur Adet
counted upon its refusing to vote the sums demanded by
Washington.

Adet had taken his soundings and his precautions. His
friends assured him that fifty-seven members of the House
out of ninety had made up their minds to vote against the
treaty. Lest he should compromise them, Adet avoided
seeing them; but he had an agent who kept in close touch
with them, M. d'Hauterive, the friend of Talleyrand. And
Benny Bache kept them up to the mark by the articles which
he published day by day against Jay, against Jay's treaty,
and against Washington, Jay's patron.

The Federalists took alarm. Hamilton knew that a negative vote in the House of Representatives would come near
killing the treaty, which the public had never accepted. He
set to work forthwith. He passed the word to the merchants of New York that they should draw up a great
petition in favor of the treaty and get it signed. He stimulated the merchants of Philadelphia to do the same. He
wrote letters to the papers; and he encouraged Cobbett.

It was the time when Cobbett was opening his shop.
Wolcott, the Secretary of the Treasury, offered him assistance. But Cobbett was too fond of liberty to agree to

fight under the orders of any leader, even if he was fighting on the same side; and Wolcott had to content himself with Cobbett's benevolent collaboration. It was, for that matter, efficacious, for never did Cobbett show himself more active or more droll.

Bache denounced Cobbett and Jay, and Cobbett denounced Bache and Adet. The House of Representatives protested against Washington and Washington protested against the House of Representatives. The crowd shouted and the merchants petitioned. Adet wrote to his Government that he was nursing his majority as a mother watches over her children, and that indeed he must, for the merchants had subscribed a fat sum.

Perhaps the merchants' sum was too fat for him, or Adet was not vigilant enough. After seven weeks of struggle, on April 30th, the House of Representatives, by fifty-one votes to forty-eight, approved the credits for the application of "Mr. Jay's infamous treaty".

The battle over Jay's treaty was at an end. America had accepted the friendship of England and her naval collaboration. French diplomacy was beaten.

But the Federalist Party was hard hit. In this long struggle Washington had lost much of his prestige; for the treaty remained unpopular. Jay's national career was finished and so was that of Hamilton. The part which they had taken in the framing and defense of the treaty had compromised them for ever. The party had compromised itself too by this understanding with England, which earned it the devotion of the merchants, Democrats though they might be, but the hostility of the patriots, though they be Federalists.

The party's organization was getting stronger and

[295]

stronger, its papers were better and better edited, its funds were growing larger and larger; but its General Staff fell to pieces, and its forces scattered. There was no hiding the fact: General Washington was worn out. He looked tired and he said he was tired. He did not want to be President any longer or let himself be elected for a third term.

If Washington retired, John Adams was going to impose himself upon his party; for he was Vice President, an outstanding patriot, and the candidate of New England, without whose support no Federalist could be elected.

But John Adams was scarcely to the liking of the more orthodox Federalists. Their party was the party of the rich and commercial class. It appealed to the practical spirit and the utilitarian sense of the country. John Adams knew little about practical life and nothing at all about commerce. He had the mind of a lawyer though he sometimes devoted himself to philosophy and sometimes even to fancy. He was an individualist; and he would have to lead the party of order and conformity.

The Federalists of the South did not like it at all. Those of New York had their doubts about it, and it made those of New England think twice. They toyed with the idea of going on with his candidacy, while getting him beaten. A few votes shrewdly spoiled would perhaps enable them to get rid of him and replace him by Mr. Pinckney, the Federalist candidate for the Vice Presidency.

But the election threatened to be indecisive. You could not permit yourself such a piece of treachery, however alluring it might be and however much you might want to indulge in it. You had to accept John Adams in order to beat Jefferson.

Thomas Jefferson was now beginning to interest himself in politics once more. For the past two years and more,

Stop de Wheels of Government

a Political Sinner.

CARICATURE OF ALBERT GALLATIN, MADE IN 1796
AND PRINTED BY WILLIAM COBBETT, AT THE TIME
OF THE DISCUSSION ABOUT THE JAY TREATY

while he had been cultivating his land, fixing his house, meditating about life and bringing up his family, Thomas Jefferson had grown in wisdom and address. From the depths of his retirement, he had achieved a masterpiece, and he had done it so well that only his cleverest enemies could have any suspicion of it. Thomas Jefferson had succeeded in cementing the opposition party which was in course of formation, and without which it was impossible for him to reach power; and he had also succeeded in remaining outside this party, which might make the tasks of government so difficult for him.

The party was formed out of the remains of the old anti-Federalist group; but Jefferson, though he had never liked the Constitution much, had never taken up a position against it, since he was in France at the critical moment and on his return he had accepted it as an accomplished fact. The anti-Federalists were on his side and would vote for him, but he was not one of them or one with them.

The party had gained consistency, thanks to the immigrants who were organized by the Democratic societies, so well led by Dallas and Bache. Everybody knew quite well that Jefferson had reproved General Washington when he condemned the Democratic societies. But never had Mr. Jefferson been a member of any one of them, and never had he had anything to do with them, except receive their homage. He was an Anglo-Saxon Parliamentarian, not a "Tammany." They would vote for him and take his side; but he would be in no way bound to take theirs.

The newspapers had given the party its line of action and its influence, and nobody had contributed more than Mr. Jefferson to shed luster on the Democratic papers, in particular the *Aurora*, to which he subscribed, which he read carefully, and for which, at his request, his friends wrote many an article. But never had he written for any paper himself — not even the *Aurora*.

Never had Jefferson put his finger in the pie, so he told other people and perhaps himself, though he had begged Madison, Monroe and his other friends a dozen times to reply in the papers to Hamilton's "heresies", and though he had himself condescended to correct the manuscripts of articles that Madison sent Bache. All the Democratic papers would be for him and would get people to vote for him; but Jefferson had nothing to do with this and was in no way responsible for it.

The party had engaged in a crusade for France, which served it as a rallying cry, and Mr. Jefferson had encouraged it by his conversation and his letters. But as Secretary of State he had always held the balance fairly between France and England, and when the critical hour came he had advised neutrality. When the crisis arose over Genet, he had been one of the first to condemn Genet, whom Bache kept on defending. All the friends of France were for him and would vote for him with enthusiasm; but Thomas Jefferson remained before all a diplomat, and though he might be close to the friends of France, he was not with them.

The great deed of daring of the party had been to attack Washington, and the party, in short, had got away with it. Bache had tired Washington out. Jefferson had not protested. He had confided to his intimates all the anxiety he felt about the ambiguous conduct of Washington under the influence of the monocrats. Everybody knew that he did not blame Bache for his campaign; thus all Washington's enemies would vote for Jefferson.

But Jefferson was a compatriot of the General's, an old friend of his, a former collaborator of his. He wrote

Washington fine letters about the growing of clover. Never would he be counted with the enemies of General Washington.

A General Staff of the party had come into being. Beckley of Virginia, the Clerk of the House of Representatives; Bache the newsman; Dallas the Secretary of the State of Pennsylvania; Gallatin the Congressman of the West; and Madison the Virginian were its section leaders. Jefferson kept in close relations with Madison, with Beckley, and with Bache, and nothing was decided in the party without his knowing about it and authorizing it with a word, a nod, or a silence. But never had he signed an order. Never had he taken any responsibility. Never had he intervened in person.

He was the oracle of the party, — not its leader. He guided the party but he did not belong to the party.

So it was that, in 1796, Thomas Jefferson became the candidate of the Democratic Party without being a candidate, and without being a member of the party.

He did not say that he would be a candidate and he never suggested that he belonged to the party. But Beckley, who did all the preliminary work, together with Bache, did not conceal from him that it would take him as its candidate, and Mr. Jefferson did not protest. In Bache's *Aurora* he read all the eulogies of Mr. Jefferson, that consistent opponent of Colonel Hamilton and General Washington, and he did not protest. He was resigned to letting Heaven and Bache and Beckley make him President of the United States, if such was his destiny.

General Washington was determined to stand in his way if Heaven permitted him. He had not lost his old affection for Jefferson — such relations as theirs can never be forgotten — but he knew what Jefferson thought about him,

[299]

and what he was doing against him, and General Washington did not want to see him become President.

Washington was himself too good a politician not to understand Jefferson's manœuver. In order to rally all liberal and patriotic minds to himself, Jefferson had kept himself aloof throughout the whole period of crisis. He was reserving himself to appear at the appropriate moment and then attract all votes towards him.

General Washington and the Federalists decided that they would not provide him with the appropriate moment. Jefferson could become a candidate, and his friends could campaign for him, only after Washington's definite refusal to run. So Washington waited before declaring himself.

June passed and then July. The torrid summer weighed on the United States and numbed everybody's mind. Washington took advantage of this to recall Monroe from France. Monroe had remained too Francophile to be of any use there. France took advantage of it to take severe measures of reprisal against the commerce of the United States. The papers bawled about this but it was too hot for anybody to get excited.

In New York Mr. Hamilton and Mr. Jay drafted, touched up, revised and perfected Washington's great farewell address to his country, which in its majesty, in its patriotism, is a kind of breviary of Federalism. The days passed slowly and at last everything was ready.

About mid-September, Washington's farewell message was sent to all the Governors of the United States, with the request that they should all issue it on the same day. On September 19, 1796, all the newspapers in America published Washington's farewell to his people. It was a noble text, moving and lucid. In it Washington denounced all the

[300]

dangers that threatened the country. He put his country on its guard against corruption within and contagion from without. He named no names, Adams no more than Jefferson; but you could clearly read between the lines that his farewell fell like a malediction upon Mr. Jefferson, the philosopher, friend of France and of the Democrats.

The newspapers took up this refrain. They assailed Jefferson. They denounced him as "a deist by profession", as a revolutionary who was a slave owner, as "a poor beggarly puff", as a bad servant of America.

So spoke Cobbett, while Bache demonstrated alike Jefferson's virtue, and his uprightness, and his services, long, loyal and tireless, to the United States. Cobbett spoke of the ruin of the United States if Jefferson triumphed, while Bache spoke of the shipwreck of the Republic if Jefferson were beaten, and if Adams were elected — Adams the aristocrat, Adams the monocrat, Adams the friend of England and the champion of rank, titles, and hereditary distinctions, Adams the grotesque, "His Serene Highness of Braintree", "His Rotundity", "Bonny Johnny Adams."

The Federalists had organized their campaign well. They held the North and they counted on keeping it. To this end they had put Pinckney out of their heads and remained attached to Adams. They hoped, thanks to Washington's farewell address and the late start of the electoral campaign, to hold Pennsylvania, pivotal State. In point of fact, their supporters were in Philadelphia and in the townships in the center of the State. On the other hand, the strength of the Democrats lay in the suburbs of Philadelphia and in distant districts, on the other side of the mountains and along the frontier, where news took a long time to arrive and the gazettes circulated rarely and belatedly.

[301]

The Federalists reckoned that the Democrats, warned too late, would be unable to put their electoral agents in motion and would thus lose the game.

They were reckoning without Beckley, Bache and Dallas. The Democratic leaders had foreseen Washington's manœuver. It was natural and to be expected. As soon as they knew that Washington's address was ready, and they could at last see the field clear for Jefferson's candidacy, they dispatched couriers. They warned the South, they warned the North.

They bent their efforts on winning Pennsylvania, which, together with Maryland, would decide the election. The North would give them but few votes: that the Democrats knew very well. The South was theirs and they reckoned that there would be no defection in it. But they needed Pennsylvania to win — and win they must.

To them a new Federalist Presidency meant a war with France, an alliance with England, and the definite, inevitable, fatal placing of Federalist officials in charge of every cogwheel of the Administration. They must avoid that at all costs. As Beckley put it, "it is now or never for the Republican cause."

Their campaign was ready, and they launched it on the spot. Bache had printed handbills. Beckley had had written by hand — for such was the rule in Pennsylvania — thousands of voting cards.[1] Two devoted Democrats promptly jumped on horseback and galloped towards the West. Avoiding townships and villages, drawing rein only at the houses of sure partisans and keeping their eyes open everywhere, they were to ride straight for the frontier, away beyond the mountains, and, once they reached the confines

[1] These served as crude ballots and contained the party's whole ticket.

of the virgin forest and the desert, then, and only then, were they to start distributing handbills and voting tickets.

Then slowly, by easy stages, they were to approach the main centers of population, scattering proclamations and addresses on their way. They must take care not to reach the towns until the day before the voting; for the Democrats wanted to avoid giving the Federalists time to answer their arguments. They could not run the risk of Hamilton launching a pamphlet or Cobbett making some thundering refutation. They had to strike men's minds just before the election and carry off their votes.

The better to do this, the Democrats had the support of Citizen Adet. As soon as they learned of the House of Representative's vote on the enforcement of Jay's treaty, the Directors had written to Adet that his official mission was ended, but that he should stay a few months longer in the United States as an observer. France would send no more Ministers Plenipotentiary to the United States until further notice — until the time came when the United States honestly fulfilled their treaty obligations towards France and made proper apologies.

Adet received this instruction at the beginning of autumn. He waited a little. He made arrangements with Mifflin, the Governor of Pennsylvania, who fixed the date of the election, and with Bache, who was to print his manifesto. Then, four days before the election, Adet sent Washington a formal letter, which he had had printed by Bache and which he at once circulated throughout Pennsylvania.

In it he presented France as magnanimous, but offended; indignant with the Government of the United States, but generous towards their people; determined to obtain justice, and ready for war if America remained in the hands of the Federalists, but resolved, on the contrary, to act fraternally if Jefferson were elected. Adet had observed the excellent use to which the English had put the fear of war in the United States, and he tried to turn it to the profit of France, and of Jefferson.

This was the last manœuver of the electoral campaign. The Federalists were indignant. The Democrats were delighted. The people were astounded. Washington was annoyed. The country as a whole scarcely took Adet's manifesto into account, for it came too late. But Philadelphia took account of it and it gave Jefferson the votes he needed.

He had a majority in the city of Philadelphia, and, as he also had a majority in the mountains, he carried the greater part of the electoral college of Pennsylvania. Beckley's campaign, Bache's efforts, and Adet's ruses had taken effect.

The Democrats imagined that Jefferson was about to be elected President of the United States.

They were reckoning without the merchants, whose solid organization saved all the coast States of the North and the Center for the Federalists. Finally, after many fluctuations — for all the States did not vote at the same time — it was found that Mr. Adams had seventy-one votes, Mr. Jefferson sixty-eight, and Mr. Pinckney fifty-four.

Adams was President, Jefferson was Vice President, and Pinckney was nowhere. The Federalists were not overjoyed; they had hoped to do better. The Democrats were much disappointed; they had counted on victory. Mr. Adams was satisfied, for he had his due, and Mr. Jefferson was delighted.

He knew that, between France and England, between the Federalists and the Democrats, between the memory of Franklin and the legend of Washington, the Government would find itself drawn and quartered. He knew that nobody could enforce both the treaties of 1778 and Jay's

[304]

treaty unless he was an angel of ingenuity, of good luck, and of good will.

He knew that a political leader was bound to be criticized whatever he did, and bound to be condemned if he did nothing during this critical period — unless it was his duty to do nothing, as was the rôle and the duty of the Vice President of the United States.

So, Mr. Jefferson hastened to send a letter of quite sincere congratulation to Mr. Adams and to beg Mr. Bache to extol Mr. Adams as soon as might be. And Mr. Bache conformed to Mr. Jefferson's desires; for, despite the defeat of his party, Mr. Bache was a happy man in 1796.

He had just had a third son. His paper was the first paper in the United States. His wife was more loving, charming and devoted than ever; and, if his party had not triumphed, it had not been crushed. Mr. Jefferson had been elected Vice President.

And that the Democrats owed to the *Aurora*, to Benjamin Franklin Bache.

CHAPTER VI

"BONNY JOHNNY ADAMS"

BENNY BACHE had fought all autumn long and he was tired of bitterness.

The winter brought back frost, good humor and health. No more yellow fever in Philadelphia, but concerts, lectures and *automates*. Mr. Pinchbeck exhibited one that could count and two that could dance. Mr. Fennel, in order to enlighten patriots, gave a course in literature. Mr. Grattan gave concerts at which you could listen to Händel; in the Medicine lecture-room there were lessons in anatomy for serious-minded people; at the theater they played "Romeo and Juliet"; Rickett had redecorated his circus; and Mr. Peale had decided to keep open his Museum every day until ten o'clock at night. At Oeller's Mr. Sicard invited you to dance, and the Irish banqueted at MacShean's Tavern.

But more diverting still was the elephant which you could see in Market Street, between Third Street and Fourth Street, for a quarter. He was an enormous elephant, such as Philadelphia had never set eyes on, and he was also a philanthropic elephant, who devoted part of his takings to the sufferers in Savannah. He set men a good example, and urged them to a little kindliness after all this hatred.

It seemed that he had succeeded, and that, in honor of Mr. Adams, suddenly the sky cleared. During the

[306]

autumn Mr. Adams had had plenty of enemies, for all his enemies had been his enemies and a good number of his friends also, though they had not dared to show it too openly. But, now that Mr. Adams was going to be President, everybody discovered his fine qualities and he had plenty of friends. Henceforth all his friends were his friends and gloried in his election; and many of his enemies had become his friends and rejoiced over his election.

"Just look at Mr. Adams," they said. "Such a fine fat fellow, and so simple! Of course, he likes the sound of his own voice and laying down the law. Of course, he likes to ride in a fine carriage; but anybody can see that it is not his own carriage. Of course, he likes to wear a sword; but anybody can see that it does not fit him, and he's always falling over it. Mr. Adams may want to be taken for an aristocrat, but he's got a big belly and a little, bald head, and he can't help being a good fellow, for all his petulance.

"He talks, he gesticulates, he gets indignant, he wheedles, he grumbles; but, whatever he does, he never puts between himself and his interlocutor that barrier of silence and distance which separates General Washington from the very people that love and adore him, and from those he seems to love himself. General Washington is very tall and Mr. Adams is short. General Washington is a soldier; Mr. Adams was never any such thing. Everything that surrounded General Washington was disciplined by him, and Mrs. Washington too. Mr. Adams has never been able to discipline either his tongue or his tastes or his actions, or Mrs. Adams either — and she's a sensible woman with a mind of her own, for that matter.

"On horseback General Washington looks like a general, and Mr. Adams like a good farmer coming home from the fair. Mr. Washington cavalcaded through the streets with his epauletted aides. Mr. Adams goes rummaging and gossiping from bookshop to bookshop, and anybody can see him in learned, voluble conversation with Monsieur Moreau de Saint Méry, the bookseller on Second Street. He is very proud of his high rank, and he is very proud of himself when he stops to think about it; but he is always thinking about so many different things, and he passes so quickly from one subject to another, that he is never proud for long at a time.

"Nobody can ever persuade or dissuade Mr. Adams, for he has too brilliant a mind and too strong a will to let himself be influenced; but he lets himself be flattered so easily that there is no need to dissuade him or persuade him — he goes where you want of his own accord. Seldom does he listen to what you are saying, but he usually understands you; and, if he refutes you violently, that is just the moment when he is closest to your points of view, for Mr. Adams is one of those men who always react against everybody around them and mostly against themselves.

"His virtue, which is great, and his honesty, which is immense, and his restlessness, which is infinite, always urge him to react, and he always does it straightforwardly, for everything about Mr. Adams is plain and honest — even his bad temper, even his vanity, even his astuteness. And, if Mr. Adams may sometimes let himself be taken in, that comes, no doubt, rather from his uprightness, which is chivalrous, than from his obstinacy, which is gigantic, or from his vanity, which is a joke."

So said the good people of Philadelphia, who knew what they were talking about, and so thought Benny Bache, who knew the President well, and to whom the President had always been kind; for Mr. Adams remained faithful to his old connections, and he did not despise journalists. Though he had never — at least to his way of thinking — been spoiled by the gazettes, he was still fond of praise and eager for approval. He read the *Aurora* carefully. It sometimes made him wince, when he was himself in question, but he often agreed with it when somebody else was.

Mr. Bache knew this and Mr. Jefferson had borne it in mind. An old political friendship and a great intimacy of mind had united Mr. Jefferson and Mr. Adams, ever since they had sat side by side in the second Congress of the United States and had drawn up the Declaration of Independence together. Then they had lost sight of one another for some time and their diverging philosophic opinions had alienated them.

But now they found themselves side by side once more. To their old friendship, to their old esteem, were added the esteem in which Mr. Adams held the office that he had just relinquished and that Mr. Jefferson now filled, and the esteem which Mr. Jefferson professed for the high post that Mr. Adams now occupied and that he counted upon occupying himself some day. Was not Mr. Jefferson, as Mr. Adams put it to him, "the heir apparent of the President of the United States", and the first in the land after Mr. Adams?

The past was wiped out, and a new friendship was established between them. This suited Mr. Adams, who loved his country well enough to want to raise it above party quarrels, and who loved himself enough to want to remain above parties. It also suited Mr. Jefferson, who, having emerged from the exile in which his disgust and his hostility towards the Federalist Party had kept him, now felt himself close to power and desired to free himself gently from the Democratic Party.

[309]

Of this party Jefferson had had need to approach power. But, if he was soon to reach power, he needed to get rid of the party as much as possible; he proposed to be the President of the whole country, not a party man. So he wanted to disarm the Federalists, and, after reducing them to impotence, he contemplated weakening the Democrats and splitting up their organization.

To make an end of the Federalists, it sufficed for him to assure himself that Washington, their most dangerous and powerful prop, would never reappear on the political stage, and that John Adams should free himself from them. Deprived of the protection of the great man, and of the advantages which the favor of the President meant to them, the Federalists would return to limbo. So Thomas Jefferson set himself to wheedle John Adams and create a favorable atmosphere for the great reconciliation.

Benny Bache served as pivot for this delicate operation. He was Mr. Jefferson's friend and Mr. Adams was well disposed towards him. Of all American journalists, he was the most prominent: the only one who had stood in the breach for eight years, the only one who had always defended the same doctrine without flinching, the only one whose traditions linked him with the earliest efforts of the American liberal party. His paper set the note for all the Democratic Press, and all the Democrats found their inspiration in his campaigns and his watchwords.

Through Bache alone could one give John Adams what he would love above all else: the impression that he had disarmed his enemies and risen like a giant above the clouds of jealousy and the storms of political rivalry. As early as November, even before the end of the electoral campaign, Benny Bache had paved the way for the operation. He had

SILHOUETTE OF DEBORAH BACHE
MADE BETWEEN 1800 AND 1805

In the collection of M. L. Vail

SILHOUETTE OF FRANKLIN BACHE
THE ELDEST SON OF BENJAMIN FRANKLIN BACHE

*This was made between 1800 and 1810 and is
in the collection of Franklin Bache*

published here and there in his paper, from time to time,
notes which said that John Adams, aristocrat though he
might be, was a good fellow and a patriot.

Then, as the weeks passed and the election was no
longer in doubt, Bache had presented a contrast between
George Washington and John Adams: between the Virginian General, booted and spurred, opulent and owner
of slaves by the hundred, and the Bostonian lawyer, plain
and simple soul; between the *Grand Seigneur* who wanted
to be a Republican but could not help being an aristocrat,
and the bourgeois who tried in vain to be an aristocrat.

"The difference is immense," said Bache in his article,
"and no friend to Republicanism would hesitate one moment in giving the preference to John Adams."

John Adams was not the man to reject this compliment.
Benny Bache had touched him in a sensitive spot, for
John Adams had never been able to help thinking that
Europe had shown a childish enthusiasm for Mr. Franklin,
at the expense of the other heroes of America, and that
America lavished a popularity out of all proportion to his
merits upon General Washington, who was a good patriot,
but not the only one.

So Adams was less surprised than many people when,
in the *Aurora* of December 21 and 23, 1796, he read a denunciation of the General which compared him with
George III. The article reproached Washington with his
arrogance and the flattery with which he surrounded himself, and it wound up: "It has been a serious misfortune to
our country that the President of the United States has
been substituted for a Providence and that the gifts of
Heaven have been ascribed to his agency. . . . If ever a
nation was debauched by a man, the American nation has
been by Washington."

[311]

There was in this language of his, as Benny was well aware, something that would shock a good many people, including Mr. Adams. But Benny knew also that Mr. Adams would find a basis of truth in it, and would see in it a retribution here below — just as Mr. Jefferson would see in it the enunciation, perhaps a little brutal, of true fact, and an interesting initiative.

Between these three heroes and the young newsman an odd interplay developed. On his return from Monticello, Mr. Jefferson paid a visit to Mr. Adams, who returned it immediately, and Mr. Jefferson was also called upon by Bache, who came with Leib, his collaborator, to present his compliments and seek inspiration. In memory of the great Franklin, Mr. Jefferson could not help being well disposed towards Bache. In honor of the principles which united them, he was bound to be cordial towards him; and this interview was the first of a long series which, from January, 1797, to August, 1798, drew together the illustrious diplomat and the young editor.

Mr. Bache did not see Mr. Adams at this time; but he watched him with care; and, if Mr. Adams did not see Mr. Bache, he read him with care.

On the day of his inauguration as President of the United States, it struck the spectators that Mr. Adams was not inspired by the pure Federalist tradition, that he did not imitate Washington too closely, and that this ceremony, in which President Washington, President Adams and Vice President Jefferson appeared side by side, had a curious air about it.

The ceremony was performed in an atmosphere of middle-class dignity and administrative majesty. For the great day John Adams had procured himself a new carriage and lackeys in livery. He himself had donned a suit of fine

[312]

buckram, a two-horned hat with a huge black cockade, and at his side a sword, which he did not usually wear.

It was in this garb that he made his entrance into the Hall of the House of Representatives, where he was to take oath. Preceded by a few police and ushers of Congress, he advanced on to the dais overlooking the semicircle of seats, where were ranged the two Houses, the Senate to the right and the Representatives to the left. On either side of him were Mr. Washington, very calm, very serene, dressed all in black, and Mr. Jefferson, also dressed in black and clad in calm and serenity. Above them, dominating the gallery where men and women spectators crowded, a bust of Doctor Franklin, with the famous motto: *"Eripuit coelo fulmen, sceptrum que tyrannis"*, thus seeming to unite in a mystical presence the four great men who had led the American Revolution and whose accord had made the American nation.

Franklin had died at his task; at his task Washington had worn himself out, and he was quitting it now to give place to John Adams, who in his sonorous voice, vibrant with pride, zeal and emotion, took his oath of fidelity to the Republic and pronounced a little address, ritual, reasonable and republican, under the good-humored eyes of Mr. Jefferson, his heir apparent, his comrade, his friend.

Behind the dais the members of the Diplomatic Corps; in front of the dais the Justices of the Supreme Court; in the hall Senators and Congressmen, and in the gallery quidnuncs and fair dames could not help being all smiles and sighs at the sight of so virtuous a spectacle. When Mr. John Adams set about leaving, preceded by his little escort of police and ushers; when they saw Mr. Washington go through the motion of getting out of Mr. Jefferson's way, and Mr. Jefferson step back with a movement full of grace and consideration, the ladies in the gallery brushed away the starting tear or even burst into sobs, Senators and Representatives grew round-eyed with curiosity, and the diplomats smirked at one another to show their understanding.

Monsieur Adet, who was a fine figure of a man, carried his head high that day, for Mr. Adams had taken care to say that he entertained sentiments towards France whose warmth he could not express. But Mr. Liston, Minister of Great Britain, who was small and ruddy, did not look so well and did not seem in such good form, for Mr. Adams had proclaimed that never would he forget the heroic struggle for the liberty of America, in which he had taken part.

However, Mr. Liston was a Scot, and, disgruntled as he was, he noticed with interest that along Mr. Adams's route unanimous and warm applause broke out, and that no sign of bitterness was to be seen even among those who had been disappointed by the election.

No anger anywhere, everywhere good humor. It seemed as though politics had suddenly decided to become very cordial and a trifle comic. Mr. Bache, in his *Aurora*, praised John Adams because he was not Washington and because he was not disposed to let himself be taken in by Hamilton. He paid Adams scores of compliments for shunning the tinsel show of monarchy and for the republican plainness with which he went to his inauguration, with only two horses to his carriage, but one servant, and no white wands, whereas General Washington always must have six horses, four lackeys, and six guards in full-dress uniform. But, thank God, we were rid of General Washington!

To him, however, as a last compliment from Mr. Bache, a last present from Mr. Jefferson's republican affection, the presses of the *Aurora* devoted a pamphlet: "Remarks occasioned by the late Conduct of Mr. Washington as President of the United States." Herein it was declared: "We avow freely that our chief object here is *to destroy undue impressions in favor of Mr. Washington.*"

What was he? A mediocre general, "a Virginia planter by no means the most eminent, a militia-officer ignorant of war both in theory and useful practice, and a politician certainly not of the first magnitude."

What did he do? He embroiled us with France, he accustomed us to the atmosphere of monarchy and corruption, he was not "an Alfred to form a nation, or a Czar Peter to visit every country and profession for improvement, or a Franklin who could be self taught, or a Howard who could feel for distant misery."

No, General Washington's "character, having been founded upon false appearance, can only command respect while it remains unknown." His "pantomime of a grave man conceals much negative intrigue." Still, though he is "wanting in great qualities", "neither has he great original vices. He neither loves anybody, nor has he been marked by malignity towards his enemies." He desires nothing very ardently except money, which he seeks covertly, and glory, which he pursues clumsily.

At the same time Bache republished the documents relating to Jumonville, which presented Washington in his youth as an imprudent and tactless officer, perhaps with the blood of the bearer of a flag of truce on his hands.

In his *Aurora* of March 6th, Bache proclaimed: "If ever there was a period for rejoicing, this is the moment. Every heart, in unison with the freedom and happiness of the people, ought to beat high in exultation, that the name of Washington ceases from this day to give a currency to po-

[315]

litical iniquity and to legalize corruption. A new era is now opening upon us."

It opened with John Adams, John Adams the incorruptible, the pacific, the virtuous, the wise.

So Bache trumpeted and the echoes answered him. Even those voices which had never desired to blame Washington repeated: "The cause of Civil Liberty owes you much, and your country still more. Hitherto you have been considered as the man whom posterity should hold up as an example to every people determined to be free. . . . But today I am constrained to expose the personal idolatry into which we have been heedlessly running."

Cobbett himself, even while he attacked Bache, added with a sneer: "This hyperbolical praise of Washington which we have recently heard might be excusable in the editor of a foreign gazette. . . . Astonishing has been the blindness of the world in everything relating to the Americans and their Revolution!"

Jefferson, Bache, Dwight, Cobbett were all at one. People had intoxicated Washington. They had spoiled him and marred him. Now it was better for everybody that he should go and that this shameless flattery of him should cease.

John Adams was of this opinion. He did not hide it from his intimates, and if he hid it from himself, it was only as a matter of dignity. But he was quite ready to admit his own intellectual superiority over Washington and his moral superiority over Hamilton.

Jefferson and Benny, for that matter, were not the kind of men to let him forget it. The *Aurora* wrote in February, 1797: "May the Vice-President of the United States disappoint his perfidious friends and prove himself as formerly a practical Republican." And in March it said: "The insidious friends of Mr. Adams, those who pretended

to support him at the late election, while they were intent
on getting Pinckney over his head, cannot forgive the President for the Republican plainness with which he attended
at Congress Hall. . . . The true dignity of a public officer in a republican Government is simplicity. Let gaudy
monarchs attempt to dazzle their slaves with tinsel show;
freemen look deeper than the surface."

So, in March, 1797, the eyes of free men smiled upon
Mr. John Adams.

And Mr. John Adams himself did his best to smile, even
though he was not very expert at it. Was this the beginning
of the reconciliation of Americans? Was this the dawn of
a new day, which was thus foretold, and also ushered in,
by the *Aurora* of Benjamin Franklin Bache?

So men might think. So men might dream.

But Bache himself was soon to doubt it.

One fine day at the end of the winter, for a little relaxa-
tion, Benny went for a walk with two friends along the
docks of the Delaware, and they decided to pay a visit to
the frigate which was under construction for the United
States fleet and was called *The United States*. The ship
was moored at one of the docks of Southwark, the southern
suburb of Philadelphia. There were workmen still on board,
hurrying to finish their job — planing, painting, furbish-
ing, preparing the emplacements for the cannon. Then they
went below to eat their dinner.

The visitors, sure that they would not now be in the
workmen's way, strolled around the ship. She was empty and
quiet, and Benny was amusing himself studying all her
well-planned, well-executed details, when the bell on the
upper deck was struck. No doubt it was summoning the
workmen back to their jobs. Benny raised his head. The

bell kept on ringing — he could not make out why. At this moment, from behind, he received a violent blow on the head, quickly followed by a second and then by a hail of buffets. He heard somebody shouting at him: "Traitor! Insulter of the President! Insulter of the people! Hireling!"

Taken by surprise, stunned, dazed, Benny could neither defend himself nor utter a sound. His friends attempted to effect his rescue, but they were held back by the ship's carpenters who had come on deck. He was in fear of his life, for the hatchway was but a few feet from him, and the side of the vessel not far away on the other hand. Finally, one of his friends succeeded in holding his assailant off for a moment, and Benny and his party managed to get on shore, pursued by shouts, hoots, and a volley of chips.

Thus the Federalists gave Benny to understand that they were in no humor for smiling and that the time for mere joking was at an end. They were ready to defend themselves against him at all costs and his very life was in danger. As for his honor, it was assailed every day in the week.

It was in this month of March that Cobbett started publishing his *Porcupine's Gazette*. Thanks to the help of the Federalists, he got a thousand subscribers at once, and at once he told Benny: "I assert that you are a liar and an infamous scoundrel." Cobbett explained day by day that Bache was a hireling of France. He abused him for his attacks on Washington, his compliments to Adams, and his devotion to France. Cobbett called Bache a "traitor", an "ill-looking devil", an "atrocious wretch", a "stinking caitiff."

Everybody was attacking Bache.

Washington himself took the trouble to reply to Bache and defended himself in a statement which was published everywhere. Hamilton kept his eye on Bache, and Pickering, the Secretary of State, had all the mail that came for him intercepted and inspected. The Federalists had no intention of letting public opinion be swayed against them and they were determined to break anybody who tried to stand up to them. Benny was the most dangerous of their enemies and the most in danger.

As for John Adams, the Federalists did not worry very much about him. John Adams was well hemmed in, and his "perfidious friends", as Benny called them, knew how to take care of him. They proceeded to do so without hindrance, since John Adams retained the Ministers whom Mr. Washington employed and whom Mr. Hamilton had always guided. Henceforth Pickering, Wolcott and Mac-Henry, at the State Department, the Treasury and the War Department, if they were Adams's Ministers, were Hamilton's lieges. Their instructions came to them from New York, from Mr. Hamilton's office, where decisions were taken both about the affairs of the Federalist Party and about affairs of State.

Thus there was unity of leadership and direction, and Mr. Adams was not very embarrassing; for his way of understanding the exercise of authority had something grandiose about it, which permitted him to close his eyes to some of the details of life and let his Ministers govern without him — so long as it was done with dignity, and his pride did not suffer, and his vanity was not affronted.

Mr. Washington had treated the United States as he treated his own estate. He had personally examined without any undue haste or hurry, without any preconceived ideas or any sense of boredom, whatever problems presented themselves, however humble, however material, they might be. He knew that, on any well-run farm, the life even of pigs has its own importance, and that they must be cared for, like everything else. He had no very keen sense of ideas. It did not annoy him or bore him to concern himself with material details. For that matter, he had always spent a good deal of his life in balancing his accounts.

Mr. Adams, probably, had never balanced any accounts in his life; for Mrs. Adams was a mistress who kept a firm hand, and the accounts of the Adams family were simple little middle-class accounts. Mr. Adams disdained them. In his private life, he was interested rather in ideas and he was interested in them also in political life.

So he never made a point, as Mr. Washington did, of looking over all his Ministers' documents. Besides, as he stood the climate of Philadelphia badly, and spent his summers in his own good home town of Braintree in Massachusetts, far away from torrid Philadelphia, his Ministers came to believe themselves top dogs and real Ministers.

They might have been somebodies, if Mr. Hamilton had let them. But, in Mr. Hamilton's opinion, he who led the party should also lead the Ministers, and through them the President. This was what Mr. Hamilton did in that year 1797, very actively, very snappily, and very happily.

Public opinion had to be kept in its place. The President had to be kept in his place. This meant silencing Bache, who had seen the Federalists' game all too clearly.

The party also had to be stiffened and given a closer organization and a keener enthusiasm. Mr. Hamilton thought in terms of an army. The ex-officers, the Cincinnatti — were they not the nucleus of the Federalist Party?

A good standing army, with a close-knit corps of officers, would be the best guarantee of order in the United States; and, if a war happened to break out, the army would cover itself with glory and the people would rally once and for all to the Federalist cause. Without desiring it too openly, Hamilton dreamed of a war which would definitely break the Franco-American link, make the country its own master, and establish a standing army. It was still rather a vague dream of his, for the people were pacific and there was nothing military about John Adams; but Mr. Hamilton followed the ins-and-outs of affairs, and he was glad to note that events were assuming a military air.

So far as England was concerned, all was peace. The American nation, though it did not like Jay's treaty, accepted it, for people were tired of debating about it. Trade with England was flourishing, and Mr. Liston, a modest, active and likeable man, knew how to win everybody's good graces. The sailors, of course, were still grumbling, for it went hard with them to admit that England should command the seas and lord it over American ships, like those of other people. But, in a great country, there was no satisfying everybody, and England's agents might well be satisfied with what they had achieved during the past three years.

In the Senate, as in the House of Representatives, the friends of England were in a majority. In the Press, the English had eloquent champions. In the Government, all the Ministers were on their side. In short, the country was getting used to hearing the praises of King George sung and the proceedings of Mr. Pitt approved.

William Cobbett, within twelve months, had gained three thousand subscribers, and William Cobbett could say openly: "Old Franklin is held up to the admiration of the people, for having wantonly and maliciously predicted, that the empire of Britain would soon fall to the ground. For my part, for this prediction of his, I call him an old *Zanga*."

In truth, Cobbett insulted Franklin to irritate Bache, and to fight against the influence of France, which Franklin had always supported so much. To Hamilton, to Cobbett, France was the *bête noire*, the red monster. To John Adams, she was the great problem, a country at once attractive and irritant. To Jefferson, she was an old memory, tender and disturbing. To Benny, she was the flame of his youth; and, to the American people, she was the source of all their passions, the stimulant of their national sentiment.

From 1630 to 1770 France had been the hereditary enemy, always present, always hated for her policy, for her religion, for her character and for her ambitions, for all that she did or wanted to do. Then she had been the great, the sole ally, the only country that cared both about the success of America and the greatness of America, the only country that saw — that insisted upon seeing — in the United States a new and original people, different from England.

France had been an incomparable flatterer — almost a dangerous one. She was one of those friends that you love so much just because they are irreparably different from yourself. Even revolutionary France had been so. Even that tremendous Revolution of hers, which turned the whole world upside down and continued the American Revolution, had so strange an aspect, so different an atmosphere, so odd a flame, that it went to the heads of patriotic Americans like some exotic liquor. It excited among the middle classes and the pious folk of the New World a mixture of holy horror and hateful fascination. To everybody — merchants, shopkeepers, officials, sailors, farmers — France was the great problem.

She was so, above all, to the Government in 1797.

The French Directory was exasperated with the United

States. They regarded Jay's treaty as tantamount to a change of sides on the battlefield. They had hoped for Jefferson's success, which might lead to a renewal of understanding, they had worked to get Jefferson elected; but everything had failed, and now there was nothing left but their desire to be revenged on the Federalists and their hope of carrying the people with them by some decisive manifestation.

Adet had been recalled. The Directory had declared that the United States must render an account for its bad faith towards France. It had suspended the maritime regulations which resulted from the treaties of 1778 and gave the United States more favored treatment than other neutrals. The Directory wanted to punish the United States and was bent upon its humiliation.

So, while in Philadelphia the delighted crowd were celebrating the French victories in Holland, and while Bache was glorifying France, in Paris the Directory notified Mr. Pinckney, the new United States Minister, that they refused to receive him. When Mr. Pinckney, who was a good diplomat, said that he was quite ready to wait, the Directors informed him that they would not let him and that he would be expelled if he did. So Mr. Pinckney went home, to convey this intimation to Mr. Adams.

This was the kind of thing that Mr. Adams relished. He reared under the spur of this outrage. He forgot all about national reconciliation, and his understanding with Jefferson, and Bache's compliments, and the eulogies of the *Aurora*. He forgot all about his calm, his greatness, and his serenity. He summoned Congress urgently, and immediately sent it a message in which he expressed, in eloquent language, his sense of wounded dignity and offended majesty.

It was like the striking of a gong throughout the Union.

Gone were cordiality, fraternity and eulogies. Federalists and Democrats reverted to all their old polemics, all their old hatred of one another.

In Congress, where they had at last a majority, the first act of the Federalists, the day after the opening of the session, was to dismiss Beckley, who had been for nine years Clerk of the House of Representatives, and also for eight years Jefferson's discreet and efficacious acolyte and the most active artisan, with Bache, of the Democratic Party. Within a couple of days Beckley had been dismissed, arming was debated, feeling was inflamed, speeches were vehement and gestures were emphatic. Congress and Mr. Adams were of one mind. There was talk of war with France.

Jefferson retired to his tent. He could do nothing and he consoled himself by assuring himself that he would have no responsibility. That did not stop him from urging his friends to assume it and encouraging Benny to do so. If Jefferson said little, the *Aurora* had a lot to say, and what it said had at once the brilliance of Bache's youth and a sibilant tone which recalled Mr. Jefferson's wisdom.

With a smile which was nothing like its smile of March, the *Aurora* reminded Mr. Adams that, if he was President, he owed it to only three votes. "President by three votes", it called him. It also called him "His Serene Highness", or "His Rotundity", or "Bonny Johnny Adams", according to whether it was commenting upon the President's address to the Senate, remarkable for its petulance, or upon some one of his actions in which his rotundity stood out in relief.

But the *Aurora* attacked him more happily when it reproached him with his recent appointment of his son, John Quincy Adams, "the heir apparent", to the post of Minister to Berlin, where young Adams would again meet Hammond and the two of them, equally in love with the British Constitution and equally mindful of British greatness, could do good work at the expense of France — and of America.

Insulted by the French, goaded by Bache, urged by his Ministers, and gently guided by Hamilton, John Adams plunged.

He plunged first upon France. He asked Congress for credits to arm, even while he negotiated, and his enthusiastic Congress begged him to arm by all means. So war seemed close at hand. On his cross-bench Mr. Robert Liston smiled and rubbed his hands.

But, at the very moment when Mr. John Adams was setting off for war, Mr. Bache published the news of the French victories. Vanquished Austria had submitted and a young general, Bonaparte, was dictating peace to Europe. Mr. Liston fell pensive and Congress turned gloomy.

Then chance brought to light, and Mr. Bache hastened to publish, the fact that Mr. Liston, the wise and discreet Mr. Liston, had dabbled in the intrigues of Mr. Blount, who planned to invade Florida and drive the United States into war. Mr. Adams plunged again and sent all the relevant documents to Congress.

Chances jarring together, in that strange summer full of shouting, heat and scandal, cast turn by turn upon the shores of America, and upon astonished Philadelphia, the queerest of reports, the most curious of documents, and the oddest of people. The *Aurora* had plenty to publish and Bache had no time to slack.

First it was Mr. Hamilton who served the turn of the *Aurora*, Mr. Bache and the Democrats. He was accused of gambling in stocks. He published a pamphlet to prove that he had never speculated, but, incidentally, that he had betrayed his wife. He did prove it, and Benny recognized the fact, publicly and politely. But John Adams did not approve.

Then it was an Italian newspaper, which translated a letter from Mr. Jefferson to one of his friends overseas, and American newspapers reprinted it. In it the sage of Monticello denounced the political decadence of the United States and the Federalist General Staff, as corrupt, corrupting, aristocratic. It was certainly what Mr. Jefferson thought, what Benny Bache had said, and what Benny Bache kept on saying in the *Aurora*, and what Mr. Jefferson advised him to say. But the public was surprised and Mr. Adams did not approve.

Then it was Mr. Monroe coming back from France, from whence General Washington had recalled him. Colonel Monroe brought back with him love of France, Liberty and Democracy, and a lively grudge against Mr. Washington, who had negotiated Jay's treaty without informing him and, according to Monroe, had made a fool of him. Banquets were offered to him, songs were sung in his honor, and in his *Aurora* Bache extolled him. From Benny Bache's press Monroe published a pamphlet against Washington and the Democrats were delighted with it. But John Adams did not approve.

Mr. Adams was not given to approving. He wanted to send ambassadors to France to settle this quarrel; but he did not know whom to send. He had thought of Jefferson, but a Sovereign does not send his heir apparent; that would be unworthy of his dignity. He had thought of Mr. Madison but Mr. Madison did not want to go. Mr. Adams had consulted his Ministers, and they had suggested some excellent, eminent persons, devoted to the party and admirably

THE PROVIDENTIAL DETECTION

Courtesy of the Historical Society of Pennsylvania

"THE PROVIDENTIAL DETECTION"

suited, from their character and their ideas, to provoke war with France at once. Mr. John Adams did not approve.

Despite his Ministers, he ended by choosing, together with Mr. Marshall and Mr. Pinckney, whom his party liked, Mr. Gerry, whom he himself liked. Indeed, Mr. Gerry was one of those people who inspire as much suspicion in their enemies as they do confidence in their friends, and for the same reasons. Mr. Gerry had always changed his mind at the critical moment. "What an honest man!" said his friends. "What a knave!" said his enemies. He had a tall figure, a sad face, and a wink in his eye. "What a hypocrite!" said his enemies. "What a strong, silent man!" said his friends. The fact was that Mr. Gerry merely suffered from a nervous twitching of the eye.

He had never succeeded very well and had never belonged to any party. That was why Mr. Adams liked him, and perhaps also because he had voted for him at the last election, although he was a close friend of Mr. Jefferson's. So Mr. John Adams appointed him, Mr. Jefferson was delighted, Mr. Bache approved, and Mr. Adams approved too.

Then the three delegates set out. No enthusiasm accompanied them. The Federalists had no confidence in this mission of theirs, and they distrusted Gerry. The Republicans liked neither Marshall, nor Pinckney, nor all this system of ambiguous negotiation. Marshall and Pinckney did not appreciate Gerry's company and Gerry was sorry to leave Mrs. Gerry.

But Mr. Adams had gone to rest in the shade of his plane trees at Braintree. Mr. Jefferson was farming at Monticello. Mr. Logan was talking under the great trees at Stenton; and Benny Bache, to escape from pestilential Philadelphia, was staying with his little family at his father's at Settle Farm. There they swam in the river in the afternoon and in the evening they listened to the singing of the tree frogs; jolly Mr. Bache told them funny stories, or little Deborah played on the pianoforte an air which they liked above all others and which she excelled at rendering, "The Battle of Prague."

Each one of them digested the scandals of the spring and summer at his ease, while for all of them was being prepared the most shattering of all scandals.

CHAPTER VII

THE TEST

THE Directory had just triumphed in Europe and over internal enemies. It was in no mood for clemency and its appetite was insatiable. The American negotiators were not going to find a favorable atmosphere.

Nevertheless, they had a friend on the spot. That good M. de Talleyrand, by a retribution of things here below, was now Minister for Foreign Affairs; and although, under the French Constitution, the Minister for Foreign Affairs had no great power, Monsieur de Talleyrand was too shrewd, and too closely linked with Monsieur Barras, one of the five Directors, not to have some power himself.

He had it, and he exercised it with discernment, for the benefit of intelligent, well-advised and open-handed people.

Everything that could be sold — armistices, peace, treaties, conventions and the rest, — Monsieur de Talleyrand sold. Germans, Portuguese, Dutch, Italians, Turks, the Pope, everybody had been in the market, and Monsieur de Talleyrand's business was doing fine.

Now Monsieur de Talleyrand had decided that the Americans should come into the market too. He felt that this was only fair and proper in the case of a people so venal, so grasping for money, and so unfaithful to their engagements. He had been confirmed in this idea by his friend, confidant and agent, Monsieur le Comte d'Hauterive, who, having spent ten years in the United States as Consul, out-

[329]

law and spy, was now returning to France to assist the French Government in the coming negotiations, enlighten the Foreign Ministry, and advise Monsieur de Talleyrand.

When Messrs. Marshall, Pinckney and Gerry arrived in Paris, they had the most astounding reception. The city was in revolution, in jollity, in delirium. The streets, full of beggars asking for alms, shouting Jacobins, and strutting dandies; and the drawing-rooms, in which women, half-naked like pagan nymphs, and officials adorned like peacocks, rubbed shoulders on floors still stained with blood and under ceilings still gilded — all this could not fail at the outset to shock Messrs. Pinckney, Marshall, and Gerry.

They were still more dumbfounded when, scarcely settled in their hotel, they were visited by thirty musicians, who came to serenade them by way of welcome and to ask them for thirty louis, because they were musicians of the Executive Body. Then they were visited by twenty fishwives, who came to present them the compliments of the ladies of the market, to kiss them, and to tell them that this was worth thirty louis, which was the custom in France.

Mr. Pinckney and Mr. Marshall, who were Southerners, listened, kissed, and paid; but Mr. Gerry, who was a Northerner and a Puritan, did not kiss and did not pay.

Finally their astonishment reached its climax when, after a pleasant and cordial interview with Monsieur de Talleyrand, they found it impossible to obtain either official recognition, or serious and regular negotiation, or any indication whatever of the Directory's intentions. True, they had visitors. A lady came to see them. She told them: "Poor fellows, the Directory is furious with you. It can't forgive Mr. Adams for his inconsiderate speeches, and you will never be received. You are lost unless you can make use of your good friend, Monsieur de Talleyrand. The only thing is that, for all his good will, Monsieur de Talleyrand can do nothing by himself. You must give him a helping hand. You must sweeten him."

Messrs. Marshall and Pinckney, who did not know French, did not understand this very well and protested. Mr. Gerry, who did speak French, preferred to say nothing, either because he understood only too well or because he did not understand at all.

After this visitor there was another, a young man, then a fat man, then another man, a banker, a business man — and always the same kind of talk, disturbing and full of commiseration. The Directory would not hear of anything, but Monsieur de Talleyrand could save the situation if he got his price. The Directory must be paid; Monsieur de Talleyrand must be paid. To wipe out the memory of Mr. Adams's arrogance, the United States must agree forthwith to a big loan. To get the negotiations started, Monsieur de Talleyrand must receive forthwith a bagatelle of a few millions. They must pay. There was nothing doing without paying.

Messrs. Gerry, Marshall and Pinckney were surprised, discountenanced, and then indignant. Messrs. Marshall and Pinckney gave up seeing Monsieur de Talleyrand, but Mr. Gerry kept in touch with him, for he at least spoke French and he had known Monsieur de Talleyrand before. But Gerry had no more success across the dinner table than Marshall and Pinckney in their solitary penitence. When he sounded the Foreign Minister, Talleyrand left him little hope. The Directory was very angry with Mr. Adams. Mr. Adams had been so blustering. Perhaps a loan would fix everything, Talleyrand said vaguely.

But Messrs. Marshall, Pinckney and Gerry would not

[331]

hear of a loan. Instead of a loan, they sent the Directory a formal note. They received a tart reply. What had become of the great fraternal principles? What had become of the union of republics? Why had the United States betrayed the cause of France and of liberty?

When the envoys persisted, Messrs. Pinckney and Marshall were told that the Directory did not want any more of them in Paris and that they must leave at once. They hastened to go, taking their notes with them.

Messrs. Marshall and Pinckney set out in April. Mr. Gerry stayed until June, dining from time to time with his good friend Talleyrand and awaiting instructions. He was melancholy and ill at ease; but he felt that it was his duty to stay as long as there was any hope of some arrangement. So he conformed to his duty, though he missed Mrs. Gerry, his wife, and even Messrs. Marshall and Pinckney, who at least spoke English.

Monsieur de Talleyrand, who had got neither loan nor sweetener, and who was finding it a stupid business, did not quite know how to get out of it. In his embarrassment, he kept Mr. Gerry as a hostage and brooded over him as over a beloved mistress. Then Talleyrand suddenly realized that, instead of a loan, he was risking a war. He made a few pirouettes, presented a pamphlet to the public and all his compliments to Mr. Gerry, and finally let him go with very friendly letters.

It was not even a cloud over Monsieur de Talleyrand's career. But it looked as though it were going to be war between France and America, the downfall of Mr. Jefferson, and the end of the Democratic Party.

The autumn had ended sadly in Philadelphia.

Once more yellow fever ravaged the city. Once more men

found themselves powerless before the scourge. In vain Mr. Rush bled his patients, in vain Doctor Wistar purged them, in vain Doctor Kuhn gave them emetics; the patients died. In vain the municipality organized a great hospital. In vain it compelled the sick to hang out little orange flags from their houses. In the stricken city the contagion spread and all the streets were adorned with red and yellow flags.

Men tried in vain, troubled in vain, toiled in vain, prayed in vain, until the day came when the north wind, the cold rain and the frost swept away the miasma.

Then the shops replenished their stocks, the burghers came back, the Government returned, and the theater reopened. The newspapers reappeared. People went back to politics. They took up again the disputes that had been interrupted yesterday, the rising hatreds, the suspended intrigues.

Benny Bache was at the heart of all the hatreds. He was hated more than any other American of that time. He was more feared, more loved, more adored than any other man of his age. People wrote to him furtively to send them his gazette under false names. They read it feverishly.

The whole burden of the struggle bore upon him. Mr. Jefferson was in his quiet corner, Mr. Monroe was living on his estate, Mr. Madison kept silent, Beckley had turned lawyer, and Doctor Logan held aloof, meditated and planned; for Stenton was still a haven of peace. All of them had a title, a fortune, or an estate to protect them. Benny had nothing.

His printing house in Market Street was in the center of the town, at the heart of its noise, its passions and its sufferings. Benny, Benny with his black eyes, his languishing woman's eyes, Benny tall and spare, Benny the newsman and the grandson of Franklin, was the sole Democrat, all of whose windows looked out on the street, and who was always in the street.

He alone was jostled, pushed, carried along by the people. He alone saw the city as it was: overwhelmed by the yellow fever or swept with enthusiasm, stricken or throbbing.

That winter the city was like himself: restless, nervous, and threatened. As early as November the storms came. At the beginning of December the frost and snow came. The Delaware froze over and ships were icebound. Trade was interrupted, food became scarce, everybody lost money, and the prisons were full of debtors. The best-known merchants of Philadelphia went bankrupt. Mr. Swanwick, the financial backer of the Democrats, was at the end of his resources. Mr. Morris, the great banker of the Federalists, announced that he was selling "his palace on Chestnut Street."

And Benny, when he made up his accounts, found that his customers were not paying him, that his subscriptions were falling into arrears, and that his advertisements were getting fewer. From St. Croix letters came to tell him that the sugar cane harvest would be bad, that matters were not going well, and that he had been wrong to quarrel with the Government. Things and people turned against him. Poverty threatened him — him, his wife, and his children. The prisons were full of debtors.

With his belt pulled tight, his mind ill at ease and his body weary, he had to stand up to the rising tide of anger. He had to help his friends in the mêlée and keep up to the pitch of the general violence. He must not slacken for a moment. He who stopped, he whose paper ceased to appear, was submerged in a few days.

No: he must fight and he must be funny. When Congressman Lyon, who came from Vermont and was not very well-mannered, but a frank Democrat, considered himself insulted in the House of Representatives by Griswold and spat full in his face, Bache had to defend Lyon. Against Cobbett, who thundered and denounced the "Spitting Lyon", against indignant high society, he had to defend Lyon, who did not know very well how to defend himself. This was no laughing matter, for the Federalists were in dead earnest. They wanted to put Lyon in prison and keep him there.

But luckily you could raise a laugh for a moment when John Adams, invited by the city "Assembly" to come and celebrate the anniversary of Washington's birth with them, replied politely and promptly:

"Gentlemen,

"I have just received your polite Invitation to a Ball on Thursday the 22nd instant, and embrace the earliest opportunity of informing you that I decline accepting it."

To these already delightful lines you need feel no compunction about adding: "It is to be hoped that the managers will not again celebrate the birthday of a President politically defunct; but that on another occasion they will confine their adulation to the living and not extend it to the dead."

For you were sure of amusing the public and exasperating the gentleman concerned. You might even hope to receive one of those anonymous letters which Mrs. Adams, in her big, regular, dignified handwriting, sent to journalists to ask them if they did not blush in the sight of God when they attacked her husband or her son.

In the delirium of the city, in prey to all the passions of politics, it was certainly not John Adams who would restore calm. President of the United States though he might be, he was the most petulant, the most violent, the most virulent of pamphleteers and debators. He could not help his feelings catching fire on the instant, or whatever he did seeming like an explosion and whatever he said bursting like a thunderclap.

Everybody in Philadelphia was engaging in polemics, everybody was fighting. But some people fought stealthily, like Jefferson; others in broad daylight from the height of a throne, like Mr. Adams; and others again fought at the risk of their fortune, their honor, and their life, and had to brave bankruptcy, poverty, hatred, blows and prison to say what they thought. This was the case of Benny Bache.

In Congress the Democrats fought to prevent arming. But they were Representatives, they had the right to do it, and for that matter the public did not know very well what they were doing. Does anybody ever know just what Parliamentarians are doing? The Government left them alone, counting upon intimidating them and hoping to win them over some day.

But in his paper Benny had attacked John Adams and in this the Government saw a crime of high treason. He defended France and in this the Federalists saw a capital outrage. He had published Monroe's pamphlet denouncing John Adams and George Washington and all the patriotic papers had shrieked that this was a civic crime. People had sworn revenge.

Benny Bache lived on Market Street, near the market, right up against the crowd. Colonel Monroe stayed on his estate, Albemarle in Virginia. He was far away from all the hubbub, far away from the Government, far away from his enemies. He kept on beseeching Benny to print his pamphlet well, to defend it well, to circulate it well. Monroe asked him for the money from its sale. He begged him to hurry up. Benny, who was short of money, borrowed some to buy paper, to print the pamphlet, to dispatch two thousand copies of it to Virginia aboard a brig. As soon as she was in the Delaware, the brig was frozen in the ice.

Monroe grumbled, Adams threatened, the crowd muttered in the street, and Benny's creditors kept their eye on him.

Mr. Pickering kept his eye on him too. Long ago Pickering had intercepted in the mails a letter from Monroe to Logan, in which Monroe praised Bache, Logan and Beckley, entrusted his interests to them, and begged them to publish his letters, and eulogies of France, and criticisms of the Government. He gave this letter to Cobbett; and, on behalf of the American State Department, the English journalist denounced to the patriotic crowd of America the American journalist who dared to talk so loud when he had so little money.

Let them rout out the scoundrel, said Cobbett; let them expel him from the Society of Sons of Saint George! Why, when they met him in the street, did the ragamuffins not spit upon him?

The ragamuffins contented themselves, one March evening, with throwing through Benny's windows three stones the size of a man's fist, which broke several panes of glass, crashed into the middle of the room, terrified the women and made the children cry. As this did not scare Benny, a few days later the *Aurora* was able to chronicle "the third attack of the kind for which Mr. Bache has been indebted to the friends of regular government."

It was not very pleasant, and Benny thought about Margaret, and the children, and ways of protecting them. There

[337]

was no way, and to console himself he had to look at his wife's proud face, which smiled with a hard line over the eyes. Margaret was proud to suffer, and Benny was proud of her, and both of them were proud of fighting.

But it is hard to be always beaten, always abused. Benny had fought to get his friend Israel Israel chosen as Senator for Pennsylvania; but the Federalists succeeded in getting Benjamin Morgan elected, and they shouted their delight and their hopes all through the city. Cobbett proclaimed: "I have already 3000 subscribers." He was about to publish *Country Porcupine.* He reported the demise of Democratic papers which were failing, one after the other. After the *Argus* came the *Northern Star;* then, Cobbett asked, "would it be the turn of the *Aurora?*" And he added:

"The most infamous of the Jacobins is

BACHE

"Editor of the *Aurora,* Printer to the French Directory, Distributor General of the principles of Insurrection, Anarchy and Confusion, the greatest of fools, and the most stubborn sans-culotte in the United States."

It is hard to see even those to whom you are united by many memories of childhood turning against you, bitterly, angrily, and giving you back a score of stings for one attack. Benny had attacked John Quincy Adams, whose father was pushing him along in his career, and who had just been sent as Minister to Berlin, after being appointed at Lisbon. That there was nothing scandalous about this — for John Quincy had brains — many people agreed, with Cobbett; but that it was rather laughable many also thought, with Bache.

But this was not the view of Mrs. John Adams, who, without signing it, and without disguising her handwriting, wrote Benny a letter so severe in its piety, so Christian in

[338]

its wrath, and standing so much on its dignity, that it must either strike him to the heart or make him burst out laughing.

"My son," she said, "has written to me: 'As for Mr. Bache, he was once my schoolmate, one of the companions of those Infant years when the heart should be open to strong and deep impressions of attachment, and never should admit any durable sentiment of hatred or malice. There is a degree of Regard and Tenderness that mixes itself in my recollection of every individual with whom I ever stood in that relation. . . . Mr. Bache must have lost those feelings, or he would never have been the vehicle of abuse upon me, at least during my absence from the country.' — Mr. Bache is left to his own reflections. This communication is only to his own Heart, being confident that the writer never expected it would meet his Eye."

Childhood, regard, tenderness — all the luxury of fine sentiments, grand words, soft phrases! How laughable it seemed, when Benny was fighting to save his life, to save his faith, to save his hope, and when he was surrounded by a mob howling day and night!

The crowd shouted in the streets. They hooted the Democrats. They hated Benny Bache.

It was then that, during the storms of winter, shrill and stark as a shriek, came the news of the "X. Y. Z. scandal."

Dispatches from Gerry, Marshall and Pinckney had arrived. Mr. Adams read them. This time it was the limit. This must be the end. In guarded words he spoke about it to the Senate. In ambiguous phrases he forewarned the House of Representatives. The Federalists smiled. The Democrats made faces. Then they asked themselves whether, once more, Adams was trying to frighten them with shadows. Carried away by their feelings, by their polemics, by Fate, they demanded to see the dispatches.

Mr. Adams let them see them. Within two days Cobbett published the dispatches. Within a week every paper in America had reprinted them. Before the end of April the whole people had read them.

Mr. Adams published them word for word, but he had deleted the names of Talleyrand's agents, out of consideration for them, out of shame, or out of that delicate sense of the dramatic which never left John Adams. Be that as it may, of all Mr. Adams's publications, the "X. Y. Z. dispatches" were the most successful and those which the people appreciated the most. The whole public was on his side.

Mr. Cobbett edited the dispatches in haste, but with care, and he adorned them with a commentary. Here is Democratic morality, he said, the thing that constitutes the strength of the Republicans and gives them that moral superiority over despots to which they owe their triumphs, their prestige, and their invincible greatness! Here is the friendship of France, which has never failed the United States, and which Monsieur de Talleyrand, having been our guest at a time when he was himself an outlaw, knows how to express better than anybody else! Here is that noble fraternity which our Democratic friends preach to us in their papers and which Benjamin Franklin Bache represents in our midst in memory of his grandfather! Here are France, Democracy, and the Franklin tradition!

The crowd shouted in the streets, they demonstrated around Congress Hall, they spat upon the *Aurora*. The Republican Congressmen bowed before the storm and held their peace.

Mr. Jefferson shook his head, for he was a philosopher,

and never did any actions of men astonish him altogether. For that matter, he had never been a lover of company, and the solitude which now spread around him was by no means distasteful to him. He rather liked this unpopularity of his, which remained tinged with respect for him, and he awaited the future with eyes downcast.

Benny Bache stared the future straight in the face, drawn up to his full height. Never had he suffered so much. Never had the ideas he loved, his memories of his childhood, his pride in his mission, the very hope of his whole life, been thus rolled in the mud, trampled upon, disfigured and torn to pieces.

He remembered Talleyrand: that beastly, dirty, loose mouth of his, that vile, shrewd, penetrating look of his, the whole keen, subtle, low personality of the man. He remembered his dress and his gestures and his instinct to get away from him. He remembered Talleyrand's manœuvers, his friendship with Hamilton, his affair with the Negress, his jests about America, and how careful he was to avoid all those who did not talk for money, who did not play for money, who did not live for money, and who did not sell themselves for money.

Benny's hatred of Talleyrand made him love France all the more, — the France that Talleyrand had betrayed, that Franklin had loved, and that Benny Bache was not going to abandon.

There was nobody left but himself and Doctor Logan of Stenton. Mr. Jefferson shook his head, and Beckley gave advice; but Logan had decided to act, and Benny was not going to wait before he spoke. Doctor Logan, who believed in God, who was a Quaker and a doctor, had decided to go to France and tell Talleyrand all there was to tell him, and then return to America and tell Adams what nobody else

[341]

would tell him. Doctor Logan believed in God, and even in men, and in his peace of Stenton.

Mr. Jefferson, Mr. Mifflin, Mr. Dallas, Mr. Beckley and Benny Bache approved Doctor Logan's decision. Let him go to France. Let him represent all of them there. Let him open Talleyrand's eyes and bring back peace. All of them supported him: he was their Ambassador. Mr. Jefferson gave him a letter, Mr. McKean signed a circular for him, Mr. Beckley and Mr. Dallas entrusted him with commissions and packets; and Benny Bache, who knew what he was risking, told Logan that in his paper he would defend whatever he did and print whatever he said.

Benny Bache was risking his life. For the people were beside themselves. The crowd shouted in the streets, they hooted the Democrats, they hated Benny Bache. They man-handled Frenchmen, they tore off tricolor cockades, they hissed the "Marseillaise." On street corners, through the markets, along the quays, along the roads, they sang "Yankee Doodle", they roared the "President's March."

One evening, when John Adams appeared in the theater, they interrupted the play and insulted the musicians to make them play "Yankee Doodle" and the "President's March." They shouted at the Democrats: "Up, stand up, you Democrats! Up with your hands, you Democrats! Up with your voices, you Jacobins! Clap! Cheer!" If anybody had refused, they would have beaten him up on the spot. If anybody had called for the "Ça Ira", they would promptly have given him a mauling. If anybody had pro-tested, they would have lynched him. It was better to yield, to wait, to live to fight another day.

It was a fight against war. Benny advised his friends to be patient, to keep calm, to put away their French cockades, to arm themselves with cudgels, to go about in groups, to

avoid disputes and brawls, and to change their lodging every
night. He was fighting against war and amid the tumult of
war he raised his voice for peace. He cried that Talleyrand
was not France and that Talleyrand himself had said that
he did not want war.

He insisted in his paper that France did not want war
with America, and that the American people did not want
war with France, and that John Adams alone was responsible, for his wild speeches had exasperated France. He proclaimed that there were still Democrats and free men in
America; and every day, on every page of his paper, in every
column of the *Aurora*, he published the toasts, the letters,
the speeches, the votes and the addresses of those who dared
to protest against war. For his part, he was not afraid to
make himself their mouthpiece.

And every day John Adams, every day Hamilton, every
day Pickering, Wolcott, Cabot and all the Federalists
opened Bache's *Aurora* to see whether he was yielding,
whether he was rallying to the opinion of the crowd, whether
they were managing to master him, whether they could
make opinion unanimous, whether he who dared to stand
up to them was not at last being submerged. The Federalist
crowd and the Federalist Government waited for Benny
Bache to break or recant.

Their preachers and their orators, their statesmen and
their ministers, all assured them that, by entering into an
infernal pact, the Jacobins and their secret societies had
handed France over to disorder and the Devil, and that they
wanted to hand America over too. In all their papers, from
all their pulpits, they cried: "Defend yourselves! Unmask
these traitors! Break those who resist!"

The crowd was enthusiastic; and the Government was
determined. The hour which Hamilton awaited had come

[343]

at last. War with France was popular, legitimate, and near at hand. They were going to carry the whole nation with them. They were going to turn it into an army, they were going to bind it to England, they were going to break all its links with France. Amid this magnificent disorder, they were going to weld an iron casing for order, they were going to reinforce law, they were going to make America that strong nation, under a strong government of strong men, which was the dream of Hamilton in his strength.

John Adams was carried away by the momentum, the mob, and his own mettle. He flung himself where he had to go. Washington proceeded there at his own calm, dignified pace. Jefferson had the sense to stand out of the way. The nation's unanimity was wonderful. It was only a matter of breaking a few more windows around the town, breaking up a few more groups, and breaking down Benny Bache.

The hunt was up after the Democrats. Cobbett wrote: "Bache knows what all the world knows and says: he is a liar, a fallen wretch, a vessel formed for reprobation, and therefore we should always treat him as we would a TURK, A JEW, A JACOBIN, OR A DOG." He was no better than a dog. "No man is bound to pay the least respect to the feelings of Bache. He has outraged every principle of decency, of morality, of religion and of nature." And in the street the little ragamuffins sang:

> "Benny Bache and his crew
> To the Devil we'll throw,
> And Randolph and Monroe."

Cobbett announced a "Gimcrack Museum", where you could see "The American Orator, representing a member of Congress in solemn debate, spitting in the eye of his opponent to clear it from the mist of prejudice"; "The American Patriot, a fine figure, sitting upon a cask of flour, begging a bribe of a French envoy"; "The Journals of the Congress at Monticello, written entirely in French"; "A French Decree, written in blood".

He added benignantly that American citizens who disliked the treatment meted out to their ambassadors and their traders had only to blame Benjamin Franklin Bache. "The reasons given by the French for using severity towards Americans are exactly those which have been dictated by *Bache* and his infamous clan. These infamous wretches it is, and it is they alone, who have set the hellhounds on to American Commerce." Hellhound for hellhound, Cobbett suggested. On to Bache with them!

The hellhounds were after Bache. At night the crowd came and broke his windows, besieged his door, and tried to smash his shutters. Neighbors and watchmen had to intervene to save him. Young sprigs of Philadelphia on horseback went and paraded before John Adams's house and then went on to Bache's to hoot him and threaten him. The militia regiment of Philadelphia, which had once sported the tricolor and vaunted its love for France, had to lay aside its cockades, and nobody boasted his love any more.

Mr. Cobbett even decided to intimidate the Irish, for they still stood out. He published in his gazette articles and speeches to prove that the Society of United Irishmen were plotting with the Democrats to set fire to the city. They were agents of France, friends of Bache. The crowd read Cobbett, and Mr. Pickering, the Secretary of State, asked him for details, and put himself politely at his disposal for discreet collaboration between them.

Mr. Cobbett had become the best of Anglo-American patriots, and as he served his King, His Majesty George III of England, so he served his President, Mr. John Adams of Braintree.

But neither Cobbett, nor his articles, nor the young sprigs on horseback, nor the hoots of the ragamuffins, nor stones through his windows, nor the threats of the crowd could stop Benny. They could kill him, of course, but his battle was his life, and, short of killing him, they could not stop him fighting.

He was poor and they tried to starve him out. Cobbett circulated the rumor that he could not pay his debts. They conspired to ruin him. The shopkeepers gave him no more advertisements, the taverns refused to take his paper, the carriers neglected to distribute it. His tradesmen and even his relatives intervened to make him abandon his campaign.

From St. Croix, Frank Markoe wrote to his sister, in the name of their dead father and mother, bidding her no longer endure a hateful and criminal way of life, but leave this madman and return to the bosom of her family, where she would find peace and dignity and an atmosphere suited to women. But Margaret pressed her lips and Benny went on with his work.

The Government was bent on mastering him.

As nobody now resisted it in Congress, the Government could do what it liked. But it did not want to make war — or perhaps it could not make war — unless the whole people followed it. It had to silence the *Aurora*.

The Government prepared for war. First Congress declared that the alliance with France was dead and buried. Then it declared that privateers could give chase to French ships. It voted that American warships should defend the trade of the United States against any interference from the French by force. It voted the raising of an army.

So war was at hand — if the people could be carried.

The Government worked upon the people. It received Mr. Marshall and Mr. Pinckney in triumph when they landed, and they paraded through the streets amid a great concourse of people, escorted by young men on horseback. The Government encouraged processions, reviews and enrollments. Every morning at six o'clock Mr. John Adams got up, took his leave of Mrs. Adams, and sat down at his desk to reply to the addresses which patriots and merchants, boys and women, in fact everybody sent him from all directions by the hundred.

Mr. Adams was quite ready for war. He told the crowd so. "The finger of destiny," he declared, "writes on the wall the word: War." He formally started his own war against Benny, since he refused to take his gazette any more. But the people were not yet ready. John Adams had to silence the *Aurora*.

The Government attacked the newspapers. It had one law voted giving it power to expel the French and discipline the Irish; it had another passed to silence impudent gazettes, the *Alien Law*, the *Sedition Law*. Henceforth newsmen who criticized the President and the Government could be put in prison and so authority would be respected and law and order would reign. Henceforth Benny Bache need not flatter himself any longer that it was only Mr. Cobbett who threatened him with prison or the gallows. So did Mr. Pickering.

The Government threatened. It had made up its mind to strike. But Benny Bache was determined to go on, whatever happened.

On June 16, 1798, having received from a "friend", who

was probably Jefferson, a long diplomatic statement of Talleyrand, not any too good or any too clear, but at least a statement which meant, beyond mistake, that France did not want war, Benny Bache published it. He put it on his front page. It was a smack in the face to the war mongers.

Mr. Adams turned crimson with rage. Mr. Cobbett vomited his hatred. Mr. Fenno started a campaign. Mr. Hamilton thought that this was about enough. Around Benny the circle closed in. This time there could be no forgiving him. His manœuver was too audacious, too efficacious, too opportune.

Fenno wrote daily articles. Cobbett printed a pamphlet. He circulated it throughout the town, he sent it out into the country, he had it stuck on farm fences. A copy was thrown into the Bache's garden. "The Detection of Bache." Cobbett declared that Bache, paid by Talleyrand, had received the paper from Talleyrand, and printed it for Talleyrand. Bache was a traitor.

An affidavit was procured from one Mr. Kidder, who had brought a document from France for Bache, and who swore that it bore the official seal of the French Ministry of Foreign Affairs. So now they were going to prove that Bache was in direct and secret relations with the French Department of Foreign Relations, that he was a spy. Now Bache could be sent to prison. In the House of Representatives, two Members denounced him as a spy, and requested he be arrested. All the Federalist papers requested it. Some already said that Benny Bache was in jail.

In company with two friends, Benny presented himself before the Mayor. He had with him two witnesses. He had in his hand a stout cudgel. He explained that he had friends in France who sent him pamphlets. One of these friends of his was Pichon, a clerk in the Ministry of Foreign Affairs, and he had probably sent Bache a pamphlet, which had not yet reached Bache. That must have been this big envelope, with the Ministry's seal. But never had Benny Bache had any relations with Talleyrand. Talleyrand would rather have the rich Mr. Hamilton than any poor newspaperman. It was a "gentleman in this city" who had given him Talleyrand's letter. Benny Bache swore to it and the Mayor attested it. They could not find him guilty. And when, five days later, he received the mysterious package that contained some pamphlets from Pichon, and had Wolcott and Pickering's signatures on the cover in which it was enclosed, Benny could laugh at them; he did laugh at them. They had to let him go and bide their time.

Benny Bache proved that Mr. Kidder had never handed him the envelope, but that a Mr. Lee, who was bringing it from France, had written to Wolcott and Pickering to denounce Bache. Wolcott had raced to New York to see Lee and his mysterious package. Then the Secretary of State, Mr. Cobbett and Mr. Fenno, without waiting for Mr. Wolcott's inquiry, had framed a campaign against Bache. Cobbett had reviled him, Fenno had barked, and Pickering had tried to catch him this time. But they had failed and Benny laughed at them.

Bache had escaped; they could not hold him as a spy. They tried to hold him as a rebel. He was summoned before the Federal judge to answer for his attacks on the President. He presented himself with Dallas and Levy. He defended himself and they set him at liberty on bail of two thousand dollars. He kept on publishing his paper.

They did not give him back his money. Soon, they hoped, he would have none left. Soon he would be in prison for the debts that he must incur and he would not be able to keep on publishing his paper.

But he still had his audacity, he still had friends, and they wanted his paper to be published.

The more his enemies attacked him, the more he had to say. The more he was persecuted, the more his gazette was read. His subscribers, whom he had once had to beg for payment, now sent him their money in advance. His debtors, who had once adopted all kinds of ruses for keeping out of his way, now came to him of their own accord and paid him what they owed. So the *Aurora* kept on appearing.

With persecution, his boldness grew; with his boldness his reputation, and with the growth of his reputation, hatred grew around him. Cobbett attacked him every day. Fenno insulted him on every page. They did not speak about him any longer as a man, they did not even speak about him as a dog; they spoke about him as something vile, stinking and rotten. But in his *Aurora* Bache replied, — for there was no silencing the *Aurora*.

They placed around him, as they had organized around Mr. Jefferson and around Doctor Logan, a Federalist guard, a regular spy service. They called it the "Corresponding Committee." But, whereas Jefferson's spies protected him while they kept their eye on him, whereas Logan's respected him while they had him under observation, around Bache there was nothing but hatred. There was nothing but the hope of seeing him weaken, the desire to see the *Aurora* fall silent, since they could not stop it from being published.

One day (Wednesday, August 8th), when Bache had gone out and was walking along Fourth Street with his friend Beckley, Fenno junior hurled himself upon him. Bache had jibed at Fenno senior for receiving money from bankers and being subsidized by gamblers in stocks, and de-

THE TIMES; A POI

The Cannibals are landing

Volunteers

Step de wheels et

de gouvernement

CARICATURE MADE IN 1798, DESCRIBING THE
POLITICAL SITUATION IN AMERICA IN
1797 AND 1798

nounced him for accepting five hundred dollars from a bankrupt. Bache had also made game of the son — "Fenno's
young lady in breeches." But Fenno's young lady wanted
revenge.

He saw Bache in the street. He kept out of Bache's way,
he walked around the block; then he sprang at Bache and
scratched his face. Benny struck at him with his cudgel.
They grappled, mauled each other, banged each other
against the wall. When they were separated, Benny had
blood all over his face, and Fenno had a bloody head.

Fenno's *Gazette* cried: "Victory!" but the *Aurora* had a
neat retort, for the *Aurora* was never afraid of anybody.
The *Aurora* appeared every day, and, by way of a salute to
the patriots, Benny was preparing a country edition to appear three times a week. He launched it at the end of July.
The *Aurora* was still shining.

A kind of false dawn whitened over the city.

After the tumult and the shouting, after the blows and
the battles, the heat fell upon Philadelphia.

In the morning it was ninety degrees; by noon it was a
hundred. The dank steam overwhelmed everybody. You
stifled at your desk, you gasped for air at home, and the
street was a furnace.

It was so hot that everybody was tired. Mr. John Adams
was tired of drafting patriotic addresses, the crowd was
tired of shouting, the newsmen were tired of fighting, the
patriots were tired of singing, the soldiers were tired of
drilling, the gossips were tired of dawdling. Life dragged.
Life was a load.

People were so tired that for a time they forgot about
the war. Adams went to rest in the cool on his own good soil
of Braintree. Mr. Liston followed him, for Mr. Liston

looked for an alliance. He talked about it to Mr. Adams.
Had not the moment now come?

No, said Mr. Adams; the moment had not yet come.
Public opinion was not yet ready. The summer was too
hot and the people too cool. It would be soon, of course,
but they must wait a bit. The *Aurora* was still appearing.

Mr. Adams was in no hurry. He was quite ready for war,
and he knew well that, in case of war, his genius would not
fail him. But the summer was very hot; France was in no
hurry to fight either, and Mr. Hamilton was in too much of
a hurry.

Despite Mr. Adams's intentions, despite the prior claims
of Generals Knox and Pinckney, Mr. Hamilton had exercised his influence upon Washington, the commander in
Chief, and upon the Cabinet, to get himself appointed second in command. Pinckney shrugged his shoulders, Knox
protested and recriminated, and John Adams scarcely fan-
cied the idea of a war carried on over his head by Washington and Hamilton.

They had stolen his war from him. Adams remembered
the *Aurora* — what it had once said about "perfidious
friends"; what it kept on saying.

The heat fell upon the town. Reek reigned in the streets
and the very animals suffered from it; but men kept on
fighting. They were raising a great army, and, prompt to
betray, prompt to run away, many of Franklin's old friends,
many of Thomas Jefferson's faithful followers, many a
devotee of liberty, talked about enrolling under the flag.
But the Federalists frowned. They looked these newcomers
over. They did not want them.

This was the army of Mr. Washington and General Hamilton: a pure army, an obedient army. It was an army to

fight France and give the Democrats stripes on their backs, not on their sleeves. It was not the army of Mr. Adams or of the lukewarm.

Mr. John Adams began to see what it was. He did not like this army. The public did not like it much either; and the *Aurora* kept on mocking at the idea of war.

It was exhausting to do anything and it was positively painful to have to crack a joke. Humid and heavy, the heat hung over the town and started killing men off. Here and there in the streets yellow flags appeared and you could hear the rumbling of the carts that carried the sick to hospital and the dead to the graveyard. One by one the fever killed the poor, chased away the rich, and terrified the weak.

But it did not extinguish hatreds. Around Stenton, whence Doctor Logan had gone, hastening to France to tell the Directory that they must avoid a war between the two republics at all costs; around Stenton and its great trees, where there was nobody left but women and children, they mounted guard and Mrs. Logan was hemmed in. Mr. Jefferson, who was being trailed himself, slipped in under cover of the mist one evening. He comforted Mrs. Logan; but she could see that he was more nervous than she was. Then, losing no time, Jefferson went back to town to pick up his spies.

Meanwhile, heedless of his own family's safety, Benny Bache, on page two of the *Aurora*, published a eulogy of Logan. The Federalists were exasperated. They felt that their war was escaping them. What was Logan doing over there? And why had they failed to stop that *Aurora* appearing?

The death roll rose in the city. In the middle of August twenty people a day were dying. Then there were forty.

[353]

By the early days of September it was eighty, and then, in a leap, a hundred and thirty.

They still went on electing people. They still squabbled around the polling booths. They still threw stones. They still exchanged blows.

But already whole streets were silent. The rich had fled to their country homes, the poor had fled where their noses led them. But they found themselves repulsed everywhere. They slept in the fields, they fed on roots, they begged at the doors of farmhouses. They were driven off with bludgeon blows; the dogs were set on them. But they dared not stay in the city for their terror was too much for them.

Some of them died of fear. Some of them died because they had passed carelessly by a silent house, whence there emerged an acrid, stinking odor, like that of coffee gone rotten. Some of them died because they had heard this frightful death described to them; and Jane Doron only just missed being buried alive because, when they were taking her to burial, the doctor, seized by a doubt, started pinching her and shaking her, and ended by awakening her.

There were so many dead everywhere. Some of them died in their hovels. Others died in their luxurious beds and rotted there alone, alone, while their servants, their slaves, their wives and their children fled as far away as they could. Some died in the street, shrieking from pain and crying for help, without anybody daring to approach them. Others, after lying in agony in the hospital for days and nights, in their delirium ran out into the street, bleeding and half-naked, and fell dead at the next corner.

You found corpses in shops that had been shut for a week. You found them along the quays. You found them in open houses where thieves had gone to strip the dying.

You found them calcined in burnt-out houses, which robbers had set on fire to wipe out traces of their crime. Everywhere you found them, everywhere you saw them, these bluish corpses, rotting, twisted and naked.

The city was benumbed, crushed. It seemed to sweat terror. No breath of wind stirred the yellow and red flags that hung from the houses everywhere. No sound any longer awakened the echoes in squares, streets and market. The shops were closed. The Government was gone. Nobody was left but the doctors, the nurses, the undertakers and the ghouls. Nobody still sang in the city but the night watchman, to tell the living that day was coming, and the dying that rest was coming.

Everything was benumbed or dead — except hatred, which could not die; except the gazettes, which kept on fighting. Cobbett insulted Benny Bache, Fenno calumniated Benny Bache, and Benny Bache replied to them. Since he had a country edition, he had to work twice as hard; but the *Aurora* still appeared.

Carey's *Recorder* ceased to appear at the beginning of September. Soon the *Gazette of the United States* suspended publication, for Fenno fell sick. The *True American*, too, had to close its office, stop its presses, and suspend its work. The editor of the *Philadelphia Gazette* persisted in struggling on, but several of his staff died. His colleague of the *Mail and Daily Advertiser* preferred to take refuge in Germantown.

Only Cobbett and Benny remained face to face. They refused to stir. They refused to be scared away. For Benny knew that he alone at this moment was keeping up the spirits of the whole mass of Democrats, and Cobbett knew that but for him the enthusiasm of the Federalists would wane, since he alone had the real berserk rage for fighting.

In the close proximity of hatred, in the intimacy of strife, in their sharing of the same danger, the two men threatened each other.

Cobbett had children and a wife. Benny Bache had children, and his dear, gentle Margaret was in bed awaiting the birth of their fourth child. It was in vain that Margaret's family wrote to them from St. Croix: "Flee that furnace, flee that Hell." It was in vain that Benny's family wrote to them from Settle: "Come here. The river is cool, the trees are green, and the air is pure. There are no mosquitoes, no yellow fever, no Cobbett. Come here. We'll swim in the river, we'll play the 'Battle of Prague', Margaret can sing 'Caro Mio Bene' again, and at night we'll talk and enjoy the cool of the evening." Margaret could not leave her bed. Benny would not leave his *Aurora.*

He would not leave it even after Margaret was delivered of her fourth son, Hartman, on September 3d. That very day he announced a great meeting of the Democrats of Philadelphia to take counsel and organize.

Benny would not leave his *Aurora* either on September 5th. That day he had caught the yellow fever. That day he published a eulogy of George Logan.

On September 10th he had to drag himself along to get his paper printed. That day there were seventy-three deaths in the town. But that was the day when Benny announced that he had obtained proof against John Adams. John Adams had lied when he alleged that the crooks who had been denounced by the American Ambassadors in France were authentic agents of the French Directory. They were nothing but blackmailers, who had nothing to do with the Government of France.

This the *Aurora* declared. This Benny printed with his dying hands. This Benny affirmed, face to face with death.

For death was coming to him. Margaret and his staff still worked at the paper. Benny still told them what to do.

Even on his deathbed, his delirium was still the delirium of liberty. He gasped for air, there was a rattle in his throat; but still he begged them to go on working.

Benny was dying; but the *Aurora* would live.

He summoned his wife. He said his last good-by to her. But it was not about himself that he spoke. He told her that she must bring up their children as free men. He told her that he was leaving her nothing but that — nothing but this charge, this suffering, this hope, this very life of his, for which he was laying down his life.

At half-past one at night Margaret Bache had a sheet printed which the newsboys, shouting through the quiet streets, sold before the dawn came — before there appeared, for the last time, Benny Bache's *Aurora*.

The friends of civil liberty, and patrons of the *Aurora*, are informed that the Editor, BENJAMIN FRANKLIN BACHE, has fallen a victim to the plague that ravages this devoted city. In ordinary times, the loss of such a man would be a source of public sorrow. In these times, men who see, and think, and feel for their country and posterity can alone appreciate the loss; the loss of a man inflexible in virtue, unappalled by power or persecution, and who, in dying, knew no anxieties but what were excited by his apprehensions for his country — and for his young family.

This calamity necessarily suspends the *Aurora* — but for a few days only. When such arrangements shall have been made as are necessary to ensure its wonted character of intelligence and energy, it will *reappear under the direction of*

HIS WIDOW

(Philadelphia 11 IX 1798; one o'clock in the morning.)

Benny Bache had died at midnight.

[357]

THE *Aurora* reappeared on November 1, 1798, and it had a great success. Mrs. Bache published it, with the help of her foreman Duane. He had talent and he had a heart; and a little later she married him.

The *Aurora* had become the first paper of America.

Mr. John Adams had reflected during the summer. He saw Doctor Logan; he received letters from Europe. He realized that France wanted peace and that Hamilton wanted war; he discovered that his Ministers were making a fool of him. He decided to negotiate with France, he broke with his Ministers and with his party.

He was — he had asked for it — beaten in the election of 1800.

Mr. Thomas Jefferson was elected; but probably he would never have managed to become President of the United States but for Mr. Hamilton, who helped him to gain a majority over the other claimant to the Democratic candidature, Aaron Burr.

So ended the great rivalry between Jefferson and Hamilton — that intimate rivalry of theirs. Such was the crown of that long hatred of theirs.

So ended the battle of Philadelphia: that battle fought between Federalists and Democrats; between Thomas Jefferson and Alexander Hamilton; between Benny Bache and William Cobbett; between the legend of Washington and

[358]

the memory of Franklin; between Mrs. Bingham's drawing-room and the great trees of Stenton.

Mr. Morris went bankrupt and they put him in prison. Mrs. Bingham died of cancer and her husband of despair. Cobbett had to go back to England, where he turned Radical. Congress removed to Washington. The French returned to France. So disappeared the Philadelphia of Benjamin Franklin Bache.

The Federalist Party foundered. It was never meant for delirium and the summer of 1798 had set it mad. It died of the yellow fever, and of Hamilton's hatred of Adams, and of its contempt for the immigrants. It died because Benny Bache, and Dallas and Beckley, and Tammany and the *Aurora* had built up a machine which could stand strain: a machine which was more enduring than the Federalists, more enduring than the yellow fever. And so the Federalist Party died.

The Democratic Party won. Dallas, and Benny, and Beckley had made it with their ink, with their sweat, with their blood; and it could stand trying times.

It could not stand quite so well the Presidency of Mr. Jefferson, who was a Virginian Liberal rather than a Democrat — but who was, when all is said and done, a great man. In any case, a Democratic Party endured, for the people had need of one, but it was no more the idealist enthusiastic party of Benny Bache and Doctor Franklin.

Before dying it had achieved the Second American Revolution: the revolution that broke Federalism and the English alliance.

It was Benny Bache who led this Second Revolution. He had not the genius of Jefferson, or that of Washington, or that of his grandfather. But, like them, he loved his country, and to him, as to them, life was really worth living only when he could stir the people, when he could merge himself into the warm mass of mankind, into their passions, into their desires. More than those other men, he suffered; for a short suffering with defeat is harder than a long suffering that finally blooms into the joy of success. Benny Bache had died — and died too soon.

Benny Bache had led the Second Revolution, together with Beckley and with Dallas. But it had slipped out of his hands. His paper was revived by another man, and this other man married his wife, this other man became the father of his children, the father of his ideas, the father of his doctrine.

There was nothing left to Benny Bache. Not even his reputation was left, not even the scandal of him. His enemies soon stopped talking about him. So did his friends. He was dead.

Mr. Jefferson shed a few tears of praise over him, for Benny Bache was the grandson of the great Doctor Franklin. But Mr. Jefferson had not much to say about him; for Benny had denounced Washington; and, after Washington's death, Washington and Jefferson were reconciled. Their misunderstanding had died with Washington's death.

There was nothing left to Benny but a few insults from Mr. Cobbett, a few compliments from the Democrats, a few regrets from his friends.

"The real friends of their country cannot but lament the loss of so valuable a citizen," said the *Boston Chronicle*.

"Let those who despised him while living, be charitable to his talents, and allow 'there died a great young man — with all his imperfections on his head.'"

Thus the *Lancaster Journal*.

And, in his gazette, Russell cried: "The memory of this scoundrel cannot be too highly execrated."

EPILOGUE

So it was. In the annals of America, Benny Bache remains the man who attacked Washington. Historians have little to say about him; but they mention him in passing rather as a vicious boy than as a man who lived his life.

At the turn of a page, in the background of a print, in a faded silhouette, you may catch a glimpse of that face of his, still pallid with youth, fever, and self-sacrifice. You may discern, in the shadow, that graceful, gauche figure of the man who first gave its form to radical opinion in the United States and fashioned the Democratic Party.

It is to his shade in the shadow, from very far away, that I dedicate this book.

BIBLIOGRAPHY AND REFERENCES

I

THIS book, I hope, is a true picture of the political party fights in the United States from 1785 to 1798.

I have spared no pains in finding the truth, and I have examined in the last five years a very great amount of published and unpublished material. A complete bibliography of this book would be larger than the book itself. It would be too large for the present economic conditions. Moreover, the book aims at being a picture, and I don't wish to overburden the reader with the weight of my references.

I am giving here simply the most useful, the most significant, and the most important of my sources: the ones which led me to my conclusions and which furnished proofs, I believe, of the soundness of my views.

For the rest the reader can go back to the bibliography of my "Esprit Révolutionnaire" (French edition), and to the bibliography of Mr. Claude Bowers' very interesting book, "Hamilton and Jefferson", both of which cover the same period.

II

The official documents of the end of the eighteenth century have been carefully studied in France, England and the United States. The writings of the leading statesmen, politicians and public men are well known and generally well edited. I have thought that some new light could now be shed on that period by a careful examination of the leading newspapers of the time, which have never been taken very seriously and have not been studied very carefully. The center of my study was the *Aurora General Advertiser*. Rather than go through many papers, as I had done before, I made a point of seeing a few, and seeing them completely. I chose the *Aurora General Advertiser*, (Republican Democratic), the *Gazette of the United States* (Federalist, conservative), the *Porcupine's Gazette*

(Federalist, reactionary), the *Lexington Kentucky Gazette* (Republican Democratic, radical), and used the other papers of the period only to confirm or check the facts I found in these four. I studied the years 1790–1800.

I was fortunate enough to find manuscripts and documents which gave additional and vitally important information on the editors and policies of these papers. Mr. Franklin Bache's archives gave me the story of Benjamin Franklin Bache in the most complete manner, from the minute of his birth to the minute of his death; the collection of Miss E. F. Ward gave me some clear and good information on Fenno; the published works of Cobbett and some of his papers at the Pennsylvania Historical Society gave me a sound knowledge of the great British pamphleteer. The Breckenridge papers and the papers of the Democratic Society of Kentucky brought much light on the *Lexington Kentucky Gazette*.

The Mason Collection, the Morgan Library, the American Philosophical Society, the University of Pennsylvania, the Cramer Collection contain some very precious documents of and on Benjamin Franklin Bache. The Pennsylvania Historical Society has the papers of his most intimate friends, A. J. Dallas, and J. Beckley (Irvine Papers, Vol. 13). The Library of Congress has recently received the papers of his intimate collaborator, Genet, and of his friend, Thomas Lee Shippen. And it was given to me to make use of these collections.

Such has been the center and the backbone of my documentation.

As far as possible, I have followed the spelling and the style of the eighteenth century for the names, without trying to modernize them, but only to make them consistent and easy to recognize, my purpose being not to write a dictionary of eighteenth-century biography, but to give a picture as accurate as possible of eighteenth-century life, psychology and history.

BOOK ONE

III

Chapter 1. The description of the Franklin family is based upon the letters addressed to Franklin by his family and his friends, which

are to be found in the collections of Mr. Mason, of Mr. Franklin
Bache, of the American Philosophical Society, of the Library of
Congress, and of the University of Pennsylvania. "The Writings
of Franklin" (edited by Smyth) and the "Letters to Benjamin
Franklin from his Family and Friends" (1859) have also been
used. Many of the details concerning Sarah Franklin's youth and
marriage are taken from "A Book of Remembrance . . . by Mrs.
E. D. Gillespie, 1901", pages 16–26.

The first quotation on page 3 is taken from the *Pennsylvania
Chronicle*, November 2, 1767. The second one from a letter of
Sally Franklin to William Franklin, October 3, 1766. The quota-
tions on page 10 are taken from letters of Mrs. Franklin to Benjamin
Franklin, August 16, 1770 (Bache Collection), June 30, 1772
(Bache Collection); from a letter of Sarah Bache to Benjamin
Franklin, December 2, 1771, and from an undated letter of the
same (Mason Collection). The quotation on page 11 is taken from
a letter of Richard Bache to Benjamin Franklin, December 24,
1774 (Bache Collection).

Chapter 2. The description of the life of the Franklin family
and of the conditions in Philadelphia from 1774 to 1776 is taken
from the letters contained in the above-mentioned archives, plus
"Writings of Franklin" (Smyth), Vol. 6; the "Diary of Christopher
Marshall"; Scharff and Westcott, "History of Philadelphia", Vol. 1,
pages 290–300; S. B. Harding, "Party Struggles over the First
Pennsylvania Constitution" in the "Report of the American Historical Association", 1894; B. A. Konkle, "G. Bryan and the
Constitution of Pennsylvania", 1922; the *Pennsylvania Evening
Post*, years 1775–1776; the *Pennsylvania Mercury*, and the *Penn-
sylvania Gazette*, 1775–1776.

For the quarrel between Benjamin Franklin and William
Franklin, see "Benjamin Franklin" by Bernard Faÿ, page 402, the
above-mentioned archives, and the "Calendar of the Papers of
Benjamin Franklin in the Library of the American Philosophical
Society", Vol. 1, page 184 and Vol. 3, page 502.

The description of the games of the children, page 16, is taken
from "Writings of Franklin" (Smyth edition), Vol. 6, page 406.
The quotation on page 19 is taken from the *Pennsylvania Evening
Post*, August 13, 1776.

Chapter 3. The description of Franklin's life in Passy and the behavior of Benny Bache is taken from unpublished documents in the archives of Mr. Franklin Bache (account books of Franklin), unpublished letters in the collection of the American Philosophical Society, and details given by Franklin in his "Writing" (edited by Smyth), Vol. 9, page 327, Vol. 7, pages 10, 346, 348 and 368, and by Parton, "Life of Franklin", Vol. 2, pages 205–206.

The description of Benny Bache's life in Geneva is taken from his papers (diary and letters) in the archives of Mr. Franklin Bache and from documents in the archives of Mr. Philibert Cramer and of Mr. Lucien Cramer. The details concerning Geneva, its college, and its revolution, are taken from "Etrennes Génevoises", 1925, pages 78–96; "Dictionnaire Historique et Biographique de la Suisse", Vol. 2, page 603; A. Galiffe, "Notices Généalogiques", Vol. 3, page 147, Vol. 5, page 365; Charles Borgeaud, "Histoire du Collége de Genève", 1909. I have also used the archives of Geneva (Registre du Conseil), and the archives of the Marignac family.

All the details concerning the revolution in Geneva are taken word for word from the diary of Benjamin Franklin Bache. The quotation on page 35 comes from a letter of Mrs. Dorcas Montgomery, November 17, 1781 (Mason Collection); and the quotation on page 37 comes from a letter of Benjamin Franklin Bache to Benjamin Franklin, February 25, 1783 (Bache Collection).

BOOK TWO

Chapter 1. This chapter is based upon the above-mentioned archives and more particularly upon the letters and diaries of Benjamin Franklin Bache (Bache Collection); the diary of Temple Franklin (Bache Collection); the letters of Temple Franklin (American Philosophical Society); the account books of Franklin (Bache Collection); the letters of Franklin and Madame Brillon (American Philosophical Society); and the "Writings of Franklin" (Smyth edition), Vols. 6, 9, and 10. See also the "Writings of John Adams", Vol. 3; the "Writings of Thomas Jefferson", Vol. 4 (Ford edition).

The quotation on page 46 comes from Benny Bache's account book, 1784 (Bache Collection). The quotations on pages 50 and 51 come from his diary, May 7, 1784, September 30, 1784, May 19,

BIBLIOGRAPHY

1784. The quotation on page 52 comes from the same, May 2, 1784.
The quotation on page 54 comes from the "Writings of Franklin"
(Smyth edition), Vol. 1, page 78. The quotations on page 56 come
from Benny Bache's diary, May 22, 1784; from the "Writings of
Franklin" (Smyth edition), Vol. 9, page 268; and from an un-
published letter of Temple Franklin at the American Philosophical
Society. The quotations on page 57 come from the "Oeuvres de
Cabanis", Vol. 5, page 519, and from an undated page of the
diary of Benny Bache. On Mirabeau and the Cincinnati, on page
58, see *Revue de Littérature Comparée*, 8th year, pages 1–28.

Chapter 2. The description of Franklin's life and activities in
Philadelphia is taken from the letters in the collections of Mr.
Mason, Mr. Bache, and the Morgan Library in New York (Letters
of Temple Franklin and Benjamin Franklin Bache), from the
"Writings of Franklin" (Smyth edition), Vols. 9 and 10, from
the "Calendar of the Papers of Franklin in the archives of the
American Philosophical Society", Vol. 3, from the above-mentioned
books of S. B. Harding and B. S. Konkle, and from the "Autobiography of Charles Biddle", pages 215–238. See also *Pennsylvania Archives*, Series 4, Vol. 4 and Series 1, Vol. 11; the
Pennsylvania Magazine of History, Vol. 12, pages 110–112, Vol. 29,
pages 14–30; and Saint John de Crèvecoeur, "Letters d'un Cul-
tivateur Américain" (1787), Vol. 2, pages 416–423.

The quotations on pages 69 and 70 are taken from Crèvecoeur,
Vol. 2, pages 416–423, and "Writings of Franklin" (Smyth edition),
Vol. 10, pages 470–474; the quotation on page 71 from the *Pennsylvania Magazine of History*, Vol. 36, pages 92–93; the quotation on pages 71–72 from "Writings of Franklin" (Smyth edition),
Vol. 9, page 506; the anecdote about Benny Bache on page 72 from
an undated diary of Benjamin Franklin Bache; the quotations on
page 74 from "Writings of Franklin" (Smyth edition), Vol. 9,
pages 359 and 588.

Chapter 3. The description of the intimacy between Franklin
and Benny Bache is taken from the papers of Benny Bache in
the collection of Mr. Franklin Bache.

The quotation on page 88 is taken from an undated diary of
Benny Bache, the quotations on pages 89–91 from the same diary
and from the "Oeuvres de Cabanis", Vol. 5, pages 245–246, 260,

266–267. The quotations on pages 93–99 come from an undated diary of Benny Bache which had to be translated and abridged.

Chapter 4. The description of Franklin's and Benny Bache's life in Philadelphia, of Benjamin Franklin Bache's love affair, and of Franklin's death are taken from the papers of Franklin, the diaries and letters of B. F. Bache in Mr. Bache's collection, and from the "Reminiscences of John Bromfield", 1852. The picture of Philadelphia is based upon Scharff and Westcott, Vol. 1, pages 433–476; Parton, "Life of Franklin", Vol. 2, pages 546–550; T. H. W. Bowles, "The Philadelphia Assembly"; and some unpublished letters of Temple Franklin and Franklin in the Mason Collection and in the archives of the American Philosophical Society.

The anecdote, page 102, is quoted from Benny Bache's diary (undated). The quotation on page 104 is taken from the "Writings of Franklin" (Smyth edition), Vol. 10, page 4. The letter of Professor Nisbet, page 105, is in the archives of Mr. Franklin Bache. The description of the death of Franklin, page 117, is taken from an unpublished letter of B. F. Bache to Miss Markoe, in the archives of Mr. F. Bache.

BOOK THREE

Chapter 1. The description of Philadelphia is based upon the advertisements published in the newspapers of that time (principally the *Pennsylvania Gazette*, the *Gazette of the United States*, the *General Advertiser*, and the *National Gazette*, years 1790–1793), and upon the book of Scharff and Westcott, Vol. 1, pages 95–269. See also "Travels of Peter Kalm"; "A Book of Remembrance", 1901, by Mrs. Gillespie, and "An Excursion to the United States", by H. Wansey, 1798, pages 97–120, and the "Voyages de la Rochefoucauld Liancourt", An 7, Vol. 6, pages 312–320, and the "Voyage aux États-Unis", Moreau de Saint Méry, 1913.

The description of Peale's Museum, pages 128–129, is taken from *Dunlap's Daily Advertiser*, January 23, 1792. The description of Geisse's Museum, page 129, from the *Pennsylvania Gazette*, July 4, 1790. The description of Mrs. Bingham's drawing-room, page 132, is taken from Wansey, pages 134–137, and the "Recollections

of Samuel Breck", pages 187 and 200–203. The quotation on page
133 is taken from an unpublished letter of Andrew Hamilton to
Richard Bache, dated November 25, 1792 (collection of Mr.
Franklin Bache).

Chapter 2. The description of Stenton and the company who
visited Mr. and Mrs. Logan, pages 134–135, is taken from the
"Memoirs of Dr. Logan", by Mrs. Logan, pages 12–15 and 38, and
from the typewritten thesis of Miss Woodfin on Citizen Genet
(University of Chicago), pages 180–200. The portrait of Hamilton
and of Hamilton's relations with Jefferson and Washington is
based upon La Rochefoucauld Liancourt, Vol. 7, page 149, and
Vol. 5, pages 41–42; John Corbin, "The Unknown Washington",
from pages 240–246, 294–297, 312–330; upon S. E. Morrison,
"Harrison Gray Otis", Vol. 1, page 141; and Senator Lodge,
"Writings of Alexander Hamilton." The description of Hamilton's
office, pages 138–139, is taken from Moreau de Saint Méry, pages
145–146. The description of Jefferson and of Jefferson's character
is taken from "Memoirs of Dr. Logan", pages 50–55; the "Journal
of Macklay", February 19, 1791; the "Writings of Thomas Jefferson" (Ford edition and Monticello edition); and from the
excellent book of Mr. G. Chinard, "Thomas Jefferson."

Chapter 3. The description of Benjamin Franklin Bache's
activities is taken from letters in the archives of Mr. Franklin
Bache. The quotation, page 147, comes from a letter from Robert
Morris to Benjamin Franklin Bache, July 28, 1790 (archives
of Mr. F. Bache). The description of the Federalist Party is based
upon Purcell, "Connecticut in Transition", pages 298–330; the
"Journal of Macklay", pages 386–400; the "Writings of Alexander
Hamilton", Vols. 9 and 10; and George Gibbs, the "Administra-
tions of Washington and Adams." The quotation on page 150 is
taken from an unpublished letter of Thomas Jefferson to B. F.
Bache, April 22, 1791, in the archives of Mr. Franklin Bache.
The description of the Democratic groups in Pennsylvania is based
upon Woodfin, pages 195 and 232; Alexander J. Dallas, "Life and
Writings"; and the Dallas manuscripts in the archives of the
Historical Society of Pennsylvania. The description of the American newspapers is based upon a study of these newspapers, of the
manuscripts of B. F. Bache (Bache Collection), of the manuscripts

of Matthew Carey (American Antiquarian Society), and on the "Notes on the American Press" by Bernard Faÿ.

The quotation on page 157 is taken from the *General Advertiser*, October 23, 1790. On Jefferson and his activities, see the Madison Papers in the Library of Congress, Vol. 4; the manuscripts of John Beckley at the Historical Society of Pennsylvania (Irvine Papers, Vol. 13; the "Writings of Thomas Jefferson" (Ford edition), Vols. 1 and 8; and the newspapers of the time (*Gazette of the United States*, August 6, 1791, *General Advertiser*, May 10, June 30, July 22, 1791, etc.). Page 165, for the criticism of Washington, see *Lexington Kentucky Gazette*, February 23 and May 4, 1793, *Philadelphia General Advertiser*, March 4, 1791, February 4 and 16, 1793. The details concerning public opinion in America in 1793 are all taken from the Philadelphia newspapers (*General Advertiser*, *Federal Gazette*, *National Gazette*, *Gazette of the United States*, etc.).

Chapter 4. This chapter is based upon the Genet Papers in the Library of Congress and the very interesting thesis of Miss Woodfin.

Pages 173–174, for the information concerning John Temple see "Writings of Thomas Jefferson" (Ford edition, pages 231–232). The details concerning public opinion in Philadelphia are taken from the contemporary Philadelphia newspapers (*National Gazette*, *Gazette of the United States*, *General Advertiser*), from the "Autobiography of Charles Biddle", pages 251–255, and from Scharff and Westcott, Vol. 1, pages 470–480. Page 175, I have attributed a great deal of importance to Jay's drafting of the proclamation of neutrality in 1793. In his recent book Mr. Thomas minimizes Jay's rôle, and, though he acknowledges that Jay sent the draft to Hamilton and that this draft on the most important points is similar to the proclamation, he claims that Randolph is the only author of the proclamation. To prove his point he says that the most recent editors of John Jay's papers discount the authorship of Jay, and that Jefferson mentions only Randolph as the author. Mr. Thomas doesn't seem to know that the intimacy between Hamilton, Jay and Washington was carefully hidden from Jefferson, who would indeed have felt slighted if he had known that the Chief Justice had been so often called upon to give his opinion on foreign affairs. For the same reason, Hamilton must have been careful to avoid mentioning Jay's interference in the matter. But we see from the correspondence of Jay, Hamilton and Washington the great rôle played by Jay in framing the foreign policy of the United States from 1790 to 1795. Through Hamilton, Washington used Jay as a regular adviser in the field of foreign policy, and consequently there is little doubt that Washington saw the draft of the proclamation of neutrality prepared by Jay. Edmund Randolph was Washington's henchman in the Cabinet and the one who followed most exactly Washington's wishes. Consequently it was easy for Washington to have him write the proclamation as he wanted it without ever having him realize that the ideas came from Jay. Page 45, Mr. Thomas acknowledges that it is rather curious to see the proclamation of neutrality prepared by the Attorney General instead of the Secretary of State. It is indeed "inconceivable." It means that the President on this point didn't trust Jefferson's judgment and chose to take a judicial point of view rather than a diplomatic one; but the highest authority on legal matters was Jay, Chief Justice of the Supreme Court of the United States, and it is consequently more than likely that Washington managed to get his opinion on the subject and to use it. The events which proceeded and the later developments (Jay's negotiating the English-American treaty) strongly confirm this view. That is why I agree with Samuel Flagg Bemis when he says, "Washington issued a proclamation drafted by John Jay." ("American Secretaries of State", Vol. 2, page 69.) The description of the Republican celebration, pages 176–181, follows Scharff and Westcott, Vol. 1, page 473, and the *General Advertiser*, May 21, 1793. Pages 183–184, the information concerning the Tammany Society is taken from Edwin P. Kilroe, "Saint Tammany", New York, 1913, *passim*. The quotation, page 184, is taken from the register of the Tammany Society in the archives of the New York Public Library (folios 1, 12, and 13). The details on the Democratic societies are to be found in Woodfin, page 487 and following; the "Autobiography of Charles Biddle", page 223; the dispatches Nos. 16 and 17 in the Public Record Office, F. O. 5.1; the minutes of the Democratic Society of Pennsylvania, at the Historical Society of Pennsylvania; the Breckenridge papers, in the Library of Congress. The quotations, pages

185–187, are taken from the *General Advertiser*, July 13, 1793. Pages 189–190, the outburst of Washington is described in the "Memoirs of Dr. Logan", pages 51–52.

On the yellow fever in Philadelphia in 1793, pages 192–194, see *General Advertiser*, August 28, to September 18, 1793; Charles Biddle, pages 254–261; Wansey, pages 125–140; Graydon, "Memoirs", pages 383–387; Scharff and Westcott, Vol. 1, pages 469–471.

Chapter 5. The description of Genet's activities is based upon Woodfin *(passim)*, the dispatches of Genet in the archives of the Ministry of Foreign Affairs, in Paris (Correspondance Politique, États-Unis, Vols. 38 and 39), and the diplomatic correspondence at the Public Record Office, in London (F.O.5.1, 5.2). The details concerning public opinion and life in Philadelphia are taken from the *General Advertiser*, January, 1793, to December, 1794.

I have also used the recent and very interesting book of Charles Marion Thomas, "American Neutrality in 1793", which gives a very good picture of the working of Washington's Cabinet, and states very ably the traditional American point of view. But the fact that he has not used the archives of the Ministry of Foreign Affairs or any other French archives, and that he has apparently ignored the French pamphlets and correspondence of the time has made it impossible for him to realize what the French attitude was from 1792 to 1800. Moreover, he does not seem to have studied the negotiations which led to, and the circumstances which accompanied the signing of the treaties of 1778. His interpretation of these treaties is consequently too literal and legalistic.

BOOK FOUR

Chapter 1. The description of public opinion in Pennsylvania is based upon the newspapers, and more particularly, the *Aurora*, the *Gazette of the United States*, the *Mail*, and the *Lexington Kentucky Gazette* (years 1793–1798); and also upon "Samuel Breck's Recollections"; the "Travels of La Rochefoucald Liancourt"; the "Voyage de Moreau de Saint Méry"; the "Mémoires du Comte de Moré", pages 145–150; William Cobbett, "Porcupine's Works", London, 1801, Vol. 7; Charles Warren, "Jacobin and

Junto", 1931, and Faÿ, "Esprit Révolutionnaire", pages 260–280.

The analysis of the political situation in Pennsylvania is based upon the papers and letters of Benjamin Franklin Bache in the collection of Mr. Bache, at the Morgan Library in New York and in the archives of Messieurs Cramer in Geneva, as well as upon Woodfin, pages 486–531; Chinard's "Jefferson", pages 297–306; "Writings of Jefferson" (Ford edition), Vol. 7, pages 1–100; M. C. Conway, "Omitted Chapters of History", pages 103–122, 190–191; Kilroe, "Tammany", pages 187–198; and the manuscript diary of Thomas Lee Shippen, in the Library of Congress.

The quotation on page 211 is taken from the *Aurora*, March 20, 1794. The quotation on page 212 is taken from "Porcupine's Works", Vol. 4, pages 9–10. The quotations on page 214 are taken from La Rochefoucauld Liancourt, Vol. 5, page 7, and "Porcupine's Works", Vol. 2, page 21.

Chapter 2. In my study of the Jay Treaty, I have followed S. F. Bemis ("The Jay Treaty"). I have used also "Edmund Randolph's Vindication" and the valuable information given to me by Mr. Frank Monaghan, who is completing a life of Jay. I have used too the Public Record Office (F.O.7), Henry Adams' "Life of Gallatin", and the "Writings of Thomas Jefferson" (Monticello edition), Vol. 1, page 274.

Page 228, the description of General Washington's carriage is taken from "Samuel Breck's Recollections", pages 188 and following. Pages 230–231, the description of John Jay is taken from Graydon's "Memoirs", page 376. The story of the publication of the Jay Treaty is based upon papers in the archives of Mr. Franklin Bache, the *Aurora* (June 29, 1795), and "The Correspondence of the French Ministers", edited by F. J. Turner, pages 738–750. The quotation on page 233 is taken from "Porcupine's Works", Vol. 2, pages 192–193. The narrative of Benjamin Franklin Bache's trip to Boston follows exactly his letters to his wife (Bache Collection).

Chapter 3. This chapter is based primarily upon "Edmund Randolph's Vindication" and M. C. Conway's book on Edmund Randolph, "Omitted Chapters of History." I don't follow Conway in all his conclusions, which I think he carries much too far, but the documents he had collected enabled him to discover many facts and to give a generally true picture of the drama. I have used also letters of and to Benjamin Franklin Bache (in the collection of Mr. Bache), the Public Record Office (F.O.5.9), letters of George Hammond, July 27, 1795, August 14, 1795, and the archives of the Ministry of Foreign Affairs (Correspondance Politique, États-Unis, Vol. 64, pages 240–250). See also Gibbs' "Administrations of George Washington", Vol. 1, pages 233–256.

The quotation on page 253 is taken from "Randolph's Vindication", page 36. The quotation on page 256 is taken from "Correspondence of the French Ministers", pages 451–452.

Chapter 4. This chapter is based upon the letters of and to Benjamin Franklin Bache in the Bache Collection (years 1795–1796); upon the archives of the Ministry of Foreign Affairs (Correspondence Politique, États–Unis, Vol. 44 and 45); "Edmund Randolph's Vindication"; M. C. Conway, "Omitted Chapters", pages 350–360; the "Writings of Thomas Jefferson" (Monticello edition), Vol. 9; Chinard's "Jefferson", pages 269–311; and the newspapers of that time.

The first quotation on page 265 is taken from the "Writings of Thomas Jefferson" (Monticello edition), Vol. 9, page 226. The second one is taken from "Randolph's Vindication", page 50. The quotation of page 224 is taken from the *Pennsylvania Magazine of History*, Vol. 9, pages 214–215. The gossip of John Adams, page 267, is taken from "Journal du Duc de Liancourt" (published by J. Marchand), pages 27–28. The quotations on page 269 are taken from the *Aurora*, November 20, 1795. The quotation on page 271 is taken from a letter of Mathilda Jones to Benjamin Franklin Bache, October, 1796 (F. Bache Collection).

Chapter 5. The picture of the plight of the Federalist Party and of the need they had of a good journalist to defend them is based upon some letters to and from Fenno (Collection of Miss E. S. Ward), the "Letters of Pickering" (Massachusetts Historical Society Collections), Vol. 7, 6th series; and the book of Mrs. E. E. F. Ford, "Notes on the Life of Noah Webster."

The description of William Cobbett's personality and career is based upon his own work ("Porcupine's Works", Vol. 4, pages 25–70), and upon the answers of his enemies, particularly Benny Bache (*Aurora*, March, April, May, June, 1796) and Matthew Carey ("A Plumb Pudding for the Valiant . . . Porcupine", 1796).

BIBLIOGRAPHY

See also the "Blue Shop . . . by James Quicksilver", Philadelphia, 1796; "The Imposter Detected . . . by J. Tickletoby"; "A Roaster . . . by Sim Sansculotte", Philadelphia, 1796; etc.

For the political situation in Pennsylvania and the campaign of 1796, see the very important letters of John Beckley to William Irvine (Pennsylvania Historical Society, Irvine Papers, Vol. 131). See also the "Writings of James Monroe", Vol. 3; the "Writings of Thomas Jefferson" (Monticello edition), Vol. 9; the "Works of Alexander Hamilton", Vol. 10; the "Life of E. Gerry", by T. Austin, page 135 and 142; Gibbs, "The Administrations of Washington and Adams", Vol. 1, pages 330–355; Charles Warren, "Jacobin and Junto", pages 66–70; "Correspondence of the French Ministers", pages 887–900, 978–985; Chinard's "Jefferson", pages 285–390; the *Pennsylvania Magazine of History*, Vol. 21, pages 392–410.

The quotation on pages 284–285 is taken from "Porcupine's Works", Vol. 5, pages 7–10; on page 235, from *ibid.*, Vol. 5, pages 198–205; on page 286, from *ibid.*, Vol. 5, pages 75–77; on page 287 from *ibid.*, Vol. 4, pages 358–363; on page 288, from *ibid.*, Vol. 4, pages 36–38; on page 289 from *Porcupine's Gazette*, May 16, 1797; on page 290, from the *Aurora*, June 14, 1797; on page 291, from "Porcupine's Works", Vol. 6, pages 288–289; on page 293 from the *Aurora*, January 5, 1796, and "Porcupine's Works", Vol. 3, page 58.

Chapter 6. The description of the political manœuvers between Jefferson, John Adams, and Benjamin Franklin Bache is based upon the "Writings of Thomas Jefferson" (Ford edition), Vol. 5, (Monticello edition) Vol. 4, page 435, vol. 8, pages 240–250, Vol. 9, page 399, Vol. 10, page 55, and Vol. 13, *passim;* Chinard's "Jefferson", pages 311–325; "Madison's Writings", Vol. 2, pages 105–110; the *Aurora*, November, December, 1796, January, February, 1797; La Rochefoucauld Liancourt, Vol. 2, pages 120–130; and the letters to and from Benjamin Franklin Bache (years 1795–1797) in the archives of Mr. Franklin Bache. Pages 307–308, the speech on John Adams is made up of sentences taken from articles published in the *Aurora*, November 12, 14, 15, 17, 18, 19, 1796, etc.; "Travels of La Rochefoucauld Liancourt", Vol. 2, page 122; "Journal du Duc de Liancourt", pages 25–33; Moreau de Saint Méry, pages 263–264; "Madison's Writings", Vol. 2, page 108; Chinard's "Jefferson", pages 321–323; "Jefferson's Writings" (Monticello edition), Vol. 9, pages 352–359, 368, 381.

The description of John Adams' inauguration, pages 312–314, is taken from La Rochefoucauld Liancourt, Vol. 7, pages 280–283, and the Public Record Office (F.O.5. 18, letter of Robert Liston, March, 1797).

The quotations on page 311 are taken from the *Aurora*. December 21, 1796, and November 23, 1796; on page 312, from "Remarks on the Late Conduct of Mr. Washington", Philadelphia, 1796, pages 4, 30, 31–32, 62, 64–65, and the *Aurora*, March 6, 1797. On page 316, from "A Letter to George Washington . . ." by Jasper Dwight, Philadelphia, 1796, pages 1 and 48 from "Porcupine's Works", Vol. 5; on page 287, from the *Aurora*, February 10, 1797, and March 20, 1797. The story on pages 317–318 is taken from the *Aurora*, April 6, 1797; the quotations on page 318 from "Porcupine's Works", Vol. 5, page 7, Vol. 6, pages 293–295, etc.; on page 321 from "Porcupine's Works", Vol. 7, pages 267–268.

The political developments of the spring and summer, 1797, are described with the help of "Jefferson's Writings" (Monticello edition), Vol. 9; Chinard's "Jefferson", pages 320–340; "Life of Gerry" by J. T. Austin, pages 84, 100, 134, 154; and the contemporary newspapers (*Aurora, Porcupine's Gazette, Gazette of the United States*, etc.). The details on the life of the Bache family at Settle Farm are taken from unpublished letters of Richard Bache, Sarah Bache and B. F. Bache in the Franklin Bache Collection; and from "A Book of Remembrance . . . by Mrs. Gillespie", pages 27–35 and T. L. Shippon's Diary (L.O.C.).

Chapter 7. The "X Y Z" scandal is described with the help of the Hauterive Papers (Mason Collection); Lacour-Gayet, "Talleyrand", Vol. 1, pages 235–245; Austin, "Life of Gerry", pages 159–200; Beveridge, "Life of Marshall", Vol. 2, pages 214–335; the letter of J. Marshall and C. C. Pinckney to Rufus King, December 24, 1795, in the newly acquired R. King Collection at the Library of Congress.

The description of the political evolution of these years, of the events in Philadelphia, and of the family life of Benjamin Franklin Bache is principally based upon the letters from and to Benjamin

BIBLIOGRAPHY

Franklin Bache (archives of Mr. Franklin Bache), upon the study of the *Aurora* and of *Porcupine's Gazette*. See also at the Massachusetts Historical Society, the Pickering Papers, and particularly 7.530, 41. 227. See also Charles Warren, pages 70–80; "Memoirs of Dr. Logan", pages 50–60; the "Autobiography of Charles Biddle", pages 275–280; Moreau du Saint Méry, pages 260–270; Vernon Stauffer, "New England and the Bavarian Illuminati", *passim*.

The quotation on page 335 is taken from the *Aurora*, February 23, 1798; on page 358, from *Porcupine's Gazette*, January 25, 1798 and March 12, 1798. The letter of Mrs. Adams, page 339, is in the archives of Mr. Franklin Bache. The quotations of pages 344–345 are from *Porcupine's Gazette*, March 17, 1798, April 20 and 25, 1798; "Porcupine's Works", Vol. 8, pages 118–120. The story of Mr. Lee, pages 348–349, is taken from "Detection of Bache" (pamphlet by Cobbett), "Porcupine's Works", Vol. 8, pages 239–250, the *Aurora* of June 21, 25, 27, and 30, 1798. The description of the assault of Fenno on Bache, page 351, is taken from the *Aurora* of August 8, 9, and 10, 1798, and *Porcupine's Gazette*, August 9 and 10, 1798.

The description of the yellow fever, pages 351–355, is based upon "Facts and Observations relative to the pestilential Yellow Fever. . . . By the College of Physicians of Philadelphia . . . Phila. . . . , 1798; "An Account of the Yellow Fever . . . by Felix Pascalis Ouvrière . . . Phila. . . . 1798"; "Memoirs of Dr. Logan", pages 76–78, the *Aurora*, August and September, 1798, *Porcupine's Gazette*, the *Gazette of the United States*, same dates, "Porcupine's Works", Vol. 9, pages 290–300, and "History of the Yellow Fever . . . by Thomas Condie and R. Folwell . . . Phila. . . ." (1799). The last days and death of Benjamin Franklin Bache are described according to his last will and the family traditions. The quotation on page 357 is taken from "Porcupine's Works", Vol. 10, pages 297–300.

Epilogue. The quotations on page 360 are taken from the *Boston Independent Chronicle*, September 13–17, 1798, the *Frankfort Palladium* of October 9, 1798, *Russell's Gazette*, September 20, 1798. For the attitude of the contemporary American historian towards Benjamin Franklin Bache, see Claude Bowers' "Hamilton and Jefferson", pages 152, 242–243, 287.

INDEX

INDEX

368; his ambitions, 124, 368; his position in Philadelphia society, 145–146, 369; Robert Morris refuses to help him in starting a newspaper, 146–147, 369; fails to get support among Federalists for his newspaper, 149, 369; encouraged, then turned down by Jefferson, 149–150, 369; launches his newspaper with the help of the American Philosophical Society and the government of Pennsylvania, 152–153, 369; works hard and is in love, 154–156, 369; faces hard competition in printing his newspaper, 156, 369–370; his fight to launch his newspaper, 156–158, 370; snubbed by high society, marries Miss Markoe, and lives as a printer, 159–160, 370; becomes the favorite printer of the immigrants, 162–163, 370; his friendship with Genet, 182–183, 371; leaves Philadelphia at the time of the yellow fever, 195, 372; is the main force left to oppose the Federalist Party, 201, 204, 372; in the shadow of defeat, renames his paper, 207, 372; his understanding of the Philadelphia crowd, 223–227, 373; publishes the Jay Treaty, 240, 373; spreads the Jay Treaty through the country, 241–249, 373; becomes the leader of the Democratic crowds, 263, 374; attains glory as a popular leader, 264, 374; his attacks on Washington make of him the leading publicist of the Democratic Party, 268–274, 374; attacked by William Cobbett, 283–285, 338, 375, 377; praises the "Learned Pig", 290–291, 375; his great fight with Cobbett, 292–293, 375; opposes appropriations for Jay Treaty, 294–295, 375; his coöperation with Jefferson, 297–299, 375–376; his rôle in the electoral campaign of 1796, 301–305, 375–376; and John Adams, 308–309, 375–376; his devotion to Jefferson, 310–312, 376; denounces Washington, praises Adams, 314–317, 376; is assaulted, 317–318, 376; the chief target of the Federalist attacks, 318–319, 376; upholds France and is attacked by

John Adams, 324–326, 376; goes to Settle Farm, 327–328, 376; his financial difficulties, his unpopularity, 333–337, 377; is again assaulted, 337–338, 377; and John Quincy Adams, 338–339, 377; fights for democracy and upholds France, 341–351, 377; fights against Cobbett, even when ill with yellow fever, 355–356, 377; fights in the face of death, and dies, 356–357, 377; triumph of the Democratic Party in 1800, which he had prepared, 359–360, 377; soon forgotten, 360, 377; his place in History as the most efficient organizer of the Democratic Party, 361, 377

Bache, Deborah (sister of Benjamin Franklin Bache), 68, 72, 223, 328, 376

Bache, Elizabeth (sister of Benjamin Franklin Bache), 68, 72, 376

Bache, Franklin (son of Benjamin Franklin Bache), 195, 207

Bache, Hartman (son of Benjamin Franklin Bache), birth, 356

Bache, Louis (brother of Benjamin Franklin Bache), 68, 72, 223, 376

Bache, Richard (father of Benjamin Franklin Bache), 20, 68, 72, 76, 111, 113, 153, 226, 328, 365, 369, 376, 377; his marriage to Sarah Franklin, 3, 6, 7; his meeting with Benjamin Franklin in England, 8; his attitude at the time of the death of Mrs. Franklin, 12; his activities in Philadelphia at the beginning of the Revolution, 16; appointed Postmaster-general of the United States by Congress, 23; dismissed by Congress, 60; fails to get a job from the new government, 114–115; moves to the country, 122; advises Benny to come to Settle Farm, 356, 377

Bache, Richard (brother of Benjamin Franklin Bache), 68, 72, 223, 376

Bache, Richard (son of Benjamin Franklin Bache), 22, 207

Bache, Sarah (wife of Richard Bache and mother of Benjamin Franklin Bache), see Sarah Franklin

Bache, Sarah (sister of Benjamin Franklin Bache), her birth, 12; her death, 19

INDEX

Democratic Party, *see* Democratic-Republican Party

Democratic-Republican Party, 160, 220, 225, 234, 243, 247, 252, 260, 261, 268, 275, 276, 285, 287, 288, 324, 327, 332, 339, 340, 342, 345, 352, 356, 358; its origins as far back as 1785, 75–78, 80–82; scattered and unorganized before 1793, 150, 369; financed by John Swanwick, 152, 369; its growth after 1793, 163–164, 370; attitude towards Genet, 196, 372; opposition to Jay, 204, 372–373; criticism of Washington, 204–205, 267, 372–373, 374; attacked by Cobbett in his pamphlets, and answers back, 291–292; opposes appropriations for Jay Treaty, 294–295; builds a machine for the election of Jefferson in 1796, 297–299, 301–305, 375–376; Jefferson's attitude towards it, 309–310, 359; Bache's rôle in building it and strengthening it, 361

Democratic Societies (in America, in general), 201, 220, 221, 268, 281; attitude towards the Federal Government, 200; attitude towards Washington, 205–207

Democratic Societies (of Virginia), 187, 371–372

Democratic Society (of Lexington, Kentucky), 187, 371–372

Democratic Society of Philadelphia, 201–202, 227; organization, aims, and proceedings, 186–187, 371–372

Deslon, Doctor (French charlatan and apostle of animal magnetism), exposed by Franklin, 55–56

"Detection of Bache" (pamphlet by Cobbett), 348

Dickinson, Miss (fashionable girl in Philadelphia), 108

Didot, François (famous French printer), 63

Directory (the government of France from 1795 to 1799), 322, 323, 329; and American envoys to France, 329–332

Doron, Jane, 354

Dorset, John Frederick Sackville, Duke of, 50

Duane, William (printer, publisher, collaborator of Benjamin Franklin Bache and second husband of Mrs. Bache), 358

Ducomb (French perfumer in Philadelphia), 216

Duer, Colonel William, his bankruptcy, 160

Dumouriez, General Charles François, 167

Dunlap's American Daily Advertiser (one of the leading newspapers in Philadelphia), 156, 368

Duparc (French hatter in Philadelphia), 216

Duponceau, Citizen Peter, 179, 186

Dwight, Jasper, 316, 376

Embuscade (French frigate), 180

Emery (French printer, intrusted by Franklin to teach Benjamin Franklin Bache), 62

England, 231, 295, 302, 321, 325, 344; and the Federalist Party, 148; and the American trade, 202–203; attitude towards the United States, 230; its handling of the Jay Treaty, 251–252; sends Fauchet's dispatch to Hammond, 255; handles with great success its negotiations with the United States, 262–263; faithfully served by Cobbett, 278–280

English Fleet, 230

English Parliament, 89

Envoys, American (to France, 1797–1798), chosen by John Adams, 327; their diplomatic failure in Paris, 329–332; and the "XYZ scandal", 339–340

Faneuil Hall (in Boston), 247

Fauchet, Abbé Claude, 118

Fauchet, Jean Antoine Joseph (French Minister to the United States), 205, 206, 207, 213, 236, 237, 263, 282; his dealings with Washington, 202; attitude towards public opinion in the United States, 219; his dealings with Secretary Randolph, 219–222, 273; his dispatches seized by the English, 254, 274; certifies to Randolph's honesty, 259–260; returns to France, 262

INDEX

Federal Gazette (Philadelphia newspaper printed by Andrew Brown), 156, 370

Federal Government, 131, 138, 153, 155; moves to Philadelphia, 121–122 (*see* also the two political cartoons, opposite pages 116 and 122, showing public opinion in New York towards their removal)

Federalist Party, 151, 160, 167, 201, 203, 205, 216, 224, 225, 229, 243, 246, 247, 248, 251, 252, 261, 263, 264, 267, 275, 276, 278, 285, 287, 320, 321, 327, 336, 339, 343, 358, 374; and the Constitutional Convention, 80–83; and the leadership of Hamilton, 138, 369; organization, aims and doctrine, 147–149, 369; and John Swanwick, 152, 369; enemies, 163–164, 372; takes part in the fight against Genet, 196, 372; and the Democratic societies, 206, 372–373; and William Cobbett, 288; in favor of Jay Treaty, 294–295; steady organization of, 295–296; opposes Jefferson, 300; in the electoral campaign of 1796, 301–305; attitude of Jefferson towards, 309–310; attacks violently Benjamin Franklin Bache, 317–319; attitude towards John Adams, 319; and the dismissal of John Beckley, 324; denounced by Jefferson, 325; its final collapse, 359

Fennel, James (actor and lecturer in Philadelphia), 306

Fenno, John (editor of the *Gazette of the United States*), 156, 157, 158, 348, 349, 355, 374; his newspaper, 148; his defense of Washington, 277, 374

Fenno, John Ward (son of John Fenno), his fight with Benjamin Franklin Bache, 350–351, 377

Fisher, Mr. (citizen of Philadelphia), 89

Flagg, Josiah (grandnephew and secretary of Benjamin Franklin), 88

Foundling Hospital (in Paris), 63

Fowler (showman in Philadelphia), 90

France, 20, 162, 179, 188, 231, 251, 257, 281, 282, 285, 291, 302, 314, 315, 318, 321, 325, 336; and Benjamin Franklin, 21, 65–66, 82, 117–118, 149; and Benjamin Franklin Bache, 23–24, 67–68, 86, 341–342; popularity in Phila-

delphia, 166–167; and Genet, 169; declares war on Great Britain, 175; gives special instructions to Genet, 181; praised in the United States, 194–195, 211–227; and the Jay Treaty, 236; bitterly criticized by Cobbett, 288–290; takes measures of reprisal against the United States, 300; and Adet's letter to Washington, 302–304; finds itself drawn into a conflict with America, 322–324; victories in Europe, 325; James Monroe's affection for, 326; dissatisfied with American envoys, 329–332; unpopular in America, 339–348; and Doctor Logan, 353; settles quarrel with America, 364

Frankfort Palladium (newspaper published in Frankfort, Kentucky), 377

Franklin, Benjamin, 7, 49, 50, 51, 80, 109, 121, 123, 125, 126, 135, 149, 155, 170, 232, 242, 268, 282, 283, 285, 287, 288, 311, 312, 315, 334, 340, 359, 360, 364, 365; and the Stamp Act, 3; and his daughter's marriage, 4; and his wife, 4, 5; dismissed from the office of Deputy Postmaster of the English colonies in America, 9; death of his wife, 12; arrives in Philadelphia, 14; his relations with William and Temple Franklin, 18–19; leaves for France, 20; sends Benny Bache to Geneva, 24, 366; and Philibert Cramer, 29; recalls Benny Bache from Geneva, 37, 366; his popularity in Europe, 41; meets Benny Bache in Passy, 41–42; signs treaty of 1783, 42; his ideas on Benny's education, 42; allows Benny to quit school, 43–44; and the eaglet which fell in his garden, 45; his pleasure at Passy, 51–52; his interest in balloons, 52–54; his views on progress, 55; his exposure of Deslon, 55–56; his advice to Benny, 56–58, 61–62, 87–97, 98–99; and Mirabeau, 58–59; his unpopularity in America, 59–60; Temple's aloofness towards him, 60–61; his sorrow on leaving Paris, 65–66; his arrival at Philadelphia, 68–70, 367; his world fame, 70–72, 367; hard work in his old age, 74–77, 367; his rôle at the Constitu-

[386]

INDEX

Kuhn, Doctor Adam (stepfather of Margaret Markoe, and one of the leading doctors of Philadelphia), 109, 117, 193, 333, 377
Kuhn, Mrs. Adam (widow of Francis Markoe and mother of Margaret Markoe), *see* Mrs. Francis Markoe

La Colombe, Louis-Ange de (aide-de-camp of La Fayette), 218
Laetitia's House (built by William Penn in Philadelphia), 125
La Fayette, Marie Jean Paul Yves Roch Gilbert de Motier, Marquis de (generally spelled Lafayette after 1792), 63, 78, 118, 176, 213, 265, 266
Lailson (circus man in Philadelphia), 128
Lancaster (Pennsylvania), 128
Lancaster Journal, 360
La Rochefoucauld, François, Duc de (French philosopher and writer), 112. (The other places where La Rochefoucauld is mentioned refer to his namesake, Duc de La Rochefoucauld-Liancourt)
La Rochefoucauld d'Enville, Duc de (friend and admirer of Franklin), 50
La Rouairie, Marquis Armand de (colonel and volunteer in the American army), 265, 266
Lay, Benjamin (religious enthusiast in Philadelphia), 126; gives away all his belongings, 84
"Learned Pig" (a very erudite pig which was shown in Philadelphia), 290–291
Lecoeur (schoolmaster in Passy), 22
Lee, Arthur, 60
Lee, Charles, 78
Lee Family of Virginia, 149
Lee, Richard Henry (President of the Congress of the United States), 69
Lee, William (American merchant), 347–349, 377
Legation of France in Philadelphia, 260
Leib, Doctor Michael (Democratic leader in Philadelphia, and intimate friend of Benjamin Franklin Bache), 163, 186, 241, 312
Lemaire (French fencing professor in Philadelphia), 216
Lepelletier de Saint-Fargeau, Etienne

Michel (violent French revolutionist), 282
"Letters of General Washington", 272
Le Veillard (mayor of Passy and friend of Franklin), 50
Le Veillard, Madame, 48
Levy (Democrat of Pennsylvania, and friend of Benjamin Franklin Bache), 349
Lexington (Kentucky), 248
Liancourt, François Alexandre Frederic de La Rochefoucauld, Duc de (also called Duc de La Rochefoucauld-Liancourt), 24, 118, 127, 217, 267, 373, 375, 376
Linnæus, or, Carl von Linné, 83
Liquors in Philadelphia, 129
Liston, Robert (Minister of Great Britain in America), 321, 325; at the inauguration of John Adams, 314, 376
Logan, Doctor George, 153, 187, 189, 270, 327, 333, 337, 350, 353, 358, 369, 372, 377; his estate and his guests, 134–135; his trip to France in 1798, 340–341, 377
Logan, Mrs. George (Deborah Norris), 134, 353, 369
Logan, James (confidant of William Penn), 134
Lombardy Poplars (in the streets of Philadelphia), 126
London, 127
Longchamps (promenade near Paris), 63
Louis XVI, King of France, 60, 162, 203, 212, 215, 282, 289; his execution, 166
Louvet de Couvrai, Jean Baptiste (French writer and revolutionist), 266
Loyalists in America, 79, 147, 250
Lyon, Matthew (Democratic member of the House of Representatives), 335

MacHenry, James (Federalist politician, friend of Hamilton, and Secretary of War under John Adams), 319
McKean, Thomas, LL.D. (Democratic politician and statesman), 163, 342
MacSheane (Irishman who kept a tavern in Philadelphia which was the center of the Irish colony), 201, 306

INDEX

Moreau de Saint Méry, Médéric Louis Elie (French politician and refugee in America), 146, 212, 217, 218, 219, 308

Moreau de Saint Méry, Madame (wife of the preceding), 217

Morellet, Abbé André (French philosopher and friend of Franklin), 59

Morgan, Benjamin (business man in Philadelphia), 337

Morris, Gouverneur (minister of the United States to France), 272; and Thomas Paine, 272–273

Morris, Robert (banker and Federalist leader), 79, 114, 131, 132, 143, 147, 149, 229, 267, 276, 334; refuses his aid to Benjamin Franklin Bache, 146; goes bankrupt, 359

Morris, Mrs. Robert (wife of the preceding), 132

Morse, Reverend Doctor Jedediah, 149

Mount Vernon, 252, 256

Municipal Council of Philadelphia, 15

Musée de Paris (free university in Paris), 51

Nantes (France), 21

National Assembly of France, 117

National Gazette (Democratic newspaper printed in Philadelphia by Philip Freneau), 150, 158, 160, 368, 370

Nehra, Henriette Amélie de (mistress of Mirabeau), 59

New Theater, in Philadelphia, 125

New York City, 73, 202; the seat of the new government in 1789, 114; and the Jay Treaty, 242–243, 245, 294, 295

New York Argus (Democratic newspaper in New York), 270, 338

New York Stock Exchange, 161

Nicolson, Sir James, discovers affair between his wife and Temple Franklin, 48–49

Nicolson, Mrs. James (wife of the preceding), and Temple Franklin, 48–49

Nisbet, Professor Charles, D.D., and Benjamin Franklin Bache, 105–106, 368

Noailles, Louis Marie, Vicomte de, 132, 176, 190, 219, 252

Norfolk (Virginia), 167

Norris, Isaac (one of the first settlers in Philadelphia), 134

Northern Star (Democratic newspaper), 338

Notre Dame (cathedral church in Paris), 63

Oeller's Hotel, Philadelphia (the fashionable hotel there from 1790 to 1799), 129, 166, 201, 237, 306; and the banquet in honor of Genet, 178–181

Order in Council (of the King of England, concerning the blockade of French harbors and neutral navigation), 251–252

Oswald, Colonel Eleazer (editor of the *Independent Gazeteer* in Philadelphia), his duel with Matthew Carey, 77–78

Pagin, "Father" (French musician and friend of Benjamin Franklin), 52

Paine, Thomas, 78, 80, 160, 185, 263; his arrival in Philadelphia, 12, 13; and Benny Bache, 271; put in jail by the French Jacobins, 272–273

Papal Nuncio, in Paris, 57

Paradis, Mademoiselle (blind musician in Paris), 52

Paris, 21, 117, 225; visited by Benjamin Franklin Bache, 63

Passy (fashionable suburb of Paris), 42, 225, 245; Franklin settles in, 22; description, 44–47; life in, 62–63

Peale's Museum, in Philadelphia (famous museum of natural history, history and art, organized in Philadelphia by Peale), 127, 128, 129, 306, 368

Pelosi, Vincent M. (printer and publisher in Philadelphia), 156

Penn, William, and the City of Philadelphia, 124–125

Pennsylvania, 179, 186, 192; government of, 127, 152, 153; politics in, 163–164, 365; in the electoral campaign of 1796, 302, 304, 375; political situation in 1797, 376

Pennsylvania Chronicle, 3, 265

Pennsylvania Evening Post (newspaper published in Philadelphia), 365

INDEX

RANDOLPH, EDMUND, Secretary of State under Washington, 205, 236, 252, 253, 263, 268, 275, 291, 374; and the Proclamation of Neutrality, 175, 370–371; and Fauchet, 219–220, 373; capacity in politics, 220–221, 373; and the Jay Treaty, 239, 251–252, 373, 374; and Fauchet's intercepted dispatch, 254–255, 374; and Washington, 256, 374; his resignation, 257–262, 374; his friendship with Washington, 265, 374; and the "Calm Observer", 271–272, 374

Recorder (a violently Democratic newspaper edited in Philadelphia by James Carey), 355

Reed, Jacob (Senator from South Carolina), 247

"Remarks occasioned by the late conduct of Mr. Washington as President of the United States" (a pamphlet against Washington), 315

Reprisal, Captain Wickes (American ship on which Franklin sailed for France in 1776), 21

Republican Party (eighteenth century), *see* Democratic-Republican Party

Revolution of Geneva, 32–34

Revolutionary Calendar, French, reprinted by Bache in Philadelphia, 215

Richardet (French innkeeper and cook in Philadelphia), 130, 201

Rickett's Circus in Philadelphia (most famous show in Philadelphia from 1790 to 1800), 108, 126, 128, 306

Rittenhouse, Doctor David (greatest American astronomer of the eighteenth century, member of the American Philosophical Society, and friend of Franklin), 135, 177; President of the Philadelphia Democratic Society, 186

Robespierre, Maximilien de, 206, 219; and Genet, 198; and Paine, 273

Roland, Manon Jeanne Phlipon, Madame (a French Revolutionary leader), 172

Rollin, Charles (French educator and historian of the eighteenth century), 87

Ross, Elizabeth (friend of Sarah Franklin and engaged to Richard Bache), 6

Rozier, Jean François Pilâtre de (French balloonist), 51

Royal Troup of Dancers, in Paris, 48

Royalists, French (in America), 216–217

Rush, Doctor Benjamin (prominent doctor in Philadelphia), 135, 193, 333, 377

Russell, John (leading Federalist editor in Boston), 277, 360, 377

SAINT CROIX (island in the West Indies), 334

Saint Germain Fair, in Paris, 48

Saint-Louis, Feast of, 34

Saint Mary's of the Irish (the Catholic Irish Church in Philadelphia), 127

Saint Olympe, Chevalier de (friend of Temple Franklin), 49

Saint Peter's Church (Cathedral of Geneva), 28

"Sansculotte, Sim", 291, 375

"Sans Culotte, Citizen", 211

Savannah (Georgia), celebrates the French Revolution, 167

Schuyler, Major-General Philip (father-in-law of Hamilton), 136

Schuylkill (river near Philadelphia), 83, 146, 154, 166, 184

Seaman, Mr. (mayor of Hartford), 244

Secheron (village near Geneva), 32–33

Seddon's (fashionable shop in London), 132

Sedition Law (voted by Congress in 1797), 347

Senate of the United States, 238, 247, 292, 313, 321, 339; ratifies Jay Treaty, 237

Sentinelle de Paris (radical newspaper in Paris), 266

"Sentinels", 162

Serre, Mrs. (admirer of Franklin in Geneva), entertains Benny Bache, 26

Settle Farm (home of Richard Bache after 1793), 328, 356; life at, 376

Shippen, Polly (fashionable girl in Philadelphia), 102, 108

Shippen, Doctor Thomas Lee (a prominent physician and Democrat in Philadelphia), 135, 364, 373

Sicard, Monsieur (French dancing master in Philadelphia), 216, 306

"Sidney", 248

INDEX

Sign of the Grape (inn in Philadelphia), 129

Simitière, Doctor Pierre Eugène du (painter and collector in Philadelphia), 108

Slavery, and Benjamin Lay, 84; and Benjamin Franklin, 116

Smith, Colonel James, 186

Society for Political Research (established in Philadelphia by Benjamin Franklin), 84, 186

Society of the Sons of Saint Andrew (the Scotch benevolent society in Philadelphia), 77, 102, 183

Society of the Sons of Saint George (the English benevolent society in Philadelphia), 77, 102, 183, 337

Society of the Sons of Saint Patrick (an Irish benevolent society in Philadelphia), 77, 183

Stamp Act, attitude of Franklin, his unpopularity in America, 3

Stenton (country home of Doctor George Logan), 134, 135, 153, 159, 327, 333, 341, 353, 369

Stevenson, Mrs. Margaret (hostess of Benjamin Franklin in London), 8

Supreme Court of the United States, 313

Supreme Executive Council of Pennsylvania, 70

Surrey (a county in England), 279, 288

Swanwick, John (wealthy Irish merchant and Democrat of Philadelphia), 163, 334; subsidizes the Democratic Party of Pennsylvania, 151–152

Swedes, in Pennsylvania, 124–125

Swiss Guards, in Paris, 63, 282

Swiss Soldiers, sent to curb the Revolution in Geneva, 33–34

"Sidney", 162

TALLEYRAND, CHARLES MAURICE DE, 217, 218, 219, 294, 330, 343, 348, 349; attitude and method, 329–330, 376; tries to intimidate the American envoys to France, 331–332, 376; and the "XYZ scandal", 340–341, 376–377

Talon, Omer (French Royalist leader, refugee in America), 132, 176

Tammany Society, 101, 215, 221, 222, 281, 297, 359, 373; origin and proceedings, 183–186, 371

Temple, Lord, 173

Temple, Sir John (Counsel General of Great Britain in New York), 173–174

"Tickletoby, J.", 291, 375

Trees of Liberty, 190, 214

Triulny (foreman of Benjamin Franklin Bache at his printing press), 163

True American (newspaper printed in Philadelphia), 355

Tuileries (royal palace in Paris), 283

UNITED STATES, see America

United States, an American frigate, 317

University of Pennsylvania, 70, 86–87, 100, 105, 153

"VALERIUS", attacks Washington, 269–270

Varinot, Monsieur Ambroise (French fireworks maker in Philadelphia), 215

Vatican (the Pope's palace in Rome), 132

Vaugirard, a suburb of Paris, 54

Vauxhall (popular theater at the outskirts of Paris), 48

Vergennes, Charles Gravier, Comte de (the last great minister of the French Monarchy), 65, 170, 289

Versailles, 21

Versonnex, village near Geneva, 32

Ville de l'Orient (French ship), 195, 201

Vioti, Giovanni-Battista (famous Italian violinist), 52

Virginia, 264; politics in, 163–164

Volney, Constantin François Chasseboeuf de (French philosopher and traveler), 218

WAR OF INDEPENDENCE, 58, 250, 281, 287

Washington, an American frigate, its launching, 19

Washington, General George, 58, 71, 118, 127, 129, 135, 142, 147, 162, 163, 164, 176, 187, 194, 201, 213, 216, 218, 219, 220, 221, 232, 237, 240, 243, 247, 248, 260, 263, 268, 284, 287, 292, 293, 296, 297, 298, 310, 326, 335, 336, 344, 352, 360, 361; and the Federalists, 80, 82; and Franklin, 114–115; his majestic

31

M